A Chronology of Film

Ian Haydn Smith

A Chronology of Film

A Cultural Timeline
from the Magic Lantern
to the Digital Screen

Contents

Introduction

When Auguste and Louis Lumière first unveiled their short films to audiences in Paris in 1895, they had no idea of how popular the medium they helped create would become over the course of the next century. 'Cinema' is an abbreviation of the word *cinématographe*, which was first used by the brothers and which had its origins in the classical Greek κίνημα (*kíne-ma*, or movement) and γράφειν (*gráphein*, to write). It was suited to the times. In an era of extraordinary scientific and technological advances, alongside giant creative strides in art, performance, literature, fashion, photography, design and architecture, cinema found a receptive and enthusiastic audience. Not that the Lumières' felt that way; they soon returned to their more lucrative photographic studio, with Louis saying, 'the cinema is an invention without any future'.

What the Lumières achieved with their ten films, single shots of everyday life, many people now replicate on a daily basis. From a trick performed by a pet or capturing a family moment, to recording an event that impacts the way people view the world, the integration of high-resolution cameras into the smartphones that millions carry around throughout their waking hours has made the 21st century the most mediated. It has also turned everyone into the kind of film-makers who pioneered the medium in its earliest days.

Progress came quick in the early years of cinema. The simple act of suturing two separate shots together, which became known as editing, cutting or montage, multiplied the possibilities of film. It also introduced the element of magic. Georges Méliès used simple cuts and multiple exposures to make figures disappear or duplicate, and backdrops to suddenly change. These cinematic illusions were eventually combined with more complex special and visual effects to create more elaborate scenarios. If these films look rudimentary against the advances made by the visual-effects industry of the 21st century, the

PREVIOUS PAGE. *Cabiria* (1914), Giovanni Pastrone, Italy
One of the first great epics of cinema proved a huge influence over subsequent large-scale Hollywood productions by D. W. Griffith and Cecil B. DeMille.

LEFT. *Star Wars* (1977), George Lucas, USA
George Lucas's effects-driven take on the matinee adventures of the 1930s helped forge the modern blockbuster. It transformed Hollywood and started one of cinema's most lucrative franchises.

LEFT. *The Passion of Joan of Arc (La passion de Jeanne d'Arc,* **1928), Carl Theodor Dreyer, Denmark**
The intensity of the French saint's last days is achieved through Carl Theodor Dreyer's use of extreme close-up on Maria Falconetti's face, which portrays the journey from fear through to a state of grace in martyrdom.

spirit remains the same. To watch one of the short films by TikTok star Zach King, who employs a combination of effects to create a multitude of illusory and comic set-ups, is to experience the same sense of wonder Méliès engendered among his audience. Like his cinematic forebear, King is also the ebullient star of his films.

As narrative cinema developed, the ability to cut between shots increased the complexity of the medium. Audiences no longer witnessed a brief representation of everyday life: a shot of people leaving work, a train pulling into a station, documentary footage of a royal coronation. Directors were able to collapse space and time. Continuity editing allowed them to move from one space to another, constructing a cohesive and cogent world for an audience. The chase scene between robbers and the law in Edwin S. Porter's *The Great Train Robbery* (1903) is an early example of continuity editing. It is the same approach that film-makers used for the car chases in *Bullitt* (1968), *The French Connection* (1971) or *Drive* (2011), or the pursuits on foot that appear in *The Third Man* (1949), *Point Break* (1991) and *Bridge of Spies* (2015).

Parallel editing was another tool in the film-makers' arsenal. It allowed for more than one action or event to unfold at the same time, or in multiple time-frames. If Porter's early Western once again featured this in its most rudimentary form, D. W. Griffith's *Intolerance* (1916), which traversed a quartet of narrative strands across four periods in history, or the increasing complexity of Louis Feuillade's crime serial of the 1910s, highlight how quickly this technique developed.

If Méliès offered audiences the wondrous with his cinema, US inventor and businessman Thomas Edison saw commercial potential in audiences' voyeuristic tendencies. Just as aspects of vaudeville entertainment and penny-dreadful fiction attracted controversy and accusations of moral degradation in the late 19th century, so cinema was initially regarded as a lower form of entertainment that appealed solely to people's baser desires. But as the medium developed and film-makers embraced its potential, it increased in sophistication. The narrative feature eventually outgrew all other forms of film-making, transforming a small collection of businesses into a global industry that would become a dominant form of entertainment throughout the 20th century.

Among its many attractions, cinema offered audiences spectacle on a scale that even the world's fairs of the 19th century could never have matched. It is unsurprising that the historical epic, emerging first from Italy with Enrico Guazzoni's *Quo Vadis?* (1913) and Giovanni Pastrone's *Cabiria* (1914), then followed by the films of Griffith, Abel Gance, Cecil B. DeMille and Erich von Stroheim, held such appeal. It was followed by the kinetic thrills of the war film, the expansive vistas of the Western and, latterly, the arrival of the modern blockbuster. George Lucas's *Star Wars: Episode IV – A New Hope* (1977) not only showcased the future of big-budget commercial cinema, seamlessly blending live action with visual and special effects, it set the template for the franchise film whose vast profits were increased with related tie-in products.

ABOVE LEFT. *The Hurt Locker* **(2008), Kathryn Bigelow, USA**
This portrait of a US Army bomb disposal expert remains one of the most noted Hollywood films about the Iraq War (2003–11) and earned Kathryn Bigelow Academy Awards for Best Director and Best Film.

LEFT. *Shoah* **(1985), Claude Lanzmann, France**
Claude Lanzmann's epic undertaking employs cinema as testimony in its recording of the persecuted, persecutors and witnesses of the Holocaust.

RIGHT. *Meshes of the Afternoon* **(1943), Maya Deren and Alexander Hackenschmied, USA**
Few experimental films have been as highly regarded or as influential as Maya Deren and Alexander Hackenschmied's exploration of the subconscious.

Equally attractive to audiences was the intimacy that films offered. The close-up brought them closer to the stars they adored, from Rudolph Valentino, Greta Garbo, Ruan Lingyu and Clark Gable to Gong Li, Brad Pitt, Kristen Stewart and Michael B. Jordan. But the close-up also accentuated emotion and experience. In Carl Theodor Dreyer's *The Passion of Joan of Arc* (*La passion de Jeanne d'Arc*, 1928) the close-up conveys the torment of the martyred saint. The primary focus of Dreyer's film is the face of lead actor Maria Falconetti, which expresses the agony of her character's fate. For the legendary Spaghetti Western director Sergio Leone, the extreme close-up was employed within a combination of shots to increase the intensity of his films.

A Chronology of Film presents a journey through the development of cinema. Like any history of the arts, it is in a state of constant flux. The narratives of the last century of film are at present changing more than ever. The role of race and gender identity has become key, both in the study of cinema's past and in the production of present and future films. The role women have played in the medium's history has long been undervalued. It is astonishing that since it began in 1929, the Academy Awards have given the Best Film prize to just one film directed by a woman: Kathryn Bigelow's *The Hurt Locker* (2008). The documentary *Be Natural: The Untold Story of Alice Guy-Blaché* (2018) highlighted the importance of one of the great pioneers of cinema, but for too long she was overlooked. She was not alone. The 14-hour series *Women Make Film: A New Road Movie Through Cinema* (2019) highlights the role female film-makers have played in the development of cinema since its inception. Narrated by Tilda Swinton, Adjoa Andoh, Jane Fonda, Sharmila Tagore, Kerry Fox, Thandie Newton and Debra Winger, it highlights how important it is to evaluate the past constantly

in looking towards the future of film, while also expanding one's range to include national cinemas whose contribution has been great but not always recognized. Just as focus on the importance of African American film-makers and practitioners in US cinema – both within the Hollywood system and beyond – has increased, so film traditions from African countries, India, Asia, the Americas, to name but a few regions where cinema has prospered creatively, are increasingly valued in an attempt to celebrate the heterogeneity of global cinema.

This volume primarily chronicles narrative feature film-making. Generally, when people talk about 'film', 'cinema' or the 'movies', they are referring to this form. In terms of the 'film industry' – the commercial side of film production – it revolves around the production, distribution, marketing and exhibition of feature-length narrative films. Experimental and documentary cinema play a significant role in cinema's past and present, but their roles exist in tandem to the behemoth of the narrative feature. For example, the occasional 'greatest films' listings by international cinema journals might list documentaries such as *Man with a Movie Camera* (*Chelovek s kino-apparatom*, 1929) and *Shoah* (1985), or even experimental films such as *An Andalusian Dog* (*Un chien andalou*, 1929) and *Meshes of the Afternoon* (1943) among the greatest achievements of world cinema. But the majority of these critics and film-makers' polls comprise narrative features.

A Chronology of Film opens in the distant past, charting the work of philosophers, scientists and artists in understanding the way people see – literally view – the world, moving on to the development of devices that experimented with light and optics. The progression from the camera obscura to the first still photography camera was gradual.

LEFT. *Andrei Rublev (Andrey Rublev, 1966),* Andrei Tarkovsky, Soviet Union
Andrei Tarkovsky's acclaimed second feature is an attempt at a grounded, realistic portrait of life in medieval Russia yet also contemplates the role of the artist in society.

OPPOSITE. *The Rules of the Game (La règle du jeu, 1939),* Jean Renoir, France
One of the great French Poetic Realist films and among the finest of Jean Renoir's career, his satire captures life among the bourgeoisie in a country on the cusp of war.

However, the speed of innovation and invention quickened in the latter part of the 19th century, in the years leading up to the first projections of moving images.

Chapter two opens with the Lumière brothers and works its way through the medium's infancy, the golden age of pre-sound cinema and ends just as the talkies gained in popularity at the end of the 1920s. Chapter three chronicles the emergence of a fully mature cinema, from Hollywood's golden age to the work of directors such as Jean Renoir, whose *The Rules of the Game (La règle du jeu,* 1939) remains one of the high points of French cinema. Chapter four charts the rise of new generations that not only challenged the language of the cinematic establishment, but employed cinema as a revolutionary tool or to kick against social, cultural and moral codes. The desire for change was everywhere, while film-makers such as Andrei Tarkovsky, with works such as *Andrei Rublev (Andrey Rublev,* 1966) and *The Mirror (Zerkalo,* 1975) elevated it to the status of high art. Although the cinema discussed in chapters five and six might have receded in its collective radicalism, it has excelled in its technological advances. The 21st century has also witnessed a growing chorus of voices that more accurately represent the world in terms of identity, across race, gender and culture.

Unlike previous editions in this series, whose sections are spread across a more expansive period, the majority of the timelines in *A Chronology of Film* cover two-year increments, allowing for a more detailed overview of the relationship between films and the eras in which they are produced. Interspersed among these entries are essays that focus on specific areas in more detail. They look at the way movements or styles of film-making have impacted cinema, focus on trends or technical innovations that have been key to its development, and highlight periods when certain national cinemas came to the fore on the world stage.

This book is far from exhaustive. The films listed across each entry, totalling more than 200, are a fraction of the hundreds of thousands that have been produced over the course of the last 125 years, and a portion of those that have been essential in shaping the medium. Many key figures are mentioned here because of their importance to the medium. This book will hopefully encourage the reader to seek out other works listed in the Further Reading section that explore individual movements, national cinemas and film-makers in more detail.

A final note on statistics. Throughout this volume, films are occasionally discussed in terms of their box-office returns. A succession of features have claimed to be the biggest global box-office success. When these are mentioned, these claims are not adjusted for inflation. However, the idea of judging a film by its commercial success is problematic. It gives no indication of its quality. Certainly, some great films have achieved significant commercial success. But so many great films fared poorly at the box office only to attain greatness with the passage of time. *A Chronology of Film* attempts to find a balance between the worlds of art and commerce, charting trends that saw certain films succeed with audiences – whether they deserved that success or not – with major leaps in the art and craft of film-making. It is not a definitive qualitative survey of cinema, but an overview of the history of a thrilling medium that continues to entertain, engage, challenge, shock and move people.

1

GENESIS
OF FILM

What would early cave dwellers have made of the millions of images that have flickered across cinema screens over the course of the 20th century?

The genesis of these moving images, which have come to dominate popular culture and influence societies at large, spans millennia, long before the first cinema, projector, camera or reel of film. It predates even the most rudimentary mechanical or technological innovations. What entertains, engages, moves, fascinates, shocks and occasionally outrages viewers when watching a film originated from the play between light and movement: the flicker of a shadow on a wall and people's capacity to glean from it some form of narrative.

In 1994, a group of speleologists exploring a cave in the Ardèche department of southern France happened upon a collection of extraordinarily well-preserved prehistoric paintings, dating from 37,000 to 28,000 BC. Among the figures of animals painted on the cave walls were creatures with six legs. This may have resulted from the painter attempting to grapple with the illusion of quick movement – the persistence of vision. But it also gave the paintings a sense of the kinetic actions of these animals. German director Werner Herzog employed state-of-the-art technology to convey this sense of movement and to help 'capture the intentions of the painters' in his 3D documentary about the paintings, *Cave of Forgotten Dreams* (2010). The paintings represent the earliest recorded example of a moving image.

If the human form is almost entirely absent from the early cave paintings, it became a dominant presence in the work of Egyptian artists, alongside animals; gods also featured, more often a combination of the two. The wall and tablet paintings featured a front and side perspective simultaneously and although individual figures appeared static, when seen as part of a group they give the impression of movement.

They featured religious processions and even more active pursuits, such as hunting. Although the paintings lacked any depth of field, some frescoes included fragments of the natural landscape – reeds from a nearby water source or a bird in flight – to add drama to the image. These ancient paintings can be divided into a linear sequence of individual frames, in the same way that narrative film is, in order to present a story. A similar effect was later achieved with Trajan's Column (AD 113) in Rome, the vast edifice constructed in honour of the Roman emperor's victories in the Dacian Wars (101–102, 105–106), depicted in a continuous helical frieze that winds its way up the column. It is also seen in the vast narrative and monumental scrolls produced in East Asia from 900, or in the Bayeux Tapestry (1066–77), the 70-m (230 ft) long embroidered cloth depicting the events that led to the Norman Conquest of England in 1066.

The experiments of ancient Greeks and Romans, from Aristotle, Euclid and Archimedes, through to Lucretius, Vitruvius, Pliny the Elder, Seneca and Heron, became interested in optics and the photosensitive properties of certain chemicals. At the same time, in China shadow plays became a popular form of entertainment, either through the use of ornately crafted, dried animal skins or early forms of paper, or through the projection of shadows on a screen. It was a tradition that travelled the world and remained popular up to the arrival of cinema. For the German film-maker Lotte Reiniger, the effect produced by shadow plays would form the basis of her exquisite animations of the 1920s. The Chinese inventor Ding Huan went further. In *c.* AD 180, he created a device that combined light and movement from the same source, using the hot air rising from a lamp to move hanging cut-out figures, presenting audiences with an early and rudimentary form of zoetrope.

Early European, Arabic and Chinese theorists made detailed notes of their studies of eclipses using what became known as the camera obscura. Key among them was the 11th-century Arabian polymath Ibn al-Haytham, or Alhazen. One of the most celebrated scientists of the Islamic golden age, he produced more than a dozen books on optics. He was one of the first to present a detailed study of a lens's ability to magnify objects and the constituent colours of natural light, and discovered the laws of refraction. The giant leaps he made advanced the study of optics and light significantly over the next eight centuries and his work influenced many European scientists following its publication in Latin in the late 12th or early 13th century.

If British scientists Roger Bacon and Robert Grosseteste developed the scientific study of light and optics in the 13th century, towards its end the Spanish physician, translator, alleged alchemist and religious reformer Arnaldus de Villa Nova brought showmanship and entertainment to audiences. One of his shows involved the actions of a group of actors in daylight being projected via a camera obscura on to a wall inside a dark room to the delight of the audience sitting there. The influential 15th-century Italian Renaissance architect Filippo Brunelleschi explored depth of field as another form of entertainment, with the development of a pinhole camera called the perspective viewer. A glass with a pinhole in it was held up against the viewer's face. On the outward side was a painted image. The viewer also held up a mirror. Looking through the pinhole, they saw a reflection of the image, which presented a 3D effect because of the depth of field the device created. A century later, while living in Rome, the Mannerist artist, sculptor, goldsmith and memoirist Benvenuto Cellini wrote about a light show that took place at the city's Coliseum. From the details he gave, it resembled a version of the magic lantern, which was developed more fully by the German scholar Athanasius Kircher, who described it in his influential volume *The Great Art of Light and Shadow* (*Ars magna lucis et umbrae*, 1646). The 17th-century Dutch scientist and astronomer Christiaan Huygens has also been credited with the development of the magic lantern, which he introduced to scientific communities and courts throughout Europe. He is also acknowledged for introducing the camera obscura to many of the great artists of the golden age of Dutch and Flemish painting.

As linear perspective became important in painting, many artists employed scientific tools to increase the accuracy of their work. The 16th-century German painter and printmaker Albrecht Dürer even made woodcuts of his drawing aids, detailing their operation in minutiae. Various historians have noted the importance of such tools in the work of Dutch artist Johannes Vermeer, given the exactitude of his portraits as well as the landscape *View of Delft* (*c.* 1660–61). British polymath Robert Hooke unveiled his Picture Box, a portable version of a camera obscura, at a lecture in 1694 in London, and it was soon adopted by many artists as a drawing aid.

In his book *The Long-Distance Artificial Eye, or Telescope* (*Oculus artificialis teledioptricus sive telescopium*, 1685), the German cleric Johann Zahn produced an extraordinary collection of designs that grappled with the potential of the camera obscura and magic lantern. His experiments with light, mirrors and lenses presaged the arrival of the camera in the 19th century. One design for the magic lantern involved the production of images on various glass slides. They could be passed in front of the lantern, giving the impression of movement.

Inventions and innovations appeared with increasing speed throughout the 18th and early 19th centuries. Phantasmagoria, employing a variety of lanterns, shadow play and magic tricks, created an eerie entertainment and became a popular form of travelling show throughout Europe. Around the same time, panoramas and dioramas became common, presenting audiences with huge vistas of landscapes and historical events – not dissimilar to the innovations with screen formats that benefited the return of historical epics in cinemas during the 1950s. Some panoramas even scrolled before an audience, giving the sensation of movement. But the ability to record real life with light-sensitive material became widespread following the work of French innovators Joseph Nicéphore Niépce and Louis-Jacques-Mandé Daguerre, and British scientist William Fox Talbot.

The similarity between many devices created evinced a forward momentum in a specific direction, all edging closer to the first appearance of the moving image. British scientist Charles Wheatstone developed the stereoscope, whose two combined images offered depth of field. Belgian physicist Joseph-Antoine-Ferdinand Plateau's

phenakistoscope and Austrian mathematician Simon Ritter von Stampfer's stroboscope employed a series of images that, when spun at speed, gave the illusion of fluid movement, not dissimilar to the flip books that also appeared in the mid 1800s. British mathematician William George Horner's zoetrope, originally named the Daedaleum, further developed the idea of the phenakistoscope by placing images on the inside wall of a horizontally rotating drum, with slits at the top that an observer could peer through and experience the sensation of movement through each of the images.

By the late 19th century, British-American photographer Eadweard Muybridge and French scientist and chronophotographer Étienne-Jules Marey were working on projects that employed multiple cameras to capture movement and project it in real time as a fluid moving image. From this bedrock, US inventors Thomas Edison and George Eastman, French inventor Louis Le Prince, French pioneers Louis and Auguste Lumière, British photographer William Friese-Greene, German film-makers Max and Emil Skladanowsky, British inventor William Kennedy-Laurie Dickson, British photographer Birt Acres and British scientific-instrument maker Robert W. Paul played a role in developing the medium that would be unveiled to stunned audiences as the world edged towards the 20th century.

ABOVE. Théâtre Optique (1892), France
An illustration of French inventor Charles-Émile Reynaud operating an advanced projection version of his invention of 1877, the praxinoscope. By the time he opened his theatre at the Musée Grévin in Paris in 1892, he had created a system of hand-painted glass images that would show actions sequentially, giving the impression of fluid movement.

700 BC–AD 1700

Projecting images. Recording experiences becomes integral to human existence, from the earliest cave paintings depicting daily life through to the representation of complex civilizations in Europe, Africa and Asia. An interest in the theoretical and practical applications of optics progresses alongside experiments with light-sensitive chemical compounds. Aristotle's early theories in his *Problems* (300 BC). explore the nature of light. These ideas would be challenged by Ibn al-Haytham, Leonardo da Vinci, Johannes Kepler and Isaac Newton over the course of the subsequent two millennia. The development of the camera obscura and magic lantern underpin the nature of the moving image in the future, as much embraced by those who wish to entertain as by those interested in research and education.

The Nimrud Lens, believed to be the oldest-known lens, is discovered by archaeologist Austen Henry Layard in 1850 in Iraq. With its one convex face, it is likely that its use was more decorative than scientific.

Ibn al-Haytham, Iraq
The 'father of modern optics', Ibn al-Haytham, also known as Alhazen, was a dominant presence in the scientific community of the Islamic golden age. A philosopher and theologist, his most enduring work is the *Book of Optics* (*Kitab al-Manazir*, 1011–21), when al-Haytham was incarcerated. Translated into Latin almost 200 years later, it became a defining work for subsequent studies in optics and is regarded as important a scientific text in this area as Isaac Newton's *Opticks* (1704).

Aristotle's *Problems* theorizes on what becomes known as persistence of vision in his discussion of after-images.

Euclid's *The Optics* discusses binocular vision, which is expanded upon four centuries later by Galen.

750–710 BC

c. **300 BC**

AD 1021

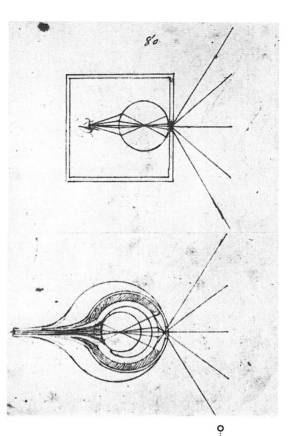

Codex Atlanticus, Italy

Leonardo da Vinci drew hundreds of illustrations of various kinds of camera obscura, such as this one created between 1490 and 1495. Many are found in the *Codex Atlanticus*, a twelve-volume series of studies published in folio form between 1478 and 1519, whose subjects range from mechanics and weaponry to musical instruments and optical devices. Unlike other scientists, Da Vinci's multidisciplinary interests always gave his studies a creative or artistic perspective. Further studies would appear in *Manuscript D* of the *Paris Manuscripts*, completed in 1509.

The *Book of War Instruments* (*Bellicorum instrumentorum liber*) is one of the earliest technological treatises of the Renaissance era by Italian engineer Johannes de Fontana. It features what is believed to be the first illustration of a camera obscura.

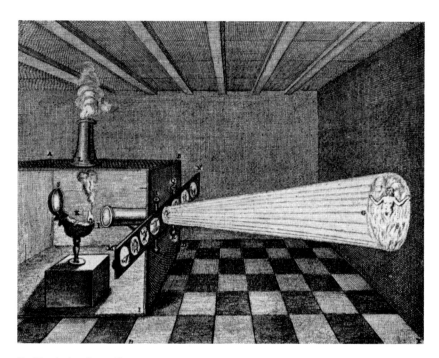

Magic Lantern, Germany

Athanasius Kircher described the magic lantern in his treatise *The Great Art of Light and Shadow* (*Ars magna lucis et umbrae*, 1646), including the addition of a revolving wheel that featured a variety of images. But it is not until the expanded edition of his book in 1671 that he includes an illustration of his device, which he calls a 'smicroscopin'. He claims the device is his own invention. The magic lantern would become as important an invention as the camera obscura in the development of moving images.

c. 1420-30   1490-95   1671

1700–1800

The age of enlightenment. Extraordinary strides are made in science, mathematics, engineering, art and philosophy. Curiosity and a desire for change helps reshape societies, culminating in the revolutions that bring independence to what emerges as the United States of America, and transforms France into a republic. It brings an end to French colonial rule in Haiti, a pivotal moment in the history of the Atlantic world. The dawn of modern India is impacted by the dominance of British rule, while Central Europe sees the beginning of a century of conflict over territorial rights. Classical music is transformed by the work of Johann Sebastian Bach, George Frideric Handel and Wolfgang Amadeus Mozart. The novel becomes a bedrock of cultural life. Exploration broadens the parameters of art and informs scientific research.

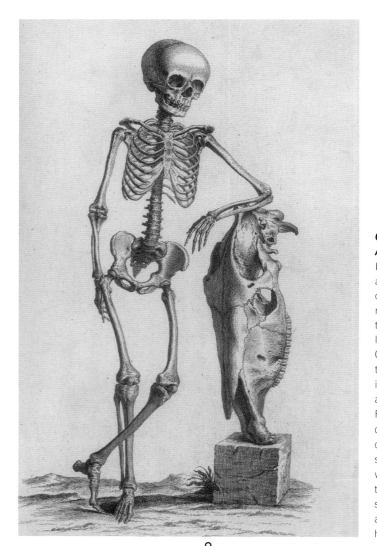

The largest encyclopaedia ever printed is commissioned by China's Emperor Yongzheng. It runs to 10,000 chapters.

Isaac Newton's *Opticks* is a key work in the study of optics and the summation of decades of study into the subject. Newton's book includes the first illustration of the dispersal of light through a prism.

Osteographia or the Anatomy of the Bones, **UK**
In much the same way that artists employed a camera obscura to accurately replicate the world around them, English surgeon and lecturer in anatomy William Cheselden employs his device to create remarkably detailed illustrations of human and animal bone structures. Focus on individual limbs is complemented by full skeletal diagrams, often performing some kind of action, from walking and carrying objects to kneeling and praying. The study is the first complete and accurate description of the human skeletal system.

1704   1725   1733

The Camera Obscura, France
The contraption held by the boy and capturing the attention of the young girl in this painting, by French portraitist Charles-Amédée-Philippe van Loo, is a camera obscura. The contraption's presence in the painting highlights the popularity of such entertainments outside of the sphere of scientific research. The *trompe-l'oeil* effect of the image existing outside of the portrait frame presages the breaking of the fourth wall that would become a staple in cinema, particularly comedy.

A Dictionary of the English Language is published by Samuel Johnson. In its first edition it includes entries on 42,773 words.

The panorama is patented by Robert Barker. In contrast to conventional paintings, the observer is required to turn in order to take in the full scope of a painted vista.

The Fantoscope, Belgium
This detailed copper engraving from 1797 presents a rapturous spectacle by Belgian Étienne-Gaspard Robert. Better known by the stage name 'Robertson', he is a professor of physics, specializing in optics, who becomes one of the most inventive European entertainers, employing all manner of visual effects to thrill audiences. Key among his arsenal is the fantoscope, which he describes in his patent of 1799 as a 'magic lantern on wheels'.

| 1755 | 1764 | 1787 | 1797 |

1800–1850

Empires rise and fall. The emergence of the camera transforms the way people see themselves and the world around them. The United States becomes a significant presence on the world stage. European and Asian empires increase their territorial gains, with Britain and Russia expanding significantly following Napoleon's defeat. Centuries of agrarian life is impacted by modernization and the First Industrial Revolution. It is driven by advances in science, although Mary Shelley's *Frankenstein* (1818) offers a timely cautionary tale about the dangers of science without ethics and is celebrated as the first great horror novel. The abolitionist movement gains traction, with countries signing accords to ban slavery. However, southern states in the United States continue the practice, increasing tensions with the north. Following the success of Haiti, many Central and South American countries seek and gain independence from colonialist rulers.

View from the Window at Le Gras, France

French inventor Joseph Nicéphore Niépce takes what has become the world's oldest surviving photographic image. A view of his estate in the Bourgogne region of eastern France, the image is projected via a camera obscura on to a pewter plate with a coating of the asphalt Bitumen of Judea. With sunlight evident on both sides of a building, it is believed that the exposure is likely to have been more than 8 hours in duration.

The Federal Procession of Philadelphia includes moving panoramas. These vast recreations of historical events or landscapes are popular. One of the longest panoramas, at nearly 400 m (1,300 ft), was a record of the procession in the Pennsylvanian capital in 1788.

1811

c. 1826

The Zoetrope, UK

William George Horner is already a celebrated British mathematician, whose method for approximating the roots of polynomial equations was unveiled in 1819, when he reveals his Daedaleum. US inventor William F. Lincoln would rename the device 'zoetrope' in 1887. A cylindrical variation of the phenakistoscope, it is capable of rotating at 14 images per second, edging closer to the speed that film frames would eventually spool through a projector.

Boulevard du Temple, Paris is taken by Louis-Jacques-Mandé Daguerre, presenting the first photographic image of people. Due to the lengthy exposure time – 10 to 15 minutes – only people who were stationary for a period of time feature in the photograph.

Fig. 99. — Phénakisticope de Plateau. (Page 125.)

The Phenakistoscope, Belgium

Belgian physicist and mathematician Joseph-Antoine-Ferdinand Plateau's device gives the illusion of movement. On one disc is a series of painted images, each differing slightly to the next. The other disc is comprised of a series of slits. Both discs are attached on an identical axis and spun counter-directionally. By looking through the slits, the illustrated object is seen to move fluidly.

The Cincinnati Panorama is unveiled. Comprising eight daguerreotype plates, each covering 3 km (2 miles) of the city's riverfront, it is a forerunner of the widescreen formats that appeared in cinemas a century later.

1832   1834   1838   1848

THE CAMERA OBSCURA

When light is projected, via a small hole, on to a wall or screen in a darkened space, an image of the outside will appear, albeit inverted and reversed. A device called a camera obscura was built specifically to achieve this effect. It became a useful tool for artists and eventually led to the invention of photographic and moving-image cameras.

Michael Powell and Emeric Pressburger's metaphysical British drama *A Matter of Life and Death* (1945) features a strange device. A man stands in a dark attic room looking at a flat white table, upon which the world outside is projected. It resembles a strange illusion, not unlike the Wicked Witch of the West's crystal ball in *The Wizard of Oz* (1939). But it is a perfect working example of a camera obscura (Latin for 'dark chamber').

There are theories that some of the caves featuring prehistoric paintings may have once allowed enough light in for an image to be projected on to a wall, which the dwellers then replicated. It would account for a horse being painted upside down in one of the caves in Lascaux, France. However, the earliest writings on this phenomenon come much later, in the text *Mozi* (4th century BC) named after the Zhou Dynasty (1046–256 BC) Chinese philosopher and founder of the Mohist School of Logic. It describes the inversion of an image that has been projected

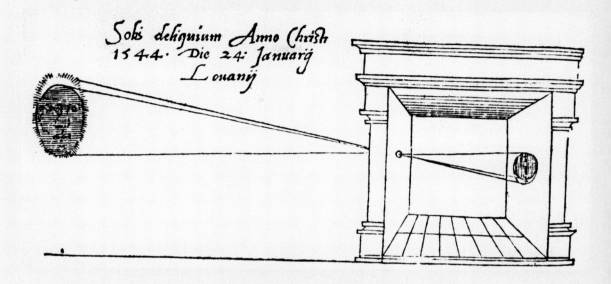

Solis deliquium Anno Christi 1544. Die 24: Januarij Louanij

through a small hole. The reasons why this happens would later be discussed by Aristotle, Euclid and subsequent Greek and Roman thinkers.

The High Middle Ages (11th–13th century) saw significant developments in the device's use, both theoretically and practically. The writings of Islamic golden age (8th–14th century) polymath Ibn al-Haytham and Song Dynasty (960–1279) scientist Shen Kuo added immeasurably to research into the study of light, the latter in his lyrically titled *Dream Pool Essays* (1088). Al-Haytham's writings in particular, once translated, proved a significant influence over European thought. The work of 13th-century English theorist Robert Grosseteste and Polish friar and mathematician Erasmus Ciołek Witelo are evidence of this. At the same time, the device was employed to observe the sun and eclipses, while Spanish physician and religious reformer Arnaldus de Villa Nova saw in it a way of entertaining audiences.

One of the earliest appearances of the device was as part of a larger illustration in an early 15th-century book by Italian engineer Johannes de Fontana. But the first published drawing of the workings of it was in 1545 by Dutch scientist, designer and cartographer Gemma Frisius. Although Italian polymath Leonardo da Vinci had drawn hundreds of designs before this, his notes on optics were not published until the late 18th century. He was first to notice the similarity between the functioning of the camera obscura and the human eye.

Across these centuries, the device was known by many names, including *obscurum cubiculum*, *locus obscurus* and *cubiculum tenebricosum*. It was German astronomer Johannes Kepler, in his treatise *Emendations to Witelo* (*Ad Vitellionem paralipomena*, 1604), who gave it the name 'camera obscura'. Kepler also realized it functioned in the same way as the human eye, but without a brain to correct the inversion and reversal of an image. The addition of a lens could do this. Through the use of lenses and mirrors, the camera obscura was able to afford greater versatility and definition with the projected image. Viewing the sun was made easier, particularly as scientists realized what damage could be done to the eye by looking directly at it. But through the writings of theorists such as French mathematician and painter Jean-François Nicéron, who detailed the advantages of using convex lenses to increase clarity and precision, as well as the creation of more portable devices, the camera obscura became a tool for artists.

If the magic lantern became the dominant device in entertaining audiences from the mid 17th century through to the late 19th century, the camera obscura's importance in the development of photography is underpinned by its use by Joseph Nicéphore Niépce, Louis-Jacques-Mandé Daguerre and William Fox Talbot. The physical setting of a cinema has changed very little from early examples of large camera obscuras: an audience sits in a darkened room as light from a small hole is projected on to a screen.

1850-1875

Wonder and war. The Great Exhibition opens in London in 1851, offering the British capital an opportunity to show the world its advances in science, technology and the arts. It is attended by Charles Darwin whose publication of *On the Origin of Species* (1859), has a seismic impact on humankind's place in natural history. Also present is Charles Dickens, who documents the best and worst of the times he lives in, particularly in focusing on the perils faced by the poor in industrialized societies. Advances in technology have also magnified the catastrophic effect of conflict, first witnessed in the Crimean War (1853–56) and then in the devastation wreaked by the American Civil War (1861–65).

o *Stereoscopic Photograph of the 1857 Manchester Art Treasures Exhibition*, UK
Stereoscopes and accompanying stereo cards, featuring right- and left-eye images of the same view that the brain then combines to give the perception of 3D depth, become popular in the mid 1800s. The most successful producer of the images is the London Stereoscopic Company, which continues to manufacture them two decades after the invention of the moving image.

The kinetoscope or 'Lantern Wheel of Light' is invented by Franz von Uchatius, an inventor and general in the Austrian army. Combining the functions of a zoetrope and magic lantern, it offers audiences one of the earliest examples of projected animation.

Roger Fenton becomes one of the first photographers to capture conflict with his images from the Crimean War.

1853 **1855** **1857**

Fading Away, UK

An early example of photomontage, this tableau image by British photographer Henry Peach Robinson was produced from five different negatives. The image displays the Gothic atmosphere that was popular at the time, as well as the influence of Pre-Raphaelite art. A family awaits the death of a beloved daughter and sister, while the Turner-esque sky reflects the characters' emotional turmoil. In its play with form, *Fading Away* presages the arrival of French cinematic conjuror Georges Méliès and the visual effects that would play a dominant role in cinema.

The Horse in Motion, USA

In 1872, the former governor of California Leland Stanford hires acclaimed English-American photographer Eadweard Muybridge to settle a wager over whether all four hooves of a horse are simultaneously off the ground when it trots. Muybridge uses twelve cameras to record a split-second sequence. Though rudimentary compared alongside his later efforts, the principle Muybridge adopts remains the same. A similar set-up would be created to capture the 'bullet-time' effects of fight sequences in the sci-fi blockbuster *The Matrix* (1999).

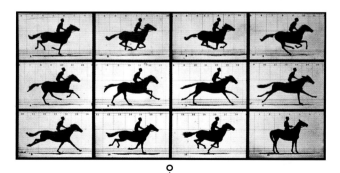

The American Civil War starts, resulting in a colossal loss of life. The photographic record of the conflict, captured by Mathew B. Brady and a small group of photographers, defines the role of the war photographer and how war is represented for the next century.

Alfred Nobel obtains a patent for his invention of dynamite.

Lionel Smith Beale creates the choreutoscope, whose frame-by-frame operation foretells the functioning of the cinematograph.

1858 1861 1866 1867 1872

1875–1890

Technology accelerates. At the beginning of the 19th century, photography was in its infancy. By the end, it is not only perceived by some to be an art form, it had become an everyday part of people's lives. The painted portraits that once hung alone on the walls of family homes are now joined or replaced by photographs. Newspapers that featured illustrations of events or people on their front pages can now send stringers out to capture them with cameras. Just as Dutch artist Vincent van Gogh challenges artistic practice through his radical vision of the world, so the darkroom allows photographers the ability to transform reality. Among these innovators are visionaries who see the potential of moving images and recorded sound.

The Phonograph, USA

By his late twenties, Thomas Edison had already established himself as an entrepreneur and inventor. In 1876, he establishes a research laboratory in Menlo Park, New Jersey.
His breakthrough invention, which makes his name, is the phonograph – a device capable of recording and replaying sound. The first version is recorded on tinfoil around a grooved cylinder. The sound is rough as the critic Herman Klein notes: 'It sounded to my ear like someone singing about half a mile away....' Subsequent models improve on the quality of the recording. This image shows Edison with the second version of the device in 1878.

Alexander Graham Bell
invents the telephone.

1876   1877

Chronophotography, France

The cardiologist Étienne-Jules Marey's interest in the functioning of the human anatomy led to a wider interest in animal movement that develops into a passion for the technologies capable of capturing it. He creates the chronophotographic gun camera in 1882, which is capable of taking twelve consecutive frames in one second. However, in contrast to Eadweard Muybridge's multi-camera set-up, Marey's device captures all the frames within one single image, such as this shot of a man pole vaulting taken in *c.* 1890.

Animal Locomotion, Plate 391, USA

In the early 1880s, Muybridge begins working out of the University of Pennsylvania photographing a variety of subjects in order to study movement. His subjects range from animals and birds to humans, such as this study of a man playing cricket. The resulting book, *Animal Locomotion – An Electro-photographic Investigation of Consecutive Phases of Animal Movements* (1872–85), features 781 plates comprising 20,000 photographs. The images remain a valuable resource for the study of movement.

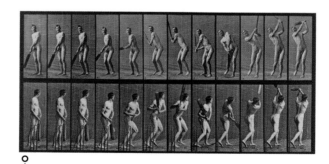

George Eastman's company begins to produce celluloid roll film for use in cameras.

Photography is more common in newspapers and periodicals.

Louis Le Prince makes the earliest extant film *Roundhay Garden Scene*, shot in the English city of Leeds.

| 1882 | 1887 | 1888 | 1889 | 1890 |

PROMOTIONAL ART

The proliferation of mass public entertainments in the 19th century, from music halls and vaudeville shows to the emergence of moving-image entertainments, meant that printed promotional material became more imaginative in its attempt to entice audiences. Paris led the way.

The earliest record of a poster, advertising the *Sarum Ordinal* or *Pye* a handbook for priests, was created *c*. 1477 by William Caxton, who was responsible for introducing the printing press to Britain. As presses became more elaborate, all-black, text-heavy posters were replaced by two- and three-tone illustrated designs.

The next important development in printing technique came in 1798, when German actor and playwright Alois Senefelder invented lithography. Borne of his frustration as a playwright over the lack of means to produce exact reproductions of an original design, it was a significant technological leap. But it was the emergence of Jules Chéret in the 1860s who brought the poster into the modern age. Born into a Parisian family of artisans in 1836, at the age of thirteen Chéret began an apprenticeship with a lithographer. From there, an interest in art took him to the École Nationale de Dessin et de Mathématiques, but the French capital's art galleries proved an equally fruitful place of learning. He spent seven years perfecting Senefelder's innovation in London. He had achieved some success before departing Paris, but that was eclipsed by the increasing demand for his services upon his return in 1866.

The Belle Époque, which coincided with the French Third Republic (1870–1940), transformed the Parisian cultural and social scene. Artists flocked to the city and previous strictly enforced codes regarding the behaviour of the sexes were relaxed. Chéret's artwork reflected the atmosphere of permissiveness, particularly in his commissions for the city's major social establishments. The women in his designs, all gay and exuberant, became known as Chérettes and were embodied by the designer's favourite model, Danish actress, singer and ballet dancer Charlotte Wiehe-Berény.

Chéret's three-stone lithograph process allowed him to break down his design into individual colours, allowing for the kind of large-scale colour printing that had previously been unthinkable. His artworks drew on earlier movements, whereas the French Post-Impressionist painter Henri de Toulouse-Lautrec, another valued poster designer, opted for a more modern look with his commissions. In the United Kingdom, Aubrey Beardsley's provocative Art Nouveau style proved influential, even holding sway over US designers such as William H. Bradley and Edward Penfield.

Chéret was responsible for promoting Charles-Émile Reynaud's Théâtre Optique (Optical Theatre) in 1892, but his association with film ended there. It was the lesser known Marcellin Auzolle who designed the poster for the Lumière Brothers' public programme of films in 1895. Across the Atlantic, the promotional material for Thomas Edison's Vitascope shows offered a similar look to Auzolle's design, with an image projected on to a screen that is watched by an audience, albeit more conservative in their response.

Posters prior to the arrival of feature-length films tended to focus on the programme of screenings or the venue itself. Many films were even screened as part of a programme of variety events and so were billed as one element in a larger listing. The establishment of site-specific screening venues, the subsequent arrival of movie palaces, the shift from one- and two-reeler films to features, as well as the emergence of stars all impacted the way films were promoted. Art movements, particularly in the early 20th century, had an immeasurable effect on poster design, as did the growing sophistication of technology and audiences' tastes. A film poster informed audiences what the film was, who was in it – or responsible for it – and conveyed the genre or tone of a film. It would eventually become the dominant form of advertising for cinema. Even with the advent of television and, subsequently, the internet, poster design played an intrinsic role in the cinema experience and reflected cultural tastes around the world.

1890–1895

The gilded age.
The phrase, coined by US writer Mark Twain sums up the United States' ascent in the eyes of the world. But Twain's term also hints at the poverty that lies beneath the glittering facade. Also tarnishing the country's image is the plight of Native Americans, with focus intensifying after the massacre at Wounded Knee in 1890. The prejudice of a nation also shames France following the outrage over the Dreyfus Affair. By the time Auguste and Louis Lumière unveil their ten short films to a paying public at Salon Indien du Grand Café on 28 December 1895, scientists, inventors, innovators and enthusiasts around the world are developing their own form of motion-picture camera and projector. The results of their experiments over the course of the next decade gradually develop the medium and inform a new grammar that turns a sideshow attraction into cinema.

Scottish-American inventor **William Kennedy-Laurie Dickson** completes work on the kinetoscope, the 'motion-picture viewer' or 'peep show' that projects images recorded by the kinetograph, the first celluloid motion-picture camera.

German inventor Max **Skladanowsky** working with his glazier father Carl and brother Emil, unveil their chronophotographic device, which is both a camera and projector.

Théâtre Optique, France
Charles-Émile Reynaud invented the praxinoscope, an improvement on the zoetrope in 1877. He opens the doors of the Théâtre Optique (Optical Theatre) to an ecstatic Parisian audience in October 1892. By the time it closes, eight years later, it has been seen by more than half a million people. Jules Chéret designs the advertising for the show, known as Pantomimes Lumineuses, and which comprises three animated shorts: *Poor Pete* (*Pauvre Pierrot*), *The Clown and His Dogs* (*Le clown et ses chiens*) and *A Good Beer* (*Un bon bock*). It is also notable for the first known usage of film perforations.

1891	1892

The Black Maria, USA

Thomas Edison is the first to realize the potential of a customized space for filming. He builds the Black Maria on the grounds of his laboratory in New Jersey. The studio is covered with tar paper to keep out extraneous light but can be opened via a retractable roof. The first film shot there features three people pretending to be blacksmiths. He unveils the first results of filming there to an audience at the Brooklyn Institute of Arts and Sciences in May 1893.

Italian electrical engineer Guglielmo Marconi conducts the first successful wireless communication.

Cinématographe Lumière, France

In what is the first poster advertising a specific film, audiences here are seen to enjoy the comic moment from the Lumière brothers' *The Sprinkler Sprinkled* (*L'arroseur arrosé*). Illustrated by Marcellin Auzolle, it depicts the gardener being splashed in the face. It is one of the ten films the brothers screen at the first performance on 10 June before a paying public. It is also the first comedy and an early example of a narrative film.

1893 **1895**

2

REVOLUTIONARY IMAGES

Historical timelines focus on key events, yet it is in the details that the complexity of human achievements emerge. By the time French pioneers Auguste and Louis Lumière unveiled their programme of ten short films to a paying audience at the Salon Indien du Grand Café in Paris on 28 December 1895, an army of individuals from around the world were developing moving-image cameras and projectors. But cinema's first decade saw the medium threatened with relegation to little more than a sideshow attraction. Even the Lumières had withdrawn from the business by 1905, returning to the more 'respectable' trade of still photography, believing there could be no future for the moving image.

If its infancy seemed uncertain to some, cinema's future was soon guaranteed not only by the medium's popularity, but by its scope.

In addition to becoming one of the 20th century's principal forms of entertainment, cinema emerged as a major art form. It also proved to be a supremely effective tool for propaganda and the dissemination of political ideology, and a weapon in revolutionary causes. But before reaching this stage, it needed a language with which to speak.

The journey from single-shot films to the complexity of features that appeared after 1912 witnessed the emergence of a grammar that allowed film-makers to collapse space and time. If a selection of the Lumières' audience did really run out of the screening room, fearing they would be run over by a locomotive when *The Arrival of a Train* (*L'arrivée d'un train à La Ciotat*) was screened in January 1896, the introduction of the edit must have confounded some. Cutting between two shots lengthened the amount of footage that

PREVIOUS PAGE. *Raja Harishchandra* (1913), **Dadasaheb Phalke, India**
As acting was not viewed as a suitable profession for women in India, male actors performed the female roles in what was the first full-length Indian feature film.

ABOVE. The Lumière brothers at work, 1892
Visionary French brothers Louis (left) and Auguste (right) Lumière in their laboratory, located in the French city of Lyons.

ABOVE. *The Four Troublesome Heads* (*Un homme de têtes*, 1898), Georges Méliès, France

Former illusionist George Méliès used a variety of camera tricks to create his story of a magician who sings along with three of his own detached heads.

could be screened as one complete film. It allowed for more than one perspective: an action could be followed by a reaction shot. It could even permit for two narratives to play out in parallel. Englishman R. W. Paul presented an early example of the continuity shot with *Come Along, Do!* (1898). It shows a couple outside an art exhibition and then inside it. It assumes an audience knows how the couple found their way in without showing it. US film-maker Edwin S. Porter went further with *Life of an American Fireman* and *The Great Train Robbery* (both 1903), using cross-cutting – cutting between shots – to show action unfolding simultaneously in two places. the various movements of a camera added to the complexity of a sequence.

There was also magic. Frenchman Georges Méliès had long been fascinated with stage magic and had opened his own theatre to present illusion shows by the time he witnessed a screening of the Lumière's films. The brothers refused to sell him a camera, so he travelled to London and purchased one from R. W. Paul. An accident that occurred while filming a street scene revealed to Méliès the potential of the medium to create illusions. Producing more than 500 films over a career that spanned 1896 to 1912, Méliès experimented with multiple exposures, a variety of editing techniques and colour tinting. He was one of the first to use a storyboard to map out his shots, particularly helpful as he appeared in so many of his own films. But beyond his technical innovations and key role in the development of visual and special effects in cinema, Méliès brought wit, playfulness and a sense of mischievousness to his work. His short *The Four Troublesome Heads* (*Un homme de têtes*, 1898) not only highlights his technical dexterity as a film-maker so early in cinema's infancy, Méliès's performance allows viewers to revel in his glee at the possibilities of the medium.

As films grew in popularity, the venues they screened in also developed. Early films were projected in halls, cafés and any venue that could be darkened and had space for an audience. Thomas Edison opened the first dedicated cinema, the Vitascope Theater, a venue in Buffalo, New York in October 1896, but site-specific venues would remain rare for another decade. As the sensation of a new experience wore off and audiences became more familiar with film, screenings would appear as part of an evening's entertainment in theatres and music halls. Audiences were still unused to spending too long watching moving images on a screen, so these films benefited from being part of a mixed programme. However, as they became longer, they required their own venues. In June 1905, businessmen Harry Davis and John P. Harris opened a small venue in a storefront in Pittsburgh, Pennsylvania. Referencing the nickname given to some dime museums – entertainment venues regarded as lowbrow distractions – in the late 19th century, these venues became known as 'nickelodeons'. They screened films on a continuous loop and audiences initially attended not to watch a specific programme, but to be entertained by whatever was screening at the time. The popularity of nickelodeons saw their numbers increase to almost 10,000 venues within five years. They ranged from makeshift operations with little more than a projector, screen and benches, to locations whose capacity ranged from 200 to 1,000 and were accompanied by live music.

The nickelodeons attracted entrepreneurs who saw a gold mine in this nascent entertainment. In 1906, German émigré and future owner of Universal Pictures Carl Laemmle opened his first cinema in Chicago. He was followed in 1907 by Louis B. Mayer, who purchased the Gem theatre in Haverhill, Massachusetts and converted it into the Orpheum theatre. He soon owned the largest chain of nickelodeons in the region. In 1910, Marcus Loew joined forces with future film moguls Adolph Zukor and siblings Joseph and Nicholas Schenck to turn the Loews cinema chain into a major franchise. By 1913, they owned the majority of the venues in New York. At the time, more than a quarter of the US population was attending film screenings every week. Production companies were coalescing into larger conglomerates and films themselves had progressed from one- and two-reelers to features. In 1914, the Mark Strand Theatre on Broadway in New York opened its doors. It seated an audience of 2,989. Five years later, the 4,000-capacity Capitol Theatre also opened on Broadway. Then, in 1927, another New York cinema, the Roxy Theatre, known as the 'Cathedral of the Motion Picture' became the world's largest cinema, holding an audience just shy of 6,000.

Screening venues around the world developed in the same way, albeit on a lesser scale. Their growth, in numbers and size, reflected the growing popularity of film. In Berlin, the Skladanowsky brothers, Max and Emil, beat the Lumières' screening to a paying audience by two months with their motion-picture show at Berlin Wintergarten theatre from 1 November 1895. The Lumières were still ahead of

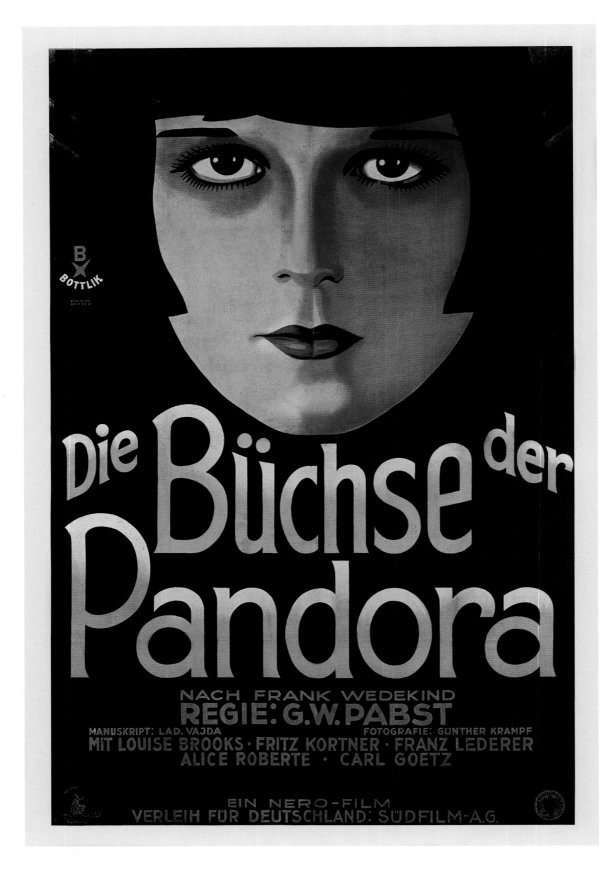

PREVIOUS PAGE. *J'accuse!*
(1919), Abel Gance, France
To attain the realism that Abel
Gance brought to his anti-war
epic, he filmed the battle of
Saint-Mihiel, shooting alongside
soldiers from the US Army.

OPPOSITE. *Pandora's Box* (*Die
Büchse der Pandora*, 1929),
G. W. Pabst, Germany
Although derided at the time
for what was seen as a poor
adaptation of Frank Wedekind's
Lulu (1895–1904) cycle of plays,
G. W. Pabst's film is
now regarded as a defining
work of Weimar cinema.

ABOVE. *Way Down East*
(1920) D. W. Griffith, USA,
D. W. Griffith's romantic drama is
best remembered for its climactic
scenes on an ice floe, with Lillian
Gish and Richard Barthelmess
performing their own stunts.

them with their first screening to any audience, having shown their films on 22 March 1895. The development of larger venues in the city continued apace, with Cines-Palast opening in 1913, which emerged from the First World War (1914–18) as the Ufa-Palast am Zoo and was then rebuilt in 1925 to accommodate more than 2,000 patrons. If the European conflict impeded the construction of cinemas in Europe during the latter part of the 1910s, film remained popular and, like in the United States, became a vast industry during the 1920s.

The progression from shorter films to features signalled a seismic shift on a creative, technological and industrial level. Film-makers such as Giovanni Pastrone, Lois Weber, D. W. Griffith, Erich von Stroheim and Abel Gance added complexity and nuance to the language, as well as pace, tension, and dramatic shifts in tone and scale. It would continue into the 1920s with directors from all around the world such as Charles Chaplin, F. W. Murnau, Fritz Lang, Victor Sjöström, Buster Keaton, Sergei Eisenstein, King Vidor, G. W. Pabst, Dziga Vertov, Marcel L'Herbier and Alfred Hitchcock.

The most significant change to any film industry prior to the surge in feature film production was the geographical shift in the United States from the East to West Coast. For the first fifteen years, the country's film business was mostly based in the east. Edison's film empire was located in New Jersey, where he had his Black Maria production studio and laboratories. But what the West Coast offered film-makers interested in moving out of the confines of the studio environment was a greater variety of landscapes and backdrops. Most important, it offered a plentiful supply of light and a climate perfectly suited to filming outdoors. It also allowed studios to escape the stranglehold of Edison's Motion Picture Patents Company, which was based on the East Coast. It would be easier to avoid legal action for infringing Edison's patents relating to motion-picture cameras.

In 1850, Hollywood was little more than a patch of undeveloped land. In the 1880s, an attempt was made to turn the area into a ranch, with little success. Its proximity to the coast and nearby Los Angeles did give it some cachet for real-estate developers and in 1902 H. J. Whitley, the 'Father of Hollywood', turned a small community into a more lucrative attraction for prospective businesses and property owners. By 1910, Hollywood merged with Los Angeles. *The Count of Monte Cristo* had been completed nearby in 1908, but the production had been started in Chicago, so D. W. Griffith's *In Old California* (1910), shot entirely in the area, holds the title of first Hollywood production. Nestor Motion Picture Company was the first studio to open in 1911. By 1915, the studios were the largest employer in the area. As the studio system created its conveyor belt of stars, celebrity lives, a roster of iconic films and immeasurable wealth, wannabes flocked to Hollywood to seek fame and fortune. It became the epicentre of cinematic entertainment, with directors such as Cecil B. DeMille and D. W. Griffith, inspired by earlier Italian directors, creating cinema on an epic scale. Griffith, ever the innovator, found the perfect balance between innovation and entertainment. The climactic chase scene in *Way Down East* (1920) is set upon an ice floe on a rapidly moving river, which thrilled audiences, posed a logistical challenge for the crew and appears more than a little dangerous for its actors. Filmed in Vermont, a small fire was kept burning beneath the camera to keep the oil from freezing and Griffith did not come away unscathed but suffered frostbite on one side of his face.

However, Hollywood was not the only home of film in the United States. Oscar Micheaux and other African American directors were making films for a black audience. There were few mainstream films made in the United States that featured black actors, and those that did unfortunately did not present them except in terms of lazy stereotypes or in marginal roles. When studios did back a film like King Vidor's *Hallelujah* (1929), which sought to redress this imbalance, it still appeared reductive in its portrayal, no matter how noble the intention behind it.

The United States was not the only national cinema to produced crowd-pleasing movies. But some countries also saw in the medium a way to explore the national psyche. German Expressionism and the subsequent *Neue Sachlichkeit* (New Objectivity) movement – best represented by the films of G. W. Pabst – reflected schisms in German society, while the results of Russian cinema's experiments with Soviet montage theory produced films that challenged the way the world was viewed. Artists from other disciplines saw huge potential in the medium too. Both the Surrealist and Dadaist movements were attracted to it. René Clair collaborated with artists Francis Picabia, Marcel Duchamp and Man Ray, and composer Erik Satie on his short *Entr'acte* (1924). In the same year, Fernand Léger, Dudley Murphy and Man Ray created *Ballet mécanique*. The so-called 'city symphonies' of the 1920s and 1930s presented lyrical portraits of metropolitan life, while artists such as Jean Epstein, Marcel L'Herbier and Jean Cocteau realized their own magical universes. In 1929, Spaniards Salvador Dalí and Luis Buñuel produced *An Andalusian Dog* (*Un chien andalou*), whose use of dream logic in connecting seemingly random scenes, some intended to shock and offend, see it ranked it alongside *Meshes of the Afternoon* (1943) and *Wavelength* (1967) as a landmark in experimental film.

Experimentation also lay at the heart of animation in its early years. The work of J. Stuart Blackton, Émil Cohl, Winsor McCay and Quirino Cristiani laid the ground for future animators. Yet for many audiences, Walt Disney's *Snow White and the Seven Dwarfs* (1937) would have been as groundbreaking as the Lumières' films were for audiences some forty years earlier. Disney's company was a little more than a modest proposal when it released its first feature. In less than a century it became one of the world's largest media and entertainment companies.

The silent era ended with the synthesis of sound and vision on the screen. The introduction of synchronous sound came at the expense of the medium's universality. Before it, films could play anywhere in the world. All that needed to be changed was the language of the intertitles (title cards). Hollywood spied the opportunity to profit from this change and the industry soon dominated global cinema output, relegating local films to their core national audience or to cinemas that specialized in foreign-language film. But this change notwithstanding, the medium continued to grow.

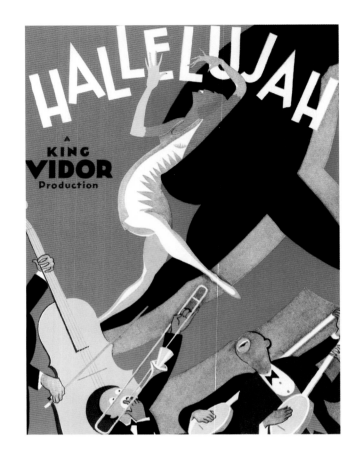

ABOVE. *Hallelujah* (1929), **King Vidor, USA**
A key scene in King Vidor's drama unfolds in a dance hall and has come to be regarded as one of the most authentic representations of the jazz scene from that era.

OPPOSITE. *An Andalusian Dog* (*Un chien andalou*, **1929), Salvador Dalí, Luis Buñuel, France**
A highpoint in Surrealist and experimental film, Salvador Dalí and Luis Buñuel's film is, by turns, irreverent, playful, shocking and inspired in its use of editing to create a stream of consciousness narrative.

UN CHIEN ANDALOU
UN FILM DE
LUIS BUÑUEL
ET
SALVADOR DALI
©1968 LES GRANDS FILMS CLASSIQUES, 16 rue de Boulainvilliers Paris 16e

1895–1900

Fin de siècle. As news spread of the Lumière brothers' success, film pioneers worldwide continue to develop their own means of capturing the moving image. Max Skladanowsky leads the way in Germany with his bioscop, while in the United Kingdom Birt Acres works with his kineopticon and R. W. Paul his theatrograph. The development of projectors and the earliest cinemas continue apace. Thomas Edison conceives of a rudimentary way to merge sound and vision with his kinetoscope and phonograph, while William Kennedy-Laurie Dickson transforms *Annabelle Serpentine Dance* (1895) into a colour film by hand colouring. To commemorate the US Presidential Election of 1896, media magnate William Randolph Hearst, who inspired the protagonist of *Citizen Kane* (1941), employs the technology to project the results on to large white canvas screens that are draped over the front of his buildings in Manhattan and other constructed platforms around the city.

***Exiting the Factory (La sortie de l'usine Lumière à Lyon)*, Louis Lumière, France**

Comprising 800 frames, shot at 16 frames a second and playing for 46 seconds, Louis Lumière's film is the first to be seen by a paying public. (Louis Le Prince's footage shot in Leeds in 1888 preceded Lumière's, but was not publicly screened.) There are three versions of the film, which are distinguished by the appearance or absence of a cart. In two versions it is pulled by either one or two horses, while in the third there is no cart.

The Gaumont Film Company becomes the first of its kind in the world.

1895

The Kiss, William Heise, USA

Stage actors May Irwin and John C. Rice re-enact an intimate moment from the Broadway musical *The Widow Jones* (1895). Filmed at Thomas Edison's Black Maria studio, it is less than 20 seconds long. The actors engage in conversation before their faces touch and the scene culminates in a kiss. Edison likely knew the reaction to the scene – and the publicity – that would ensue over the perceived moral degeneracy of the new medium. The film foresaw the power of cinema in relation to sexuality.

Alice Guy-Blaché, France

Entering the film industry as Léon Gaumont's secretary, Guy-Blaché becomes the first female film director with *The Cabbage Fairy* (*La fée aux choux*, 1896), which is also the first narrative film. A year later, she takes over production at Gaumont, which she runs for a decade. In her last year she directs the studio's largest production *The Life of Christ* (*La vie du Christ*, 1906), which has more than 300 extras. Marrying production manager Herbert Blaché in 1907, the couple move to the United States to oversee Gaumont's New York operations before striking out as independents in 1910.

Pathé Frères is founded by siblings Charles, Émile, Théophile and Jacques Pathé, who transform cinema into an industry in France. By the early 1900s, it is the world's biggest film-equipment and production company.

The Vitagraph Company of America is founded by directors and producers J. Stuart Blackton and Albert E. Smith. Within a decade it would become the most prolific film-production company in the United States.

1896

1897

CAPTURING REALITY

Cinema began with images that recorded everyday life. The first audiences watched single shots, each less than a minute, of moments such as workers leaving a factory. These early examples of documentary were known as actuality films.

Over the course of a decade, actuality films developed into a form reporting on events. In 1908, the French film company Pathé invented the cinema newsreel with the *Pathé-Journal*. The company opened an office in London in 1910 and became an essential news provider, particularly during the First World War (1914–18). British Pathé, as it became known, presented news reports from around the world to cinema audiences until 1970. It was such a recognizable format that Orson Welles incorporated a fictional version of it at the start of *Citizen Kane* (1941).

The development of non-fiction film gathered speed in the 1920s. It played a significant role in defining the concept of Soviet montage theory in post-revolutionary Russia. Dziga Vertov's startling use of editing to present a day in the life of a city in *Man with a Movie Camera* (*Chelovek s kino-apparatom*, 1929) is a landmark in the advancement of film-making technique, a key work in the possibilities of non-fiction narrative film and part of a group of films from this era that presented unique portraits of metropolitan life.

Other 'city symphony' films include *Manhatta* (1921) and *Berlin: Symphony of a Great City* (*Berlin – Die Sinfonie der Grossstadt*, 1927).

Another film-maker, Robert J. Flaherty, also made great strides with a form of ethnographic studies. The most famous of these was *Nanook of the North* (1922). A portrait of an Inuit man living with his family in the Canadian Arctic, Flaherty's film, which was later grouped under the category 'salvage ethnography' was a combination of observational filming and sequences that had been staged by Flaherty with the aim of capturing aspects of Nanook's life. The film was made at a time when the notion of documentary had yet to exist and so the distinction between fiction and factual film-making had not been set.

The first use of the word 'documentary' was by pioneering film-maker John Grierson in a review of Flaherty's later *Moana* (1926), concluding that the film had 'documentary value'. Grierson became a key figure in the development of documentary in the United Kingdom. After his groundbreaking film *Drifters* (1929), about

ABOVE. *Nanook of the North* **(1922), Robert J. Flaherty, USA**
Robert J. Flaherty requested that he film Nanook killing a walrus with a harpoon rather than his rifle, to accentuate the importance of cultural traditions in his daily life.

OPPOSITE. *Harlan County USA* **(1977), Barbara Kopple, USA**
Barbara Kopple and her crew's presence on the frontline of the Kentucky miners' strike was believed to have reduced the amount of violence used by the mining companies.

Britain's North Sea fishing industry, he played a vital role in Britain's GPO Film Unit, which was influential in the 1930s. The unit came under control of the Ministry of Information in the Second World War (1939–45) and was renamed the 'Crown Film Unit'. During this period, film propaganda became more sophisticated, employing factual documentary material to further a specific cause or ideology. At the same time, film-makers such as Humphrey Jennings experimented with the documentary form to startling effect.

In the 1950s and 1960s, the developing technology made film equipment lighter and more mobile, allowing film-makers greater ease of use. *Cinéma vérité*, or 'direct cinema', emerged during this period. Developed by Jean Rouch in France, who was inspired by the work of Vertov, and in the United States by film-makers such as Albert and David Maysles, Richard Leacock and D. A. Pennebaker, it presented a less formal approach

to documentary film-making and aimed at peeling away the veneer of daily life. Simultaneously, film-makers such as Frederick Wiseman pushed the limits of observational film-making, often spending months with a subject in order to capture their lives or work.

Since the 1970s, television has dominated the documentary landscape, while those making documentary films display a range of styles. They run from Barbara Kopple and her crew living with striking miners in Kentucky to capture their travails for *Harlan County USA* (1976) and Errol Morris's controversial use of re-enactment for *The Thin Blue Line* (1988) to Nick Broomfield's documentary portraits in which he is as much sometimes a subject as the people he profiles, to Michael Moore's *Fahrenheit 9/11* (2004), a subjective assessment of George W. Bush's administration, which became documentary cinema's first blockbuster box-office success.

1901–1905

A new century. Britain's longest-reigning monarch Queen Victoria dies in 1901. She witnessed the massive expansion of her country's empire, an industrial revolution that transformed the world and technological innovations in almost every aspect of daily life. Her successors would see a world rapidly transformed by suffrage, conflict and revolution. The Russian monarchy gradually accepts a changing world. But not quickly enough. The country is attacked in the East by Japan and from inside by a rising political movement. Future leader Joseph Stalin's escape from a Siberian gulag and return to his native Georgia to stir up political activity draws the attention of Vladimir Lenin, who is exiled in Switzerland. The rebellion aboard the battleship *Potemkin* outside the then Russian port of Odessa in 1905 proves a pivotal moment in deciding the fate of Tsar Nicholas II.

Scrooge; or Marley's Ghost, Walter R. Booth, UK

Produced by British film pioneer R. W. Paul and shot at his Animatograph Works, the first British film studio, in north London, this 5-minute film is the first adaptation of Charles Dickens's beloved novella *A Christmas Carol* (1843). Presented in twelve tableaux, or scenes, it features special effects – particularly the impressive superimposition of Marley's face over a door knocker – as well as one of the first uses of a dissolve between scenes rather than a straightforward cut. It is the first film to employ intertitles.

Ferdinand Zecca's *History of a Crime* (*Histoire d'un crime*) is one of the first films to feature a flashback.

The Great Train Robbery, Edwin S. Porter, USA

Shot on location, employing composite editing (intercutting more than one narrative) and exploring the possibilities of cross-cutting, Edwin S. Porter's *The Great Train Robbery* is a landmark in the development of narrative cinema. The final shot of the film, in which one of the killed robbers appears before the audience, aims a gun at them and fires, is an early example of breaking the fourth wall – the invisible divide between the fiction of the drama and the audience.

1901

1903

○ **_Rescued by Rover_, Cecil M. Hepworth and Lewin Fitzhamon, UK**

The most narratively complex film produced to date, _Rescued by Rover_ is an early example of continuity editing. The shots are edited in a way to give audiences a sense of the space of the world the action unfolds in. It presumes an audience's understanding of action that takes place off screen, allowing for the collapse of time – a journey taking a moment when in reality it would take longer. Cecil M. Hepworth and Lewin Fitzhamon also make use of lighting to affect the tone or tension in a scene.

The Wright brothers, Orville and Wilbur, achieve the first engine-powered air flight near Kitty Hawk, North Carolina.

Marcus Loew founds his theatre chain in Cincinnati, Ohio.

William Fox opens his first nickelodeon in Brooklyn, New York.

The Manaki brothers – Yanaki and Milton – become the Balkans' first film-makers.

Entertainment industry bible _Variety_ is launched by Sime Silverman in New York.

Alfred Stieglitz and Edward Steichen open what will become known as the 291 photography gallery on New York's Fifth Avenue.

1904 **1905**

MAGICAL CINEMA

The first film-makers soon saw the potential to transform the everyday into a place of wonder. From the earliest visual conjuring through to the creation of worlds with computer-generated imagery, the only limit to what can be created lies with the imagination.

OPPOSITE. *A Trip to the Moon* (*Le voyage dans la lune*, 1902), Georges Méliès, France
George Méliès's most celebrated film blends special effects, such as steam escaping from the moon's craters, with visual effects and animation to create a 14-minute masterpiece.

LEFT. *The Wizard of Oz* (1939), Victor Fleming, USA
This popular film presented audiences with a resplendent Technicolor fantasy whose state-of-the-art visuals still employed some of the techniques used earlier by Méliès.

The manipulation of images can be traced to photographic experiments in the 18th century. Multiple exposure of one frame or overlaying a number of negatives to create a single image were early examples, employed by pioneers such as British Pictorialist photographers Oscar Rejlander and Henry Peach Robinson. US film-maker Alfred Clark was one of the first to cut two pieces of film together to create a desired effect, for *The Execution of Mary, Queen of Scots* (1895). At the moment of the Scottish queen's beheading, Clark stopped filming, kept everyone stationary save for the actor playing Mary, whom he replaced with a dummy, and started shooting again. In the resulting film, the beheading is remarkably convincing.

Clark's film, with its use of a dummy, employs a special effect – the term given to physical effects used during filming. Effects that are achieved through the manipulation of film or, more recently, the use of computer programs, are known as visual effects. Most films that require effects will generally employ both, as was the case with the first wizard of cinema, Georges Méliès. The prolific French film-maker apparently stumbled upon his first effect when the film in his camera momentarily jammed while filming a street scene. On projecting the film, he saw that a van suddenly transformed into a hearse, pedestrians instantaneously changed direction and women became men. This accident resulted in Méliès's increasingly ambitious series of short films, playing cinematic tricks to audiences and creating the largest early body of visual and special effects sequences.

The next two decades saw improvements in the use of effects such as matte paintings – the creation of backdrops that give a sense of another world or a vast space – particularly through the work of US director Norman Dawn, who was also responsible for the earliest use of rear projection in films. In Germany, Eugen Schüfftan created a process that allowed actors to appear in scale on miniature sets through the use of mirrors. Known as the Schüfftan process, it was developed for Austrian director Fritz Lang's *Metropolis* (1927). The optical printer, a projector connected to a camera, which was originally used to produce multiple copies of a film, was developed by US special-effects pioneer Linwood G. Dunn and eliminated the need for effects to be produced in-camera. His work, alongside matte painters and stop-motion animators, achieved the effects produced in *King Kong* (1933). He also worked with US film-maker Orson Welles and US cinematographer Gregg Toland to achieve some of the deep focus shots for *Citizen Kane* (1941).

Colour brought its own challenges. Chromakey compositing followed in the 1940s, which used a blue screen background to allow one shot of a character to be superimposed over another. It was pioneered by Dunn in the 1930s, but primarily used for screen-wipe effects in films. US special-effects artist, Lawrence 'Larry' W. Butler displayed its potential with the magic carpet sequence in *The Thief of Bagdad* (1941). That film was co-directed by British film-maker Michael Powell, who would make the most of visual-effects technology for his acclaimed ballet sequence in *The Red Shoes* (1948).

Visual and special effects over the next few decades added enhancements to this technology. However, the appearance of digital technology in the 1980s transformed the cinematic landscape. Canadian film-maker James Cameron's *The Abyss* (1989) pushed the boundary of what could be achieved with computer-generated imagery (CGI), which he then took further with *Terminator 2: Judgment Day* (1992), while US film-maker Steven Spielberg merged animatronics with CGI for *Jurassic Park* (1993). The astonishing technological advances that produced the first-ever computer-animated feature film, Pixar's *Toy Story* (1995), would eventually erase the line between live action and animation.

1906–1910

Birth of an industry. The film industry emerges out of a disparate collection of small film companies. Thomas Edison leads the way in 1908 by forming the industry cartel the Motion Picture Patents Company, which vertically integrates production, distribution and exhibition of films. It is a model that US studios will follow until prevented by law in the late 1940s. A similar structure is intended for European film production by the Paris Film Congress when it meets in 1909. But its aim is undermined by US interests. D. W. Griffith enters the film industry in 1908, first as an actor and then as a director for the American Mutoscope and Biograph Company. In 1910, he shoots *Old California*, one of the first films made in Hollywood. The same year, Hollywood is consolidated with the city of Los Angeles and soon after witnesses the migration of almost every major US studio to it.

The Story of the Kelly Gang, Charles Tait, Australia

Premiering at Melbourne's Athenaeum Hall on 26 December 1906 and running at just over an hour, theatrical entrepreneur Charles Tait's retelling of the Australian outlaw Ned Kelly's exploits becomes the world's first feature film. All complete versions of the film would eventually be lost. It is the best example of the popular bushranger genre. Tait's film is followed by Michel Carré's *The Prodigal Son* (*L'enfant prodigue*, 1907), the first European feature film, and J. Stuart Blackton's *Les Misérables* (1909), the first US feature.

Alfred Dreyfus is exonerated of treason, ending a shameful episode in modern French history.

1906

Fantasmagorie, Émile Cohl, France

Émile Cohl begins his career as a mentee to cartoonist and satirist André Gill. He enters the film industry in 1907 as a way of supplementing his income. Initially hired as a scenarist, the success of Blackton's *The Haunted Hotel* (1907) results in Cohl's commission to create an animated film. Following a stick man's various encounters and occasionally featuring live action of the animator's hand, drawing the animated images, *Fantasmagorie* is immensely popular.

Max Linder, France

A star of French theatre, Max Linder first appears on film in a short for Pathé in 1905. He quickly becomes a leading actor, playing a debonair, man-about-town character. His screen persona 'Max' is cemented with his appearance in the comedy *The Skater's Debut* (1907). Displaying traits that would later influence Charles Chaplin's tramp character, Linder becomes a favourite with audiences and the first film star. He moves to the United States in 1916, but fails to repeat his success. He returns to Paris and in 1925 commits suicide.

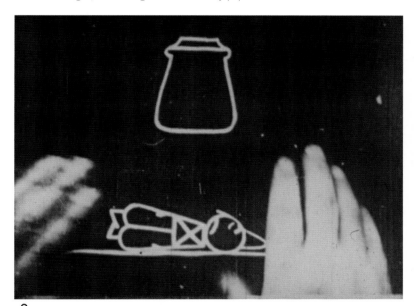

Guglielmo Marconi initiates transatlantic radio communications between Ireland and Nova Scotia.

Gilbert M. 'Broncho Billy' Anderson – soon to become the first Western film star – directs *Mr Flip*, the first movie to feature a pie in the face, a staple of future comedy films.

The Ballet Russes performs for the first time, under the directorship of Sergei Diaghilev and featuring Vaslav Nijinsky.

Pablo Picasso and Georges Braque create the first works of Analytical Cubism.

Frankenstein is one of the first horror films ever made. J. Searle Dawley directs the adaptation of Mary Shelley's novel of 1818 for Edison Studios.

1907   1908   1909   1910

1911–1912

The hubris of humankind. The rapid advances of the industrial revolution and more recent leaps in technological innovation come to symbolize the superiority of humankind in the world. But such achievements prove powerless in the face of nature. The success of Roald Amundsen's expedition to the South Pole in December 1911 appears less triumphant in the aftermath of the failure of the *Terra Nova* Expedition led by Robert Falcon Scott. The wrecking of the RMS *Lusitania* off South Africa's Cape Point in April 1911 presages the sinking of the RMS *Titanic* a year later, after it collides with an iceberg in North Atlantic Ocean and results in the loss of almost three-quarters of its passengers and crew. The 710 survivors arrive in New York three days later aboard the RMS *Carpathia*.

Svetozar Botorić directs the first Balkan feature *Karadjordje*.

Defence of Sevastopol (*Oborona Sevastopolya*) is the first Russian feature film, directed by Aleksandr Khanzhonkov and Vasili Goncharov.

The first Italian feature, *Dante's Inferno* (*L'Inferno*), is directed by Francesco Bertolini, Adolfo Padovan and Giuseppe de Liguoro.

Der Blaue Reiter (The Blue Rider) art group unveils its first exhibition, at the Moderne Galerie in Munich.

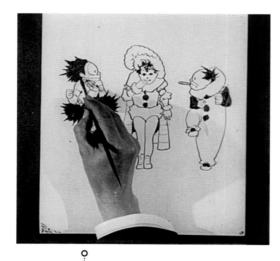

Little Nemo, **Winsor McCay, USA**
In 1905, artist Winsor McCay creates his most famous comic character Little Nemo, as a full-page strip in the Sunday edition of the *New York Herald*. The following year, his son introduces him to a flip book and McCay develops an idea for an animated film. The resulting short comprises of 4,000 drawings on rice paper that are then photographed by J. Stuart Blackton at the Vitagraph Studios in Brooklyn. What sets McCay's film apart is the level of detail McCay brings to each drawing.

1911

**The Musketeers of Pig Alley,
D. W. Griffith, USA**

Film-maker D. W. Griffith's reputation as an innovator is already high. He is one of the first directors to employ a close-up, in *The Lonedale Operator* (1911). *The Musketeers of Pig Alley* is one of the first gangster dramas. With it, Griffith pioneers the use of follow focus, a device that allows for easier manual focusing by the focus puller, a key assistant to the camera operator and cinematographer.

Universal Pictures is formed when entrepreneurial cinema owner and director of Independent Moving Pictures Carl Laemmle joins forces with Powers Motion Picture Company, Champion Film Company, Rex Motion Picture Company, Nestor Film Company and New York Motion Picture Company.

Photoplay, USA

Fan-based movie magazine *Photoplay* was not the first of its kind. Stuart J. Blackton brings *Motion Picture Magazine* out at the beginning of 1911. *Photoplay* is initially little more than a promotional tool for films, but it soon develops into the leading fan magazine for cinema entertainment in the United States. Throughout the 1920s and 1930s it is considered hugely influential. It set the template for the celebrity-oriented magazines that followed. The Photoplay Magazine Medal, introduced in 1921, provides a model for the Academy Awards.

1912

THE RISE OF THE FILM STAR

Cinema regarded the promotion of stars a way of attracting audiences. As the medium developed into a vast industry, it streamlined the process to produce stars whose screen appeal met the demands and desires of the audiences who paid to see them.

In the first decade of cinema, actors remained mostly anonymous. The shock of the new and exciting storylines were enough to sate most cinemagoers' appetites. But as the medium entered its second decade, it became clear that certain actors were attracting a following. Canadian-American actor Florence Lawrence was acknowledged for a long time as the first 'name' star. Her work at Biograph Studios, often under the direction of D. W. Griffith, earned her the moniker the 'Biograph Girl'. She then moved to the Independent Moving Pictures Company whose owner Carl Laemmle was looking for a 'star'. Before he released their first film together, Laemmle arranged a publicity stunt announcing that his new star had been run over and killed by a streetcar. However, Laemmle then placed advertisements in newspapers saying 'We nail a lie', proclaiming that Lawrence was still alive and would appear in his next production *The Broken Oath* (1910). The stunt worked and Lawrence's fame was sealed.

Recent research has shown that Max Linder had made a name for himself in France before Lawrence's ascendancy. His series of comedy shorts in which he embodied a debonair character made him a popular presence on French screens. His cinematic alter-ego would influence Charles Chaplin's development of his tramp persona. Had Linder travelled to Hollywood soon after achieving fame, he might have established himself as a star there. But by the time he made his way to the United States many studios already had their comedy stars and Linder's fame ebbed.

Chaplin, Mary Pickford and Douglas Fairbanks represented the most powerful stars in Hollywood at the dawn of the 1920s and their joining D. W. Griffith to form the studio United Artists was evidence of their influence. But as the major Hollywood studios grew in size and power, they exerted increasing control over stars, the films they appeared in and even their private lives, to ensure that audiences only ever saw the image of the stars the studios wanted portrayed.

BELOW. *The Goddess* (*Shen nu*, 1934), Yonggang Wu, China
Echoing the 'fallen woman' trope, this was one of the final and most acclaimed roles for Ruan Lingyu – known as the 'Garbo of the Orient'.

The most popular actors were not just the leads in films, they become an investment for studios and represented a lifestyle that could be sold to audiences; their charisma and charm could power a film to huge commercial success, anchoring the revenue of an entire industry.

The impact stars had on the lives of audiences and fans could be significant. When Italian actor Rudolph Valentino died in 1926 at just thirty-one years old, his funeral procession through New York was witnessed by more than 100,000 onlookers. Such fervour was not just limited to Hollywood. In China, the actor Ruan Lingyu was a hugely popular screen presence. Her role in *Spring Dream of an Old Capital* (*Gudu chun-meng*, 1930) made her a star at the age of twenty. But in 1935, at the age of twenty-four

and following extensive media intrusion, she committed suicide. Her funeral procession was reported to have been 4.8 km (3 miles) long, with even *The New York Times* referring to it as 'the most spectacular funeral of the century'.

In Hollywood in the 1950s, certain stars began to use their popularity and box-office draw to gain more power and independence. As the studio system weakened, the role of agents became pivotal in shifting the balance of power towards their clients. This accelerated in the 1980s, with many stars employing a small industry of agents, managers and even production companies to identify projects that would serve to develop their careers and ensure their fans and audiences in general kept returning to see them on the screen.

BELOW RIGHT. Studio portrait of Florence Lawrence (1908), USA
The first star of US cinema is seen here in a publicity shot taken by Frank C. Bangs, a former actor and noted Broadway photographer whose work with film stars became the model for early Hollywood portraiture.

1913–1914

War ahead. The Ottoman Empire is losing grip on its territories and various skirmishes across Europe underpin a growing sense of unease between nations. Commenting on the build-up of arms by nations, London's *The Daily Chronicle* notes: 'It requires no gift of prophecy to foretell that this mad competition in military expenditure will end in disaster.' Focus is centred on the Balkans. On 28 June 1914, while inspecting forces in Sarajevo, Archduke Franz Ferdinand of Austria, the heir to the Habsburg Empire, is assassinated by nineteen-year-old Serbian nationalist Gavrilo Princip. A series of crisis talks unfold in the corridors of European power. On 28 July, Austria-Hungary declares war on Serbia. In just over a month, Europe and countries surrounding the continent are at war. Shortly after, the United States declares itself a neutral player.

Raja Harishchandra, **Dadasaheb Phalke, India**

Inspired by Alice Guy-Blaché's *The Life of Christ* (*La vie du Christ*, 1906) former printer Dadasaheb Phalke sets up his own production company. He makes a trip to London, where he meets Cecil Hepworth, receives a introduction to the film-making process and purchases filming equipment. His ambition is to tell the story of Harishchandra, the legendary Indian king of the Ikshvaku dynasty, who appears in classical Indian texts. It becomes India's first feature film and is met with positive reviews and modest commercial success.

Suffragette Emily Davison throws herself in front of King George V's horse Anmer at the Royal Derby in Epsom and dies four days later.

Igor Stravinsky's ballet *The Rite of Spring* premieres at Paris's Théâtre des Champs-Élysées and causes a riot by an outraged audience.

Charles Chaplin begins making films with Mack Sennett at Keystone Studios in California. His first film is *Making a Living*.

1913

Lois Weber, USA

An innovator whose role in the development of film language has been underappreciated, Lois Weber is the first US woman to direct a feature-length film, *The Merchant of Venice* (1914). At the height of her career she is involved in most aspects of production and possesses a cinematic vision second only to D. W. Griffith during the 1910s. Producing hundreds of films, she introduces significant innovations, such as pioneering the split screen, as seen in her drama *Suspense* (1913).

Les vampires, Louis Feuillade, France

Louis Feuillade directs more than 700 films in twenty years. A journalist with literary aspirations, he submits scripts to Gaumont to supplement his income. By 1906, he is directing films. His early years were dominated by comedies, but he establishes his reputation with crime tales. In particular, his serials *Fantômas* (1913–14), *Les vampires* (1915–16) and *Judex* (1916) are a success. Feuillade not only thrills audiences with his tales of master criminals and vengeful phantoms, his visual style influences future directors of the genre, such as Fritz Lang and Alfred Hitchcock.

Giovanni Pastrone's *Cabiria* is released and its innovative use of moving camera and epic scope influences the subsequent work of D. W. Griffith and Cecil B. DeMille.

Babe Ruth makes his debut for the Boston Red Sox baseball team.

1914

1915–1916

The cost of war. Over two decisive years, and across all battle fronts and occupied territories, millions perish as a result of conflict, famine and illness. Allied forces suffer huge losses at Gallipoli, against a Turkish army led by the country's future leader Mustafa Kemal Atatürk. The death toll from the battles of Verdun and the Somme run into the hundreds of thousands on both sides. Divisions between Turkish and Armenian troops result in the demotion of the latter under Turkish command and, eventually, the state-ordered genocide of the Armenian population. Britain tests an early prototype of a tank, while German Zeppelin airships carry out bombing raids on London. In response to the escalation of conflict, D. W. Griffith releases his pacifist epic *Intolerance: Love's Struggle Through the Ages* (1916), which is seen by some as penitence for the racist tone of his previous feature *The Birth of a Nation*.

Franz Kafka publishes his novella *The Metamorphosis* (*Die Verwandlung*).

Japanese actor Sessue Hayakawa becomes a heart-throb and matinee idol following his performance in the box-office hit *The Cheat*.

○ *The Birth of a Nation*, **D. W. Griffith, USA**
D. W. Griffith's revisionist epic opens to commercial success. Showcasing the film-maker's radical strides in technical innovation it sets the standard for what will become the classical Hollywood style. But the film's heroic portrayal of the Ku Klux Klan, racist stereotyping of African Americans and radical alteration of history attracts controversy. It is seen as responsible for the resurgence of a near-moribund Klan and the burning crucifix, a fiction created for the film, becomes a symbol of power for white supremacists.

1915

The Tramp, Charles Chaplin, USA

Uncredited as director, Charles Chaplin's short, his sixth for Essanay, introduced the iconic character he is forever associated with. Chaplin had played a variation of the character in the Mack Sennett productions *Mabel's Strange Predicament* and *Kid Auto Races at Venice* (both 1914). His roles in both those films were played solely for comedy, whereas in *The Tramp* Chaplin introduces a sentimental, bittersweet side to the character. He will continue to play the role until *Modern Times* (1936).

Mary Pickford, USA

'America's Sweetheart' Mary Pickford makes a swift ascent after entering the film industry. Her popularity at a time when actors' names were not featured on billboards found her described as the 'Biograph Girl', named after the company producing her films. A stint at Universal Pictures and on Broadway is followed by a contract with Adolph Zukor and what would become Paramount Pictures. That move sees her earn the largest salary of any star in Hollywood when in 1916, Pickford signs a new contract with Zukor.

The Easter Uprising in Dublin is quashed, with many of the republican ringleaders executed.

***The Battle of the Somme* documentary**, shot by Geoffrey Malins and John McDowell, is an early example of film propaganda and is seen by a British audience of more than twenty million people in its first six weeks of release.

1916

THE CINEMA OF SPECTACLE

As films increased in length, they grew in scale. Stories from the Bible and events in history became the source for the cinematic spectacle, sweeping dramas that employed casts of thousands and required the construction of sets that resembled small cities.

The popularity of epics has fluctuated over the decades, but whenever cinema has been threatened, they have returned to prove that nothing compares to the big screen when it comes to scale. The earliest spectaculars came from Italy. Enrico Guazzoni's *Quo Vadis?* (1913) was one of the first, employing a cast of more than 5,000 extras. It represents a pattern that has become familiar in cinema – if it works, remake it. Having already featured as the source for Lucien Nonguet and Ferdinand Zecca's short of 1901, Henryk Sienkiewicz's novel of 1896 was adapted into another pre-sound version in 1924 and then for Mervyn LeRoy's large-scale Hollywood production in 1951.

Guazzoni's film was followed by Giovanni Pastrone's even more audacious *Cabiria* (1914), which influenced Cecil B. DeMille and D. W. Griffith, as shown by the similarity of the latter's set designs for the Babylon sequences of his epic *Intolerance: Love's Struggle Throughout the Ages* (1916). If these directors were most closely associated with the Hollywood epics of the 1920s – and DeMille would return to the epic in the late 1940s and 1950s – their counterparts in Europe were Abel Gance in France and Fritz Lang in Germany.

Although epic cinema is primarily recognized for presenting certain tropes, it can be widened to encompass a variety of genres. It would be difficult not to regard *Gone with the Wind* (1939) as anything but an epic. Likewise, the vastness of Italian film-maker Sergio Leone's sprawling *Once Upon a Time in the West* (*C'era una volta il West*, 1968) is equalling deserving of the term. But US film-maker George Steven's modern-day *Giant* (1956) also evinces an epic quality, while the weighty themes

and visual majesty of US director Paul Thomas Anderson's *There Will Be Blood* (2007) might also be regarded as an epic.

Viewed in more classical terms, drawing on biblical or historical events, the epic remained relatively quiet for the first two decades of sound cinema. The threat of television saw it return, with some films playing out on an even larger scale. If many of the films from this era harked back to the silent era, particularly DeMille's second version of *The Ten Commandments* (1956) and German-Swiss film-maker William Wyler's *Ben-Hur* (1959), some directors saw in the epic an opportunity to contrast a study of humanity within the large perspective of history. British film-maker David Lean achieved this with *Lawrence of Arabia* (1962), contrasting the battles T. E. Lawrence engaged in during the First World War (1914–18) with more intimate moments that attempted to understand the man and the inner conflicts that drove him. US film-maker Stanley Kubrick also employed these

contrasting perspectives in his First World War drama *Paths of Glory* (1957), the Roman drama *Spartacus* (1960) – his most classically epic film – and his later Irish historical drama *Barry Lyndon* (1975). However, it was with his oblique exploration of outer space *2001: A Space Odyssey* (1968) that Kubrick took the epic, whose key component is traditionally the concrete presentation of past events, and turned it inside out in order to engage with the question of who humans are.

Advances in technology have allowed film-makers to create worlds that no longer require a cast of thousands or the construction of vast edifices. British film-maker Ridley Scott's *Gladiator* (2000) might best epitomize the modern epic, whose scale is achieved through a combination of physical construction and visual effects. Almost all modern epics are achieved by this process, from the fantasy worlds of *Harry Potter* and J. R. R. Tolkien to the most recent biblical dramas.

1917–1918

Peace in sight. German antagonism towards the United States, through their aggressive strategies in international waters and attempts to draw Mexico into conflict with their neighbour, finally see the previously neutral state enter the war on the side of the Allies. Following the abdication of Tsar Nicholas II of Russia, Vladimir Lenin arrives from Switzerland to rally the masses against the state and its involvement in the war. Bolsheviks gain ground in elections as the Allies attempt to ensure Russia keeps the Eastern Front open against the Germans. But Lenin's ascension and the signing of the Treaty of Brest-Litovsk removes the Soviet government from the war. Nevertheless, with US involvement, the German alliance falls apart and the war ends on 11 November 1918. With it, the map of Europe is changed and the empires that ruled the majority of the world at the beginning of the 20th century either crumble or reveal fissures that will eventually see their demise.

Thomas Edison's monopoly over the film industry is broken when the US Supreme Court rules against his Motion Picture Patents Company over copyright infringement by Universal Film Manufacturing Company. It disbands the following year.

German film company Universum Film-AG (UƒA), which will prove to be a dominant force in the 1920s, is founded in Berlin.

The Apostle (*El Apóstol*) directed by Argentinian Quirino Cristiani becomes the world's first feature-length animated film.

The Butcher Boy, **Roscoe Arbuckle, USA**
Roscoe 'Fatty' Arbuckle became a star in Mack Sennett's Keystone Cops comedies before he turned to directing himself in comedies. Arbuckle also saw talent in others. Buster Keaton meets Arbuckle shortly before *The Butcher Boy* begins shooting. It is the first of the director-star's comedies for the Comique Film Corporation and he casts Keaton as one of the customers in a general store. The newcomer shoot his scenes in one take and Arbuckle hires him as an actor and gag writer.

Thaïs, **Anton Giulio Bragaglia, Italy**
Although the Futurist film movement never quite takes off in the way that German Expressionism does in the post-war era, in terms of visual style it is no less radical. With an ostensibly conventional plot, featuring Thaïs Galitzy's predatory countess seducing married men until tragedy ultimately destroys her, Anton Giulio Bragaglia's film dazzles. Futurist artist Enrico Prampolini's wildly imaginative set designs will influence the look of German Expressionist films.

1917

Eyvind of the Hills (Berg-Ejvind och hans hustru), Victor Sjöström, Sweden

A driving force during the golden age of Swedish cinema in the 1920s, Victor Sjöström garners praise with his imaginative horror film *The Phantom Carriage* (*Körkarlen*, 1921) and US dramas such as *The Wind* (1928). Based on a play of 1911 by Jóhann Sigurjónsson, *Eyvind of the Hills* tells the story of 18th-century Icelandic outlaw. Shot over the course of spring and summer in Sweden, it is notable for its portrayal of the natural world.

The Spanish flu makes its way around the world, affecting approximately a quarter of the world's population. The pandemic kills millions.

Warner Bros releases its first feature film, *My Four Years in Germany*, a fictional account of James W. Gerard's experiences as US ambassador to Germany in the lead up to his country's entry into the First World War.

1918

1919–1920

A divided Europe. Thirty-two nations involved in the First World War (1914–18) convene in Paris to discuss reparations and the future of the continent. The Central Powers of Austria-Hungary, Germany, Bulgaria and the Ottoman Empire are not invited. The subsequent Treaty of Versailles proves crippling to the German economy and is seen by some to sow the seeds of fervent nationalism and encourage the popularity of the Nazi Party. Also absent is the Russian Soviet Federative Socialist Republic, which had signed a peace treaty with the Central Powers in 1918. It is still fighting a war with internal forces opposed to Bolshevik rule and other countries that either border the communist state or fear it represents a threat to international stability. Germany and the soon-to-be Soviet Union's woes notwithstanding, both countries lead the way in furthering film as an art form over the course of the next decade and developing cinema as a perfect tool for propaganda.

The Homesteader, Oscar Micheaux, USA

Oscar Micheaux's adaptation of his novel of 1917 is the first race film made by African Americans for an African American audience. He hires Charles Lucas and two actors from the Lafayette Players Stock Company, Evelyn Preer and Iris Hall, to play his leads. The film is a success and establishes Micheaux as the leading black film-maker of his time. He remains outside the mainstream of the almost entirely white industry, which allows his work to avoid lazy stereotyping.

The US Congress passes the 18th Amendment in January, which prohibits alcoholic beverages.

The 19th Amendment that makes it illegal to deny women the right to vote, is passed six months later.

New York's Capitol Theatre opens. It is the largest cinema in the world with 4,000 seats.

1919

United Artists, USA

By 1919, Charles Chaplin, Mary Pickford and Douglas Fairbanks (left) are huge stars, and D. W. Griffith (right) is one of Hollywood's most respected film-makers. Chaplin struggles to get his new feature made with First National Pictures, while Pickford and Fairbanks's contracts with their studios are expiring. Griffith, meanwhile, is moving between studios. Realizing their potential as a combined force, on 5 February the four incorporate United Artists. Although the shared interest in the company lasts just four years, United Artists creates the model for future star-producers seeking independence from studios.

The Miracle Man, George Loane Tucker, USA

George Loane Tucker's film establishes Lon Chaney as the most chameleon-like actor of pre-sound cinema. Tucker's feature debut *Traffic in Souls* (1913) was one of the first films to feature innovative use of camera movement. He would complete one more film, *Ladies Must Live* (1921), before his untimely death at the age of forty-nine.

Ireland proclaims independence from the United Kingdom. The Irish Republican Army commences its war of independence against British Forces in Northern Ireland.

Adolf Hitler gives one of his first public addresses to an audience in Munich, outlining his twenty-five point Nazi Party programme.

1920

GERMAN EXPRESSIONISM

Part of a wider art form prevalent in northern and central Europe at the outset of the 20th century, German Expressionist cinema sought to explore characters' damaged psyches – and by extension a nation in a state of disarray – through the way they perceived the physical world.

The First World War (1914–18) had separated Germany politically, socially and creatively from its neighbours. From 1916 to the end of 1920, there was a ban on all imports, which prevented foreign films from screening domestically. It resulted in a large group of German film-makers striking out on a singular path. Expressionism was harder to define than other cultural movements that preceded it, but the film-makers who embraced it drew upon the full panoply of its influence, from visual and performance art to design and architecture. They also drew on pioneering work in psychoanalysis. The films they made did not just explore their characters' torment, but a nation torn apart – physically and psychologically, as well as politically and socially – by war.

Stellan Rye and Paul Wegener's *The Student of Prague* (*Der Student von Prag*, 1913) offers an early example of what was to come. The tale of a sorcerer who tricks a student (Wegener) and steals his mirror image to produce a *doppelgänger*, Germany's first art film balanced the unsettling thrills of horror with deep-seated concerns over national identity as Europe headed towards an era of great change. *The Golem* (*Der Golem*) followed in 1915. Directed by Wegener, it continued to explore the possibilities of cinema, but the film-maker would more fully realize his vision with his remake *The Golem: How He Came into the World* (*Der*

OPPOSITE. *The Cabinet of Dr Caligari (Das Cabinet des Dr Caligari*, 1920), **Robert Weine, Germany**
The town where Caligari's somnambulist wreaks havoc is less an Alpine idyll than a projection of one insane man's most dreaded fears.

LEFT. *Nosferatu (Nosferatu, eine Symphonie des Grauens*, 1922), **F. W. Murnau, Germany**
The fear induced by Max Schreck's strange misshapen monster is accentuated by F. W. Murnau's employing his shadow as no less a terrifying presence in the film.

Golem, wie er in die Welt kam) in 1920. That was also the year that signalled the arrival of German Expressionism as a powerful creative force in cinema and was best exemplified by Robert Weine's *The Cabinet of Dr Caligari (Das Cabinet des Dr Caligari*).

Weine's film uses the framing device of a patient in a psychiatric institute telling the story of a mad hypnotist who controls a somnambulist and uses him to commit murders. Screenwriters Carl Mayer and Hans Janowitz were both pacifists in the First World War and the film is an examination of authority and unchecked power. Weine employs a wildly imaginative style to conjure up the world the patient describes. The sets featured oddly angled buildings and uneven surfaces, while the cinematography accentuated the contrast between light and shadow. Weine even had the set painted with additional 'shadows' to accentuate the chiaroscuro effect. The movements of Conrad Veidt's somnambulist were choreographed to heighten the otherworldliness of the character.

The film was followed in the same year by Wegener's *Golem* and Karl Heinz Martin's *From Morn to Midnight (Von morgens bis mitternachts*). Fritz Lang drew on German Expressionism for his fable-like *Destiny (Der müde Tod*, 1921) and would feature elements of it in later films, particularly *Metropolis* (1927) and *M (Eine Stadt sucht einen Mörder*, 1931). F. W. Murnau created one of the most noted Expressionist films with *Nosferatu (Nosferatu, eine Symphonie des Grauens*, 1922). His use of shadow to instil fear in audiences would become a staple of horror films. With his first Hollywood film *Sunrise: A Song of Two Humans* (1927), Murnau drew heavily on the mood associated with German Expressionist cinema.

The influence of the films upon the international film-making community was twofold. Directors such as Alfred Hitchcock embraced the style immediately. He visited Murnau on set in 1924 and his films, from *The Lodger: A Story of the London Fog* (1927) through to *Psycho* (1960), highlights its effect upon him. But the emigration of so many film-makers and technicians following the rise to power of the Nazis saw the people responsible for the creation of German Expressionism working in a variety of national cinemas. The impact was felt strongly in Hollywood, first in the horror films of the 1930s and then with film noir in the following decade.

1921–1922

Life and laughs. As Vladimir Lenin consolidates control over Russia and fends off attacks from the White Army and its international supporters, the theorist and film-maker Lev Kuleshov oversees a new generation of ideologically minded students at the Moscow Film School. They include Sergei Eisenstein and Vsevolod Pudovkin, whose work promotes the Soviet worldview. It is a stark contrast to Hollywood output, which is dominated by its comedy stars. Charles Chaplin makes the transition from short comedies to features with *The Kid* and is second only to *The Four Horsemen of the Apocalypse* at the US box office for 1921. Harold Lloyd, who like Chaplin develops his own unique comic persona, had experimented with test screenings – showing initial versions of a film to an audience in order to gauge whether they work. It pays dividends with *A Sailor-Made Man* (1921), which is intended to be a two-reeler but is instead turned into a successful feature. It is a practice that studios continue to use.

The Sheik, George Melford, USA

This was a watershed year for Rudolph Valentino. Cast mostly as a gangster in his early years, his role in *The Four Horsemen of the Apocalypse* makes him a star. But it is his switch from Metro to Famous Players-Lasky for whom he plays the lead in *The Sheik* that catapults him into the stratosphere. He becomes Hollywood's most exotic lead and his erotic appeal has women fainting in the aisles. It establishes his persona of lover/adventurer that he would exploit before his untimely death in 1926.

Mao Zedong becomes a founder member of the Communist Party of China and sets up a branch in Hunan.

1921

Häxan, Benjamin Christensen, Sweden/Denmark

Benjamin Christensen's stylized documentary, interspersed with fictional horror sequences, presents an account of the occult and superstition throughout history. Inspired by a 15th-century text *Hammer of Witches* (*Malleus Maleficarum*), the film's four parts detail how societies have often used disease or mental illness as an excuse to persecute individuals. Also known as *Witchcraft Through the Ages* and with the director playing Satan, it is the most expensive Swedish production of the time, attracting much controversy when it opens.

The Toll of the Sea becomes the first colour feature film made in Hollywood.

Benito Mussolini's fascist blackshirts march on Rome.

James Joyce's *Ulysses* is published in its entirety in Paris by Sylvia Beach. It follows the obscenity trial that resulted from its publication in serial form in the United States.

Dr Mabuse the Gambler (*Dr Mabuse, der Spieler*), Fritz Lang, Germany

The first in a trilogy of films about a criminal mastermind, Fritz Lang's 271-minute-long thriller begins production as Norbert Jacques's source novel is still being serialized. The film and its malevolent character attract different readings. Some see anti-Semitic traces in the portrayal, but Lang's sequel *The Testament of Dr Mabuse* (*Das Testament des Dr Mabuse*, 1933) makes the link to the Nazis stronger. Later Lang said that Mabuse was modelled to reflect Friedrich Nietzsche's idea of the Übermensch.

1922

1923–1924

The jazz age. With memories of the war receding and the rise of ideologies in Europe notwithstanding, jazz music continues its ascent, initially in the United States but soon spreading far and wide. More than just a musical form, it has a profound impact on culture in general, from fashion and dance styles to art, cinema and even classical music. In early 1924, George Gershwin premieres his composition *Rhapsody in Blue* in New York. Along with Edgard Varèse's *Amériques* (1918–21), it is both a paean and theme to the city, capturing its cadences and cacophony, and what Gershwin refers to as 'metropolitan madness'. The city's bars and clubs, particularly those in Harlem, become the epicentre of this jazz world. Prohibition may have banned alcohol in the United States, but crime syndicates make it easily available from speakeasies.

Eastman Kodak introduces 16 mm film, a cheaper gauge format that will become instrumental in the burgeoning field of experimental and independent film-making.

The Hollywoodland sign is erected above the Hollywood Hills as a way of advertising real estate in the area. It is intended to stay for eighteen months, but instead remains there. When it is rebuilt in 1949, the sign loses the suffix 'land'.

Adolf Hitler fails in his attempt to start a political coup in Munich. A year later, he completes his lengthy political tract *Mein Kampf* (My Fight).

○ *The Ten Commandments*, Cecil B. DeMille, USA
Unlike Cecil B. DeMille's similarly titled epic of 1956, this version only features the second book of the Old Testament as a prologue to the main action, which unfolds in the present. Nevertheless, it is the scale of this section that draws huge audiences to see it, with the parting of the Red Sea presenting one of the most memorable visual effects of the silent era. The contemporary tale draws on the themes that appear in Exodus, as well as the Ten Commandments.

1923

The Last Laugh, F. W. Murnau, Germany

An ageing doorman at a top hotel loses his job. From this simple premise, director F. W. Murnau and screenwriter Carl Mayer choose not to use intertitles, instead conveying the nuances of the narrative through performance and camera movement. Working with cinematographer Karl Freund, Murnau uses various techniques, from placing a camera on a bicycle to having it attached to a high wire over the set, which take viewers into the psychological maelstrom of Emil Jannings's protagonist.

Greed, Erich von Stroheim, USA

A director with ambitious vision, Erich von Stroheim had already been fired from previous productions when he began shooting his adaptation of Frank Norris's novel *McTeague* (1899). The film is one of the first to be shot entirely on location, including two gruelling months in Death Valley. The film-maker's preferred original cut runs to 8 hours and features daring stylistic choices. However, it is cut to 2 ½ hours by the studio. The missing footage subsequently becomes one of the holy grails from this era of Hollywood.

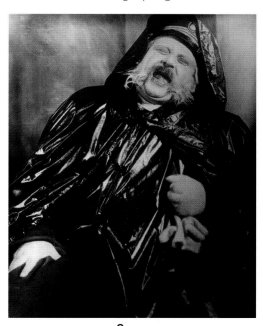

Fernand Léger unveils his Dadaist post-Cubist Futurist experimental art film *Ballet mécanique* at the International Exposition for New Theatre Technique in Vienna.

Vladimir Lenin dies and against his final wishes Joseph Stalin assumes power.

Aelita: Queen of Mars (*Aelita*) is directed by Yakov Protazanov. In addition to being one of the first science-fiction features, it exhibits the propagandist style synonymous with this period of Soviet cinema.

1924

SOVIET CINEMA

The Russian Revolution not only brought in sweeping social and political change, its impact upon culture was hugely significant and on cinema seismic. What had been a fledgling art form in the country soon transformed into a tool for the promotion of ideology. It inspired an approach to cinema that would expand the grammar of film.

Prior to 1917, Russian cinema had yet to flourish. The Lumière brothers travelled to Moscow and St Petersburg in mid 1896 to exhibit their films. But it would be another decade before the first narrative film, Vladimir Romashkov's *Stenka Razin* (1908), reached the screen. The first Russian feature, Aleksandr Khanzhonkov and Vasili Goncharov's *Defence of Sevastopol* (*Oborona Sevastopolya*), followed in 1911. Film production increased in the early years of the First World War (1914–18), mostly to disseminate anti-German propaganda. Yakov Protazanov and Alexandre Volkoff's *Father Sergius* (*Otets Sergiy*, 1918) was the last film made before Vladimir Lenin took power.

The new regime saw cinema as the perfect medium to spread its revolutionary message. A state-controlled film organization was established, as was the world's first film school in Moscow. One of its earliest tutors was Lev Kuleshov, who had covered the civil war as a documentary film-maker. He was interested in the theoretical aspects of cinema and in particular the power of editing. He believed that cutting between two shots was not just a physical process. Each shot expressed something specific, but by placing two shots together a film-maker could communicate something new. To explain his reasoning,

Kuleshov made a short film in which the image of a man's face (popular actor Ivan Mosjoukine) followed shots of a bowl of soup, a young girl in a coffin and a woman on a chaise longue. Audiences believed that the man's expression changed in reaction to each shot, displaying hunger, grief and desire. Yet the shot remained the same. The 'Kuleshov effect', as it became known, was an early example of the Soviet theory of montage. The directors who emerged in the 1920s took this notion further, theoretically and in practice.

The most important figure of this era was Sergei Eisenstein. His book *The Film Sense* (1942) presented the summation of his experiments in cinema, while his first films had a far-reaching impact on the medium. His use of montage in his three key films of the 1920s, *Strike* (*Stachka*, 1925), *Battleship Potemkin* (*Bronenosets Potemkin*, 1925) and *October 1917 (Ten Days that Shook the World)* (*Oktyabr*, 1928), was radical and the antithesis of the more classical editing style used in Hollywood. But it suited the politically provocative and confrontational approach to film that defined notable Soviet cinema of the 1920s. It echoed the Constructivist style of artists such as Aleksandr Rodchenko. Eisenstein cut shots together to

increase their visceral power and to emphasize an ideological perspective. This is evident in the Odessa Steps sequence in *Battleship Potemkin*, based on a real-life massacre of civilians by Tsarist troops, and which typifies the film-maker's approach to editing.

At the same time, Dziga Vertov's work in documentary, particularly on the *Kino-Pravda* (film-truth) series that he began in 1922, challenged the nature of non-fiction film. It culminated in the 'city symphony' *Man with a Movie Camera* (*Chelovek s kino-apparatom*, 1929), whose avant-garde style embraced montage theory to create a radical portrait of a day in the life of a city.

The extreme nature of the films made during this decade eventually saw them rejected by the establishment in favour of Socialist Realism, which dominated Soviet film from the 1930s and is exemplified by the rousing drama of *Chapaev* (1934) and Eisenstein's *Alexander Nevsky* (*Aleksandr Nevskiy*, 1938). But like German Expressionism, the formal aspects of Soviet montage theory were embraced by directors worldwide to convey meaning through an edit and, as world events in the 1960s challenged societal norms, by film-makers who once again saw the potential of cinema to foment revolution.

1925-1926

The film factory. By 1925, Hollywood has not only established itself as the epicentre of the US film industry, it is regarded by many as the global capital of film production. Films are being produced at a fast rate throughout Europe, but the movie business in Hollywood is streamlined to ruthless effect. It is dominated by five major studios: Warner Bros, Fox (later 20th Century Fox), RKO, Metro-Goldwyn-Mayer (MGM) and Paramount. There is also the 'Little Three' of United Artists, Universal and Columbia. All follow the assembly-line system of film-making pioneered by US film-maker Thomas H. Ince. In 1912, Ince purchased a large area of land in the Santa Monica Mountains that he turned into a sprawling studio – initially known as 'Inceville' – that featured sound stages, costume departments, production offices, film laboratories and catering facilities. It becomes the standard for all studios.

F. Scott Fitzgerald publishes his jazz age novel *The Great Gatsby*.

Adolf Hitler resurrects the Nazi Party.

Benito Mussolini becomes dictator of Italy.

The New Yorker publishes its first issue on 21 February.

John Logie Baird successfully transmits the first television images.

○ *The Joyless Street* (*Die freudlose Gasse*), G. W. Pabst, Germany
Known in the United States as *The Street of Sorrow*, Georg Wilhelm Pabst's drama details the life of an impoverished neighbourhood. Established star Asta Nielsen and Greta Garbo, in her second major role, play two women whose lives are adversely affected by their circumstances. A significant departure from the German Expressionist style, the film is regarded as a prime example of the *Neue Sachlichkeit* (New Objectivity) movement, which sought to explore social issues impacting Weimar Germany.

1925

The Adventures of Prince Achmed (*Die Abenteuer des Prinzen Achmed*), Lotte Reiniger, Germany

The oldest surviving animated feature film perfectly captures the silhouette animation technique created by director Lotte Reiniger. Employing a similar style to Wayang shadow puppets, which emanated from Java in Indonesia, Reiniger collaborates with experimental film-makers Walter Ruttmann, Berthold Bartosch and Carl Koch – her husband – on constructing characters and environments from cardboard and thin sheets of lead, to create fluid stop-motion animation.

The General, Buster Keaton and Clyde Bruckman, USA

Buster Keaton's most ambitious film, loosely based on an event that took place during the American Civil War (1861–65), gives the writer-director-actor an expansive backdrop to create a series of complex set-ups, culminating in the destruction of a real bridge and train engine. The film's budget almost doubles, and audiences' lacklustre response results in its commercial failure, which costs Keaton his creative freedom in Hollywood. Subsequent appraisals of the film recognize it as Keaton's finest.

Rudolph Valentino dies prompting an outpouring of grief and hysteria from fans. An estimated 100,000 people attend his funeral procession in Manhattan, New York.

1926

1927–1928

The world turns. While *The Jazz Singer* (1927) marked the most significant change in commercial cinema since its inception, with audiences clamouring to see the 'talkies', political forces are transforming the direction of societies. Soviet film-makers celebrate the seismic events surrounding the October Revolution of 1917, but the inception of Joseph Stalin's Five-Year Plans, beginning in 1928 and focused on industrial and economic regeneration proved disastrous for rural communities and also cloaked Stalin's desire to rid Soviet society of kulak (peasant farm owners) as a class. In Germany, the French may have removed their troops from the Ruhr in late 1925, but their occupation – the result of Germany defaulting on reparations payments – escalates nationalist sentiment and the rise in popularity of the Nazi Party. After gaining control of Italy, Benito Mussolini, a future Nazi ally, looks to Ethiopia to extend his control. Elsewhere, relations between Japan and the West grow tense as the country attempts to assert control over East Asia.

Napoleon (Napoléon vu par Abel Gance), Abel Gance, France

Abel Gance's account of the French emperor's early years was meant to be the first of a sprawling six-part cinematic portrait. However, the difficulty he faced in completing the first film, which runs to more than 5 hours, left this as the only completed entry. Nevertheless, the resulting film is admired for its narrative prowess and technical innovation, which includes the use of Polyvision – the name given to the format that employs three projectors across a triptych of screens to capture the film's climactic battle.

The Academy of Motion Picture Arts and Sciences is founded by the head of MGM, Louis B. Mayer.

Alfred Hitchcock directs his first thriller *The Lodger: A Story of the London Fog*.

The first transatlantic telephone call is made between New York and London.

1927

Metropolis, Fritz Lang, Germany

A tale of revolution borne out of the disparity between a wealthy ruling elite and dispossessed working masses in a future city, Fritz Lang's epic is one of the most expensive films produced in the silent era. He worked with visual-effects specialist Eugen Schüfftan, whose process involving mirrors to allow actors to appear as part of miniature sets was named after him. Initially polarizing critics, it draws admiration from Nazi propagandist Joseph Goebbels, who seeks to employ Lang, but he emigrates to the United States a year after the Nazis came to power in 1933.

Sunrise: A Song of Two Humans, F. W. Murnau, USA

Those who see pre-sound cinema of the late 1920s as the apotheosis of the medium's artistry often cite F. W. Murnau's first Hollywood production as evidence. The tale of a farmer seduced by a woman from the city to leave his wife and child is presented through the expressionistic use of light and stage settings to create a visual tone poem that reflects the yearning, pain and torment of its protagonists. It is celebrated for its use of long camera tracking shots.

Women in Great Britain achieve equal suffrage to men; anyone over the age of twenty-one can vote.

Tafari Makonnen is crowned King of Ethiopia. Two years later he is made emperor and takes the name 'Haile Selassie'.

Walt Disney's *Steamboat Willie* opens, which marks the first appearance of Mickey Mouse.

1928

INNOVATIONS IN SOUND

The challenge of integrating the moving image with sound preoccupied engineers and scientists long before Al Jolson sang to his mother in 1927. The relationship between the two is a story of developing technologies that continues to the present.

In the late 19th century, US inventor Thomas Edison developed the kinetoscope and cylinder phonogram in tandem, bringing them together for the kinetophone in the same year that the French film-makers Lumière brothers unveiled their film programme. Like the subsequent cinemacrophonograph and Phono-Cinéma-Théâtre, which were both exhibited in Paris at the turn of the century, they were rudimentary forays into pairing sound and film. But precise synchronization lay some way off.

The major breakthrough arrived with advances in sound-on-film technology. A number of innovators, primarily Frenchman Eugène Lauste and Finn Eric Tigerstedt, had attempted to find an effective way of recording sound on film, but attracted little commercial interest. In 1919, US inventor Lee de Forest succeeded in creating a composite print – motion-picture film with a soundtrack photographically recorded on to a side strip. Sound was recorded synchronously during filming to ensure it corresponded to the image. At the same time, experiments were carried out with sound-on-disc technology – sound recoded on to a disc and played on a phonograph turntable connected to a projector. This system produced clear sound, but synchronization was more problematic. After a brief competition between the studios over which system should be used, further advances to sound-on-film technology resulted it becoming the industry standard.

Having developed a universal system, the next challenge lay in deciding whether synchronous sound was necessary. By the late 1920s, the finest film-makers had pushed cinema to unparalleled heights. The interplay between actors and the camera, and the complexity of production design and editing produced films whose sophistication and ingenuity seemed to know no bounds. Introducing sound would have a paralyzing effect. The technology was in its infancy and so recording required complete silence. Cameras and all equipment would be soundproofed, resulting in limitations on their movement, while actors were required to

ensure their dialogue was spoken in the direction of the microphone. The sequence in *Singin' in the Rain* (1952) when Gene Kelly and Jean Hagen are filming a swashbuckling adventure but have problems recording a love scene because of microphone placement captures the problems actors and film-makers faced. Not only that, but as Hagen's squeaky voice makes clear, actors who appeared captivating in pre-sound films found their careers threatened by the new innovation if their voices were not good enough.

Sound also proved to be expensive. Every cinema had to be refitted to accommodate the new technology. But what if it was, like some critics claimed, a passing fad? Fox had screened a number of newsreels to a New York cinema audience in mid 1927, as well as the comedy short *They're Coming to Get Me*, which featured synchronized dialogue. Some feature films, including Frank Borzage's *7th Heaven* and F. W. Murnau's *Sunrise: A Song of Two Humans* (both 1927) had also appeared with a synchronous music soundtrack, which included a selection of sound effects. But if there were doubts over audiences' willingness to embrace the new technology, they were answered by the success of Warner Bros Al Jolson vehicle *The Jazz Singer* (1927). The film only featured a few scenes of synchronized dialogue, but audiences flocked to see it. Sound films increased in numbers and over the course of the next decade, cinemas around the world were adapted to accommodate what would become the standard.

The technology gradually improved. The introduction of multichannel sound in 1937, high-fidelity or hi-fi stereo and magnetic strips in the 1950s, Dolby sound in the 1970s, Dolby Stereo and THX in the 1980s, Dolby Digital in the 1990s and Dolby Atmos in the 2000s brought to cinema a level of technological sophistication in sound to match advances in the moving image. Today, if a pin drops on screen it is not just possible to hear it with perfect clarity, a film-maker can choose the exact location within an auditorium that the sound will come from.

ABOVE RIGHT. *Apocalypse Now* (1979), Francis Ford Coppola, USA
Among the innovators of sound, Walter Murch, who realized the possibilities of technology to add to the film-going experience, is referred to as the 'Godfather of Modern Sound'. His contribution to *Apocalypse Now* is crucial to the film's effectiveness.

RIGHT. *The Jazz Singer* (1927), Alan Crosland, USA
It was not the first film with synchronous sound, but the success of Al Jolson's musical made it a landmark in the development of cinema.

1929–1930

A perfect escape. As the impact of the global financial crisis spreads, cinema offers a diversion for audiences from their woes. In 1930, John Wayne appears in his first major role in Raoul Walsh's Western *The Big Trail*, shot in the early widescreen format of 70 mm Grandeur film. A burgeoning landscape of experimental and non-fiction cinema sees Luis Buñuel attract the rancour of the Catholic church with his satirical *L'âge d'or* (1930), the follow-up to *An Andalusian Dog (Un chien andalou*, 1929), his collaboration with Salvador Dalí. In the United Kingdom, John Grierson establishes the nation's documentary scene with *Drifters* (1929), while in the Soviet Union brothers Dziga Vertov (formerly David Kaufman) and Mikhail Kaufman push the possibilities of Soviet montage theory with their portraits of metropolitan life over the course of a day and a season with *Man with a Movie Camera* (*Chelovek s kino-apparatom*) and *In Spring* (*Vesnoy*, both 1929).

Blackmail, Alfred Hitchcock, UK

Europe's first successful 'talkie' begins production as a silent film, but British International Pictures wants to catch on to this new trend and so they produce two versions, one of which featured synchronous and non-synchronous sound. Ever the innovator, Alfred Hitchcock introduces ways to stylize the use of sound, most notably the repetition of the word 'knife' in a breakfast scene the night after a man is killed by Anny Ondra's protagonist.

The first Academy Awards ceremony takes place, lasting just 15 minutes.

Popeye and Tintin appear in print for the first time.

The stock market crashes on Wall Street, sending shockwaves around the world, which causes a global depression.

1929

The Blue Angel (Der blaue Engel), Joseph von Sternberg, Germany

This adaptation of Heinrich Mann's novel *Professor Unclean* (*Professor Unrat*, 1905) began a collaboration between Joseph von Sternberg and actor Marlene Dietrich that spanned seven films. It made her a star, thanks in part to her rendition of the song 'Falling in Love Again'. Von Sternberg had returned to Germany because of the commercial failure of his films in Hollywood. Aware of *The Blue Angel's* potential, Sternberg took his star to the United States and completed their second film *Morocco* (1930) before *The Blue Angel* had opened Stateside.

All Quiet on the Western Front, Lewis Milestone, USA

Abel Gance's *J'accuse!* (1919) which featured sequences shot on real battlefields, may lay claim to being the first major anti-war film, but Lewis Milestone's adaptation of Erich Maria Remarque's novel of 1929 chose the perspective of the enemy in order to eschew jingoism in favour of a nuanced portrait of the human cost of conflict. The film was the first to win both the Best Picture (then Outstanding Production) and Best Director Academy Awards.

The Motion Picture Production Code is introduced, creating a self-regulating office of censorship in Hollywood.

1930

3

AN ART FORM
CONSOLIDATES

The introduction of sound technology into cinemas around the world increased throughout the 1930s. Some countries initially adopted sound-on-disc systems, such as Poland. But sound-on film would eventually become the standard. In the United Kingdom, the speed of changing cinema technology was similar to the United States, with the majority of venues refitted by the end of 1930. In France, silent cinema remained the predominant form of projection as late as 1932. Meanwhile, in Japan more than a third of all films produced in the country in 1938 were still shot without sound. One reason for this can be attributed to the popularity of the *benshi*, a narrator who performed alongside a film as it screened.

The introduction of sound had repercussions for international production. Countries could no longer recoup revenues from overseas sales because language was now a factor. The change also had an impact on certain genres, arguably none more so than comedy. The silent era had been a golden age for comic actors with great physical dexterity. French actor Max Linder, the first film star, led the way. Charles Chaplin drew on Linder's comic persona for his own tramp character and became the first global star. Audience's appetite for comedies found him joined by Roscoe 'Fatty' Arbuckle, Harold Lloyd, Mabel Normand, Harry Langdon, Buster Keaton and countless other comic performers. The arrival of sound did not cause an abrupt end to the careers of most silent comedians. However, Langdon's star did diminish rapidly, with producer Hal Roach apparently describing his style as 'not so funny articulate'. In the case of Keaton, a comic genius who at the height of his success boasted complete creative control, his move to MGM in 1928 saw him flounder and never fully recover. Lloyd remained a popular figure into the 1930s, but his go-getting persona proved out of touch with the times and so he appeared in fewer films. Chaplin successfully made the transition, but his first 'proper' sound film did not appear until 1940. If *City Lights* (1931) was a silent film in every sense, *Modern Times* (1936) featured little more than sound effects and a smattering of dialogue – none of it spoken by Chaplin's Tramp, save for some gibberish in a musical sequence. *The Great Dictator* (1940) was when Chaplin finally embraced sound for the entirety of a film. But his star was so great and his willingness to adapt, albeit at his own convenience, assured his continued success. Likewise, Stan Laurel and Oliver Hardy, who had been popular stand-alone acts before joining forces in 1927, succeeded in taking their act into the sound age and remained popular well into the 1940s.

Many studios saw the arrival of sound as an opportunity to introduce new blood – actors who were as adept at using language as their bodies to elicit laughs. The Marx Brothers were one of the first sound-era comedy acts to achieve great success. A popular stage act in the 1920s, the siblings (Chico, Harpo, Groucho, Gummo and Zeppo) initially appeared in film versions of their shows. With *Monkey Business* (1931) they left their stage antics behind and cemented their popularity with *Horse Feathers* (1932). *Duck Soup* (1933) proved less successful with audiences, but it showcased their inventiveness in balancing slapstick and comedy set pieces with linguistic dexterity. Alongside them was Mae West, a vaudevillian performer whose crossover into cinema introduced more risqué humour that would eventually be censored with the arrival of the Motion Picture Production Code in the mid 1930s.

As the success of *The Jazz Singer* (1927) proved, the musical was an obvious genre for studios to focus on to promote the new technology. Even early sound films that were not musicals, such as the crime drama *Lights of New York* (1928),

PREVIOUS PAGE. *Modern Times* (1936), Charles Chaplin, USA
Charles Chaplin's last outing as his beloved tramp was also his most pointed critique of a progressively mechanized world where humans literally become part of an industry's machinery.

RIGHT. *Duck Soup* (1933), Leo McCarey, USA
Attracting mixed notices on its release, *Duck Soup* has come to be seen as the Marx Brothers at their most anarchic, offering up a constant barrage of verbal and visual comedy.

LEFT. *Snow White and the Seven Dwarfs* (1937), William Cottrell, David Hand, Wilfred Jackson, Larry Morey, Perce Pearce and Ben Sharpsteen, USA
'Disney's Folly' not only became the box-office draw of 1938, it earned the admiration of directors as diverse as Charles Chaplin and Sergei Eisenstein.

OPPOSITE. *Casablanca* (1942), Michael Curtiz, USA
Producer Hal B. Wallis was the driving force behind this perfect example of studio film-making at the zenith of Hollywood's Golden Age. It was also effective as US wartime propaganda.

the first all-talking drama, featured a musical sequence. MGM's *The Broadway Melody* (1929) cemented the popularity of the genre and became the first sound film to win the Best Picture Academy Award. Its show-business plot would also become a staple of musicals over the course of the next decade. Not that the genre's journey was frictionless. The number of song-and-dance films that opened in the first years of sound more than sated audiences' appetite and, by the end of 1931, interest in the musical dwindled, and production was dramatically reduced. Many of the early musicals were also shot in colour, but even that innovation began to tire audiences and they looked elsewhere for entertainment, most notably the nascent gangster and horror genres.

With the onset of the Great Depression, the musical offered the most extravagant escape and by 1933 the genre was popular again. Busby Berkeley was a key figure in revitalizing it. He created rapturous spectacles through ambitiously choreographed dance numbers. Films such as *42nd Street*, *Gold Diggers of 1933* and *Footlight Parade* (all 1933) featured a variety of stars, but the set pieces were what drew audiences. The dance partnership of Ginger Rogers and Fred Astaire picked up the mantle in the mid 1930s and became two of the most enduring stars of Hollywood's Golden Age. The popularity of the musical waned again towards the end of the decade, only to see its fortunes revive, alongside the biblical epic, in the late 1940s and early 1950s, offering a spectacle that cinema's most significant threat, television, could not match.

While Hollywood's growth as an unstoppable commercial force continued throughout the 1930s, various national cinemas forged their own paths in addition to producing films to challenge the cultural hegemony of the US film industry. In the Soviet Union, film-makers embraced Socialist Realism, which would remain popular into the 1960s and continue to exert an influence until the collapse of Eastern Bloc countries in the late 1980s. An expression of socialist ideals that cut across various disciplines, the films presented a highly idealized portrait of life under communist rule. There was a strong element of romanticism to them, particularly in their depiction of significant historical figures or portraits of the proletariat.

A different strain of romanticism ran through French Poetic Realism. The films were mostly set among the working class and portrayed the hardships of everyday life. Their atmosphere drew on German Expressionism and in their moral ambiguity presaged film noir in the 1940s and 1950s. Early examples ranged from Jean Grémillon's *Little Lise* (*La petite Lise*, 1930) and the Jean Vigo's *L'Atalante* (1934) to Jacques Feyder's *Le grand jeu* (1934). Later in the decade, Jean Renoir dominated with *The Crime of Monsieur Lange* (*Le crime de Monsieur Lange*, 1936), *La grande illusion* (1937), *La bête humaine* (1938) and *La règle du jeu* (1939), while Marcel Carné was celebrated for his *Port of Shadows* (*Le quai des brumes*), *Hôtel du Nord* (both 1938) and *Le jour se lève* (1939). Jean Gabin appeared in many of the most popular films, but it was his work with Julien Duvuvier, particularly his role in *Pépé le Moko* (1937), that most perfectly captured his swarthy handsomeness, roguish charm and air of danger.

Just as Gabin's anti-hero was ducking the law by hiding out in the labyrinthine kasbah of Algiers in Duvuvier's romantic crime drama, audiences around the world were mesmerized by Walt Disney's animated feature debut. When he announced that production was to begin on

ABOVE. *Pépé le Moko* (1937),
Julien Duvuvier, France
Jean Gabin plays a criminal on
the run from the French police
and seeks haven in the Casbah
quarter of Algiers. The film is
credited with having inspired *The
Third Man* (1949) by British
film-maker Carol Reed.

Snow White and the Seven Dwarfs in June 1934, Disney was met
with doubt and ridicule. Starting out as a cartoonist after the First
World War (1914–18), Disney moved from New York – where most
cartoonists plied their trade – to Hollywood in 1923. The Walt Disney
Company was created shortly after and in 1928 Mickey Mouse made
his first appearance. The character's third animated short, *Steamboat
Willie* (1928), became the first post-produced sound cartoon. By
1934, Disney had established his brand of wholesome, emotionally
engaging animation. He saw *Snow White* as the next step. The film's
initial budget of $250,000 disappeared quickly and the project earned
the nickname 'Disney's Folly', with industry insiders believing it
would bankrupt the animator's company. *Snow White* eventually cost
$1,500,000, but it was a sensation and a resounding commercial
success. The critical acclaim for the company's subsequent feature
animations, *Pinocchio*, *Fantasia* (both 1940), *Dumbo* (1941) and
Bambi (1942), was not immediately reflected at the box office, but
the films' longevity, with audiences happy to watch them more than
once, was key to the company's success. Other studios followed suit,
creating their own animation departments. But none held such a
distinctive place in the collective psyche as Disney.

Escalating tensions between countries in the 1930s saw an
increase in film's use as a tool for propaganda. It had proven
effective on a limited scale during the First World War, but the Soviet
embrace of cinema highlighted the medium's potential. Under Joseph
Goebbels, the minister of Nazi propaganda, cinema became a weapon
for disseminating hatred of anything that opposed, undermined or
was different to the Nazi image of the Aryan ideal. It was at its most
effective with Leni Riefenstahl's *Triumph of the Will* (*Triumph des
Willens*, 1935) and *Olympia* (1938), and its most abhorrent with the
hateful and anti-Semitic *Jew Süss* (*Jud Süss*, 1940). Once the Second
World War (1939–45) began, Allied Forces also used the medium
to promote its cause. In the United States, Hollywood was prevented
from advocating any active involvement in the conflict until after the
bombing of Pearl Harbor in 1941. Forces in favour of following an
isolationist policy fought to prevent films depicting the Nazi regime in
a negative light. In September 1941, a Senate subcommittee went
so far as to launch an investigation into whether Hollywood was
campaigning to bring the United States into the Second World War
by inserting pro-British and pro-interventionist messages in its films.
Some studios did. Warner Bros produced *Confessions of a Nazi Spy*
(1939) while MGM released *The Mortal Storm* (1940). The message
delivered by Joel McCrea's journalist to the world via radio from a
London besieged by German bombers at the end of Alfred Hitchcock's
Foreign Correspondent (1940) was all too clear.

Once the United States entered the war in 1941, like other
Allied nations, its cinema covered the conflict from the front and
at home. Film-makers such as John Ford, John Huston and Frank
Capra produced a series of documentaries that detailed the battles
around the world and Capra's *Why We Fight* (1942–45) series was
the most comprehensive. At the same time, war was incorporated
into genre cinema, most notably *Casablanca* (1942), a swooning

adventure-romance that transformed Humphrey Bogart's image from the stone-faced gangster of 1930s thrillers to an unconventional heart-throb. But its popularity was dwarfed by William Wyler's *Mrs Miniver*, the year's most successful film. Even Goebbels conceded its success in the battle of hearts and minds saying: 'There is not a single angry word spoken against Germany; nevertheless, the anti-German tendency is perfectly accomplished.'

British cinema also featured dramas that rallied morale during the war, from *The Next of Kin* and *Went the Day Well?* (both 1942) to *Millions Like Us* (1943) and *This Happy Breed* (1944). Pioneering film-makers Michael Powell and Emeric Pressburger went further. Their films *49th Parallel* (1941) and *One of Our Aircraft Is Missing* (1942) were accomplished examples of cinematic propaganda. But what they released next incurred the wrath of Prime Minister Winston Churchill. Their adaptation of David Low's satirical cartoon strip *The Life and Death of Colonel Blimp* (1943) was not anti-British, but it suggested that the upper echelons of British military command needed to understand that they were fighting an enemy unlike anything they had engaged with before. Powell and Pressburger's first colour film, it was heavily edited but still stands out from the films of that era. Their production company The Archers, alongside Gainsborough Pictures, which popularized a series of bodice-ripping period dramas, and the beloved series of comedies produced by Ealing Studios, were responsible for a renaissance in British film that ran throughout the 1940s and into the 1950s.

Italian cinema under Benito Mussolini resulted in a series of dramas focusing on the lives of the bourgeoisie, derisively known as *telefoni bianchi* (white telephones). The end of the war saw a surge in Neorealist film, which focused on the plight of the poor and whose manifesto would become a beacon of inspiration for and influence over a wide array of subsequent film movements, from Parallel Cinema in India and the French New Wave to Brazil's Cinema Novo. It lasted less than a decade, with Vittorio De Sica's character study *Umberto D.* (1952) regarded as the last pure example of a Neorealist film.

One of the first Neorealist films was Luchino Visconti's *Obsession* (*Ossessione*, 1943), an adaptation of James M. Cain's novel *The Postman Always Rings Twice* (1934). Cain's crime story was also adapted by Tay Garnett in 1946, for a drama starring Lana Turner and John Garfield, which would come to be seen as one of the definitive film noirs. Less a genre or movement than a style, the term 'film noir' was coined by the French critic Nino Frank in 1946. It describes a group of films that spanned the 1940s and 1950s and which demonstrated similar traits in terms of visual style, character, plot and worldview. The line between protagonist and antagonist was often unclear, with both male and female characters displaying moral ambivalence. Sex and greed were major factors. The narratives frequently featured detectives whose working practices could be dubious, dupes who fell for get-rich-quick schemes or for femme fatales who manipulated situations to their advantage, heroes who were often compromised and few people who were truly innocent. Reflecting the tone of the narratives, film-makers drew on the

TOP. *The Life and Death of Colonel Blimp* **(1943), Michael Powell and Emeric Pressburger, UK**
Prime Minister Winston Churchill actively pushed for production on Michael Powell and Emeric Pressburger's first colour feature to be stopped. He failed, but it was forty years before audiences saw the original version.

ABOVE. *Double Indemnity* **(1944), Billy Wilder, USA**
Billy Wilder's fractious collaboration with acclaimed crime writer Raymond Chandler notwithstanding, their adaptation of James M. Cain's novel is one of the key film noirs of the 1940s.

chiaroscuro style of German Expressionism, creating a world of light and shadow. The films began to appear in the early 1940s and would continue to the late 1950s. There is debate over the first noir, with films from the 1930s such as *Fury* (1936) and *You Only Live Once* (1937) displaying traits. It is notable that these films were directed by Fritz Lang, one of the key directors of German Expressionist cinema. Lang, like so many film-makers and technicians opposed to Nazi rule, fled to Hollywood and their influence is most clearly seen in these films. But the classic period stretches from Boris Ingster's *Stranger on the Third Floor* (1940) to Orson Welles's *Touch of Evil* (1958). If Billy Wilder's *Double Indemnity* (1944) is the sterling archetype of the genre, films such as Edgar G. Ulmer's *Detour* (1945), Joseph H. Lewis's *The Big Combo* and Robert Aldrich's *Kiss Me Deadly* (both 1955) showed how noir was employed on low-budget features, as well as accentuating the sadism of characters and engaging with the escalating Cold War (1947–91) and edging into the surreal.

Japanese cinema was second only to the United States in terms of its output during the silent era. It spanned the successful *jidaigeki* (period dramas) and films advocating social reform to avant-garde titles such as Teinosuke Kinugasa's *A Page of Madness* (*Kurutta ippêji*, 1926). In the years before the Second World War a number of key directors rose to prominence, including Yasujirō Ozu, Mikio Naruse and Kenji Mizoguchi. The conflict halted much film production in the country, but by 1950, the cinema had not only entered a golden age, it was increasingly feted around the world. In 1951, Akira Kurosawa was awarded the Golden Lion, the top prize at the Venice Film Festival, for his feature *Rashomon* (*Rashōmon*, 1950). It was a watershed moment in the international recognition of Japanese film and focus on both Kurosawa's work and Japanese cinema in general grew over the course of the 1950s. By 1960, Japanese society had undergone a radical transformation, which was reflected in the cinema of a new generation of film-makers. What these new films had in common with their US counterpart, as well as other cinemas around the world, was the ubiquity of a new phenomenon: the teenager.

Teen culture emerged in the post-war period and exploded in the 1950s, at the same time that other elements of popular culture were gaining ground throughout society. Music gave a generation a voice, while cinema reflected a shift in attitudes. In James Dean it found its icon. *Rebel Without a Cause* (1955) offered up an angst-driven study of generational difference and the desire to break free from outdated attitudes. That Dean died shortly after the film was released – after completing just three features – only added to his aura. He became the image of cool, whose spirit of rebellion can be found in the early films of Nagisa Ōshima, actor Zbigniew Cybulski's protagonist in *Ashes and Diamonds* (*Popiól i diament*, 1958) and Albert Finney's working-class anti-hero in *Saturday Night and Sunday Morning* (1960).

Dean's importance in cinema also stems from his performance style. He represented a radical new way of acting that would challenge the conventions of classical screen performance. Inspired by the theories of Konstantin Stanislavski and expounded in the United States by the teachings of Stella Adler, Lee Strasberg and Sanford Meisner,

ABOVE. *Rashomon (Rashomôn,* 1950), **Akira Kurosawa, Japan**
Director Akira Kurosawa's film was adapted from Ryūnosuke Akutagawa's story *In a Grove* (*Yabu no Naka*, 1922) not his tale *Rashomon* (*Rashōmon*, 1915). The film was many international audiences' first encounter with Japanese cinema.

LEFT. *Rebel Without a Cause* **(1955), Nicholas Ray, USA**
Like Marlon Brando, James Dean challenged the classical Hollywood acting style with his portrait of an angst-driven teenager searching for his place in the world.

directors such as Nicholas Ray and Elia Kazan cast actors willing to go beyond the norm in embracing roles. Nowhere was this more apparent than in Marlon Brando's early screen performances. Most notably, the actor's appearance in Kazan's *On the Waterfront* (1954) distilled the essence of this new style, heightening the intensity of each scene and drawing out nuances of his character Terry Molloy with every movement and expression.

If the 1950s ended with the arrival of the French New Wave, challenging much that had come before it, wider shifts in societal attitudes raised questions regarding what was permissible on the screen. Attitudes to sex and moral certainties that were previously held as sacrosanct were being challenged. Not just from outside the establishment but also from the rising tide of independent film productions. Powerful voices inside the system acknowledged change was coming. Billy Wilder's *Some Like It Hot* (1959) was released without the approval of the Motion Picture Production Code, which had been Hollywood's moral arbiter for three decades. The film featured cross-dressing, sexual innuendo and references to homosexuality. But it went on to become the third-largest grossing film of the year and is now seen as one of the key films in ushering in a new age in cinema.

ABOVE. *Some Like It Hot* **(1959), Billy Wilder, USA**
Shifting seamlessly between gangster drama and screwball comedy, Billy Wilder's gender-bending film brought out the best of Marilyn Monroe and cemented the director's fruitful relationship with star Jack Lemmon.

OPPOSITE. *On the Waterfront* **(1954), Elia Kazan, USA**
Interpreted as Elia Kazan's response to critics of his testimony before the House Committee on Un-American Activities in 1952, *On the Waterfront* is widely admired for Marlon Brando's influential central performance.

1931–1932

The Depression. The impact of the Wall Street Crash of 1929 ripples outwards, sending countries spiralling into depression. It coincides with the rise of political extremists, most notably in Germany. Anger over the repercussions of the Treaty of Versailles (1919), along with the failing Weimar Republic, result in the Nazi Party gaining 19 percent of the popular vote to become a strong and vocal presence in the Reichstag. In the United States, the rise of organized crime throughout the 1920s, partially as a result of Prohibition, sees the gangster drama become a popular genre at the box office. Thomas Edison, one of the pioneers of cinema dies at the age of eighty-four, as does F. W. Murnau, the director of *Nosferatu* (*Nosferatu, eine Symphonie des Grauens*, 1922), who is killed in a car crash at the age of forty-two.

Mass flooding in China creates one of the largest natural disasters in human history, while Japan's military incursions into Manchuria increase in scale.

Chicago mobster Al Capone is sentenced to eleven years for tax evasion, nearly half of it served on the island prison of Alcatraz.

Dracula, Tod Browning, USA

Tod Browning began his career as an actor in single-reel comedies, but gained a foothold as a director in the 1920s through his collaboration with Lon Chaney. Their now-lost feature *London After Midnight* (1927) is Browning's first take on the vampire genre, which he would more fully realize four years later with his loose adaptation of Bram Stoker's novel. Bela Lugosi, who appeared in Browning's previous *The Thirteenth Chair* (1929) and had already portrayed Dracula in a successful Broadway stage production, was cast in the title role. In contrast to Browning's usual professionalism, the production is reportedly chaotic, with German cinematographer Karl Freund playing a significant role in the film's completion. Nevertheless, it is an immediate success and, along with James Whale's *Frankenstein* (1931), makes Universal Studios the home of gothic horror during the 1930s. Browning's next film *Freaks* (1932), MGM's attempt to cash in on the popularity of horror, would become one of the most original and controversial films of the era.

1931

M (*Eine Stadt sucht einen Mörder*), Fritz Lang, Germany

Fritz Lang's first sound film opens with Peter Lorre's child killer wandering the streets of a German city. His compulsion to kill children holds society in the grip of fear and panic. The police are under pressure to catch him and the criminal fraternity, seeing their activities curtailed by the law's ever-stricter controls, take matters into their own hands, capturing the killer and holding a kangaroo court to pass sentence on him. The film transforms from a dark thriller into a moral conundrum that explores how justice defines what society is. Lang challenges viewers to feel sympathy for Lorre's psychologically disturbed character and uses sound expressionistically to ratchet up the film's tension.

Love Me Tonight, Rouben Mamoulian, USA

Whatever constraints some film directors experienced working with the cumbersome technology that produced synchronous sound, they presented no obstacle to Rouben Mamoulian. Born in Georgia, he moved to the United States in 1923 and in 1927 shifted his attention from theatre to film, becoming one of the first directors to work solely in sound. *Applause* (1929), *City Streets* and *Dr Jekyll and Mr Hyde* (both 1932) all showcased Mamoulian's willingness to play with form, but *Love Me Tonight* went further. From its opening sequence, creating an overture of sounds from the increasing cacophony of a waking Paris street, the film is a dazzling display of cinematic verve. It was the third on-screen pairing of Maurice Chevalier and Jeannette McDonald, playing a poor tailor and the princess he falls in love with, but the real draw is Mamoulian's inventiveness.

The Kingdom of Hejaz and Nejd is renamed the Kingdom of Saudi Arabia, while Iraq becomes an independent state, free from British rule, following a League of Nations mandate.

Franklin D. Roosevelt defeats Herbert Hoover to become US President and will be the last to serve more than two terms in office.

Aldous Huxley publishes his dystopian novel *Brave New World*.

1932

CLASSICAL HOLLYWOOD

The early years of sound saw Hollywood increase its dominance over cinema, not only determining for a significant number of the world's cinemagoers what they would see, but the style and form of what was produced.

ABOVE. *The Public Enemy* (1931), William A. Wellman, USA

William A. Wellman's violent drama cemented audiences' enthusiasm for the gangster film, following the success of *Little Caesar* (1931), and made a star of James Cagney.

LEFT. *It Happened One Night* (1934), Frank Capra, USA

Frank Capra's romantic comedy was the first of only three films to date to win the five main Academy Award categories: film, director, leading actor and actress, and screenplay.

By the early 1930s, Hollywood was fully established, comprising the five major studios (Paramount, MGM, Warner Bros, 20th Century Fox and RKO), and smaller – though still significant – studios that included Universal, Columbia and United Artists. Disney was gradually gaining momentum during the decade, but it would take some time to transform into the dominant powerhouse it has become. Together, the studios created the star system – grooming actors to play the role created for them on the screen and in life. Each star was contracted to a specific studio and had little say over what films they appeared in. Control of those films, with a few exceptions, lay in the hands of producers not directors. The way films were made was part of a system. The classical Hollywood style required that editing be invisible, with each shot conforming to a certain pattern so that audiences were never aware of the film-making process. The Motion Picture Production Code, initially overseen by Will H. Hays (it became better known as the Hays Code), the head of the Motion Picture Producers and Distributors of America, determined what was acceptable for audiences to watch. He was replaced in 1934 by Joseph Breen, who for two decades proved to be more draconian. But a changing world and audiences tastes in the 1950s and 1960s saw the code eventually replaced with a certification system and the power of the studios was undermined by the Supreme Court's decision in 1948 to halt the studio-theatre monopolies of the industry.

By the mid 1930s, Warner Bros was known as the home of gangsters thanks to a series of hard-hitting dramas that focused on the world of organized crime. The series began with *Little Caesar*, starring Edward G. Robinson, which opened in January 1931. It was followed, three months later, by William A. Wellman's *The Public Enemy* (1931). The other acclaimed gangster film from this period, Howard Hawks's controversial production of *Scarface* (1932), was released by United Artists. It was Wellman's film that caught audiences' imagination. James Cagney was originally cast in the supporting role of Tom Powers's friend Matt Doyle. But as sound recording had improved, Wellman swapped Cagney and Edward Woods's roles, no longer needing the latter's clear enunciation and preferring Cagney's kinetic energy. It made him a star and he would subsequently appear in other iconic gangster roles, in *Angels with Dirty Faces* (1938), *The Roaring Twenties* (1939) and the last gangster film from this classic era, *White Heat* (1949). Unsurprisingly, many of the films fell foul of the Hays Code and had to be re-edited before they could be screened.

Frank Capra's sprightly romantic comedy *It Happened One Night* (1934) was one of the last to be released before the imposition of the Motion Picture Production Code the same year. It is one of only three films to win the five major Academy Awards: Best Picture, Best Director, Best Actress, Best Actor, Best Adapted Screenplay. Claudette Colbert plays a socialite who has married against her father's wishes. Running away from home, she encounters Clark Gable's recently sacked journalist, who agrees to help her reach her husband provided she gives him an exclusive story. But as they travel together their attraction to each other grows. One of the eight films on which Capra worked with noted screenwriter Robert Riskin – a seemingly harmonious working relationship, their personalities clashed because of their political leanings – the director constructs an elegant comedy with a series of memorable set pieces. The most notable is the 'walls of Jericho' scene, when Gable and Colbert's characters spend a night together in the same room. The film began a run of acclaimed films for Capra, who became the golden goose at Columbia and one of the most admired Hollywood film-makers of the 1930s.

1933–1934

Rise of Nazism. Franklin D. Roosevelt and Adolf Hitler take office as leaders of the United States and Germany. Whereas Roosevelt aims to heal an ailing nation and promote economic recovery through communal activity and a radical programme of nationalization, Hitler promotes the concept of an Aryan elite and begins his purge of Germany's political and social landscape. His ideas coalesce in annual rallies held in Nuremberg, which Leni Riefenstahl films in 1934. A number of artists, film-makers and scientists, many of them Jews fearing for their lives, leave Germany and Austria for France, Britain and the United States. Émigré film-makers include Billy Wilder, Emeric Pressburger, Max Ophüls, Fritz Lang and Robert Siodmak. The persecution of the kulak dissidents and rural communities in the Soviet Union and its satellite states goes unnoticed by most journalists.

Footlight Parade, Busby Berkeley, Lloyd Bacon, USA

Hollywood escapism was never more glamorous or outrageous than the series of musicals associated with Busby Berkeley. From his work choreographing shows on Broadway, Berkeley honed in on the way groups of dancers could form geometric shapes, a style that transferred perfectly to film. *Footlight Parade*, co-directed by Lloyd Bacon, presents the perfect distillation of this style, with James Cagney's hell-for-leather producer overseeing a show-stopping musical that culminates in three climactic dance numbers.

Hitler is appointed chancellor by President Paul von Hindenburg and, after a fire at the Reichstag, passes decrees that increase his power.

The Holodomor famine-genocide in Soviet-controlled Ukraine comes to light when British journalist Gareth Jones files his first report.

1933

Ciapaiev (Chapaev), Georgi and Sergei Vasilyev, Soviet Union

Vasily Chapaev was a Red Army commander, born into a peasant family, who distinguished himself in the Russian Civil War (1917–23). Although they shared the surname, directors Georgi and Sergei Vasilyev were not related. They met while working in the same editing room at Moscow's Sovkino studio. Because of its subject matter, *Ciapaiev* was a high-profile production. Embracing the Socialist Realist style, it presented its hero as a man of the people. More than thirty million people watch the film in its first year of release.

Dust storms create havoc in the United States, sweeping from the Great Plains to the East Coast and displacing hundreds of thousands of families.

The Long March by the Red Army of the Communist Party of China begins. Led by Mao Zedong, the army embarks on a nine-month, 9,000-km (5,600 mile) trek to the northern province of Shaanxi to escape Kuomintang forces.

L'Atalante, Jean Vigo, France

One of the high points of French Poetic Realism, *L'Atalante* is also the only feature by the gifted film-maker Jean Vigo. It is a deceptively simple love story between a canal barge captain and the young woman he marries, bringing her aboard the barge to live with him. The film explores their hopes and the realities of life on the margins, but exudes a lyricism and heightened aestheticism that gives weight to even the smallest moments.

1934

1935–1936

Global unrest. Adolf Hitler's power increases as Germany descends into a police state. Military sanctions are ignored as the army and air force increase in numbers and factories ramp up the production of munitions. The Berlin Olympics offers another opportunity for the Third Reich to project its image of strength to the world. The Spanish Civil War commences. In the United States, Mikio Naruse's *Wife! Be Like a Rose!* (*Tsuma yo bara no yō ni*, 1935) is the first Japanese sound film to screen commercially. Warner Bros attempts to sidestep criticism over the glamorization of criminals in their gangster dramas, as seen by James Cagney's switch from playing a criminal to take the lead role as a government agent in *G Men* (1935), a thinly veiled slice of FBI propaganda.

The 39 Steps, Alfred Hitchcock, UK
Based on John Buchan's novel, *The 39 Steps* was the ideal vehicle for Alfred Hitchcock, who revelled in suspense. He conjures up a cat-and-mouse espionage thriller in which Robert Donat's Richard Hannay is mistaken for a murderer and embroiled in a plan to steal highly sensitive secrets. For all its action set pieces, the film succeeds because of the subtlety of character development, from the moving scene between Hannay and Peggy Ashcroft's unhappy farmwife to the interplay between the hero and Madeleine Carroll's resourceful captive-turned-ally.

Libya is born when Italy merges the colonies of Tripolitania and Cyrenaica. At the end of the year Italy invades Ethiopia.

The Nuremberg Laws are introduced. They deny Jews the right of German citizenship, while marriage between Jews and Aryans is prohibited.

1935

Modern Times, Charles Chaplin, USA

As its title suggests, *Modern Times* finds Charles Chaplin's tramp lost in a world of rampant industrialization, where human beings are no longer regarded as individuals, but cogs in a machine designed to produce profits for the few. The film's potent critique of capitalism gone awry notwithstanding, Chaplin creates a series of inspired comic set pieces that highlight his ingenuity as a film-maker and deft comic timing as an actor. Although it employs a panoply of sound effects and sparse fragments of dialogue, *Modern Times* is a silent film in everything but name.

Devdas, Pramathesh Barua, India

Based on the novel by Saratchandra Chatterjee, *Devdas* had been adapted as a silent film in 1928. Pramathesh Barua's Bengali version, along with his Hindi and Assamese versions of 1936 and 1937, remain the defining adaptations. They tell the story of childhood friends Devdas and Paro, whose affection turns to love as they grow up. Barua also played a titular role. As director, he encouraged a naturalistic style of acting and his screenplay tweaked Chatterjee's ending, offering audiences a critique of class division in India.

Jesse Owens wins a historic four gold medals at the Summer Olympics in Berlin, but Hitler leaves the stadium.

King Edward VIII abdicates, making his brother George VI the British monarch.

Gone with the Wind by Margaret Mitchell is published in the United States.

The Cinémathèque Française film archive is founded in Paris.

1936

ABOVE LEFT. *Once Upon a Time in the West (C'era una volta il West*, 1968), Sergio Leone, Italy/USA

Less political than the director's subsequent *A Fistful of Dynamite (Giù la testa*, 1971), Sergio Leone's operatic account of how the frontier was civilized is nevertheless pointed in its critique of unbridled capitalism. Henry Fonda's cold-blooded psychopath remains one of the most surprising transformations of a classical Hollywood star.

LEFT. *Stagecoach* (1939), John Ford, USA

The finest example of the Western in its most classical form, *Stagecoach* established John Ford's reputation as a master of the genre and made a star of John Wayne.

THE WESTERN

Although it may have originated as a thrilling way of portraying the battle between right and wrong, the Western developed into a morally complex genre that embraced political upheaval in a shifting cultural and social landscape in the United States and beyond.

The genre is almost as old as cinema itself. British pioneers Sagar Mitchell and James Kenyon produced *Kidnapping by Indians* in 1899 and the template of the classical Western was forged by Edwin S. Porter with *The Great Train Robbery* (1903). Westerns were popular in the pre-sound years but began to attract sizeable audiences from the 1930s. The films played out a Manichean battle between civilization and wilderness: the settlers, frontier people and the forces protecting them against all outsiders, from Native American tribes presented as hostile 'Indians' to outlaws.

By the late 1930s, the Western was hugely popular and John Ford was the director most closely associated with it and his drama *Stagecoach* (1939) is a perfect example of the genre at its purest. The main actors do not so much play characters as they do archetypes, representing the individuals who helped shape the myths of the West – a land that promised prosperity. John Wayne's Ringo Kid initially appears to be the villain, but he characterizes the spirit of adventure needed to exist in this world. The real enemy – the tribes attacking the stagecoach – are an anonymous

obstruction to progress. This misrepresentation was challenged by US cinema from the late 1960s, with white people and the armies that protected them made into the aggressors, in films such as *Soldier Blue* (1970).

The line between hero and villain became less clear as the genre developed. Even Wayne, the most iconic Western star, saw his persona take on darker moral hues in films such as *Red River* (1948) and *The Searchers* (1956). This ambiguity became pronounced with the emergence of the Spaghetti Western in the 1960s. With it appeared a new, more ambivalent hero, personified by Clint Eastwood's Man with No Name, in Sergio Leone's trilogy *A Fistful of Dollars* (*Per un pugno di dollari*, 1964), *For a Few Dollars More* (*Per qualche dollaro in più*, 1965) and *The Good, the Bad and the Ugly* (*Il buono, il brutto, il cattivo*, 1966). If the landscape of the classic Western was best represented by Monument Valley, this variation on the genre, mostly shot in Spain and Italy, looked more parched and unforgiving. It was hard to tell the difference between the good and the bad, and every character had an ugly side. The Spaghetti Western proved popular, with more

than 600 films produced across the span of two decades. Most were set in the United States or neighbouring countries, whereas subsequent offshoots of the Western genre came from further afield.

The Ostern offered an Eastern European take on the Western. Not to be mistaken with Red Westerns, a variation on Spaghetti Westerns that were produced in East and Central European countries but were set in the United States, Osterns took place in the wilderness of the eastern USSR and mostly unfolded during the Russian Revolution (1917–23) or the subsequent civil war. Bollywood also embraced the Western in Masala films, colourful entertainments that employed a magpie approach to genres and styles, incorporating Western tropes into classic song and dance narratives. Early examples include *Sholay* (1975) and *Amar Akbar Anthony* (1977).

US cinema has employed staple elements of the genre within a modern context. Although different in style and tone, *Brokeback Mountain* (2005), *No Country for Old Men* (2007) and *Hell or High Water* (2016) are all variations of the Western.

1937–1938

Aggression and atrocities. Adolf Hitler officially withdraws from the Treaty of Versailles (1919). Japan increases its aggression towards China, which includes the bombing of Shanghai and atrocities committed over the course of one month in Nanking. Joseph Stalin begins his Great Purge, which leads to the deaths of more than 700,000 Soviet citizens. Sergei Eisenstein regains the favour of the Soviet leader by directing *Alexander Nevsky* (*Aleksandr Nevskiy*, 1938), a heroic portrait of the 13th-century Russian prince's defeat of an invasion by the Teutonic Knights of Novgorod. It initiates a collaboration between him and composer Sergei Prokofiev, who would provide the score for the first two parts of Eisenstein's *Ivan the Terrible* (*Ivan Groznyy*, 1944/58) trilogy. Orson Welles makes a name for himself with his radio adaptation of *War of the Worlds* (1938), which plays in real time and panics some Americans, believing that Martians had invaded the United States.

Make Way For Tomorrow, Leo McCarey, USA

This Paramount production, directed by Leo McCarey, never pulls its punches as it details the impact of the Great Depression on an elderly couple and the indifference meted out to them by their loved ones. When Barkley and Lucy Cooper's house is foreclosed and he is unable to find employment because of his age, they turn to their family, who force them to separate and live with different children. The siblings' acknowledgment of their callousness ultimately comes too late.

La grande illusion, Jean Renoir, France

The futility of war, class, anti-Semitism and racial prejudice are explored through the prism of Jean Renoir's prisoner-of-war drama, one of the key works of French Poetic Realism. Set during the First World War (1914–18), it opens with Pierre Fresnay's aristocratic Captain de Boëldieu and Jean Gabin's working-class Lieutenant Maréchal shot down and captured by Erich von Stroheim's upper-class German officer Rittmeister von Rauffenstein. The film warns of the rise of fascism in Europe and the need for a class-consciousness that could overturn it.

The Basque town of Guernica is destroyed by the Luftwaffe at the behest of Francisco Franco's Nationalist faction, and is immortalized by Pablo Picasso's painting.

NKVD Operative Order 00447 sanctions the execution or imprisonment of more than 250,000 kulak dissidents and other individuals opposed to Stalin's regime.

1937

Germany annexes Austria.

Enormous reserves of oil are discovered by US geologists while searching for water in the deserts of Saudi Arabia.

Prime Minister Neville Chamberlain returns from a meeting with German and French leaders in Munich, declaring 'peace for our time.'

○ *Bringing Up Baby*, Howard Hawks, USA

Although it failed to ignite the box office when it opened, Howard Hawks's frenetic screwball comedy is regarded as one of the best examples of the genre. It finds the life of Cary Grant's palaeontologist David Huxley descending into chaos after he encounters Katharine Hepburn's Susan Vance, an eccentric society heiress, who has to look after a tame leopard named 'Baby'. Hawks encouraged his actors to race through their dialogue, and combined with his frenetic direction, this adds to the film's gradual increase in mayhem and hilarity.

1938

COLOUR

Colour film did not just allow cinema to mirror the world, it also gave directors the opportunity to employ it in expressive ways to heighten the intensity of a drama through the accentuation of a certain palette or by desaturating an image.

From Dorothy's sparkling red shoes in *The Wizard of Oz* (1939) and the shades of green in *Vertigo* (1958) to the way red transforms a landscape in *The Red Desert* (*Il deserto rosso*, 1964) or midnight blue reflects longing in *Moonlight* (2016), colour possesses the transformative power to elevate the ordinary. For a director like Aki Kaurismäki, a colourful backdrop not only enlivens a scene, it acts as an ironic counterpoint to a character's predicament. For Wong Kar-wai, the use of red in his period drama *In the Mood for Love* (*Faa yeung nin wa*, 2000) underpins the intensity of the emotions at play, whereas Pedro Almodóvar employs primary colours to accentuate the heightened state of his dramas. His use of red represents different

emotions, from desire in *Live Flesh* (*Carne trémula*, 1997) or a passion for life in *All About My Mother* (*Todo sobre mi madre*, 1999), to retribution in *Volver* (2006) and as a contrast to the protagonist's grief and remorse in *Julieta* (2016).

The easiest form of colouring in early cinema was attained by tinting film. Soaking it in dye, to stain the emulsion, the process was used to safeguard against piracy. But this range could be used by film-makers as a signifier. Blue represented night and yellow daytime. Various tints differentiated between interior and exterior shots, or distinguished between a series of timelines. It was followed by the more elaborate process of hand colouring, exemplified by the imaginative worlds Georges Méliès created.

Experimentation with colour film stock began decades before its widespread introduction into cinemas. Edward Raymond Turner developed the additive colour system in 1899, promoting his results with a short film in 1902. The process, which used conventional black and white film and colour filters in filming and projection, was rudimentary at best. The more complex subtractive colour system, developed by Kodak and known as Technicolor (not to be mistaken with its later iteration), was employed by Wray Physioc for his feature *The Gulf Between* (1917). Hollywood subsequently began to consider the potential of colour after the Technicolor Motion Picture Corporation released the Anna May Wong vehicle

The Toll of the Sea (1922). Douglas Fairbanks employed the process for his swashbuckling adventure *The Black Pirate* (1926). The star, who also produced the film, saw the appeal of a colour version of the genre that he had come to dominate. He funded the experiments, sure that an audience would be drawn to the novelty of a colour adventure. The gamble paid off and the film was a success.

Colour musicals made a splash at the same time that synchronous sound in cinema was becoming more widespread. But it was not until the late 1930s that prestige productions embraced its use. As film-makers' confidence in using colour increased, they became more daring.

Musicals like *Meet Me in St Louis* (1944) and *An American in Paris* (1951) made great use of colour, creating a world at once recognizable and larger than life. Elsewhere, Michael Powell and Emeric Pressburger employed colour to heighten the emotion and expressiveness of the dramas they produced during the 1940s. In the 1950s, directors such as Douglas Sirk, Elia Kazan and Nicholas Ray used colour to balance the darker themes they explored in their melodramas. By contrast, more recent war films, perhaps best exemplified by Steven Spielberg's *Saving Private Ryan* (1998), have drained the screen of colour in order to give the illusion of authenticity and recall news footage.

1939–1940

A high for Hollywood. Yet 1939 is seen by many historians as Hollywood's most successful year, producing a wide range of films that have since come to be regarded as classics. The Spanish Civil War ends after three years of bitter conflict with General Francisco Franco assuming power. Britain and France officially recognize his regime. Germany peacefully enters Czechoslovakia, but Britain and France declare war following the invasion of Poland. In the early months of 1940, European allies gradually fall to Hitler's forces. In Hollywood, producers are pressured not to attack the Nazi regime, while some businessmen, including Henry Ford, and noted aviator and Nazi supporter Charles Lindbergh publicly campaign for a stance of non-intervention by the United States. Leon Trotsky is murdered by a Soviet agent at his home in Mexico City in 1940.

Cardinal Eugenio Pacelli is selected as the 260th pontiff, Pope Pius XII, and adopts a more sympathetic stance to the fascists.

Britain and France declare war on Germany, while the United States declares its neutrality.

○ *Gone with the Wind*, Victor Fleming, USA
This adaptation of Margaret Mitchell's novel of 1936 set in the US Civil War (1861–65) was the brainchild of independent producer David O. Selznick. He delayed production for two years to secure Clark Gable for the role of Rhett Butler. More than 1,400 hopefuls auditioned to play Scarlett O'Hara before Selznick chose Vivien Leigh. The film was the biggest box-office success of the era. It won ten Academy Awards, including Best Supporting Actress, making Hattie McDaniel, who played house servant Mammy, the first African American to win an Oscar. The film's regressive approach to race has subsequently attracted ire.

1939

Ninotchka, Ernst Lubitsch, USA

Ernst Lubitsch began his career in Germany and then moved to the United States in the 1920s, where his professional life flourished. *Ninotchka* was co-written by Walter Reisch and the soon-to-be successful film-making team of Billy Wilder and Charles Brackett. It cast Greta Garbo as a Soviet agent who arrives in Paris to carry out her superior's orders, but finds herself seduced by the West and Melvyn Douglas's suave aristocrat. Lubitsch presents one of the earliest negative portrayals of Joseph Stalin's Russia and made the most of Garbo's on-screen charisma.

Winston Churchill replaces Neville Chamberlain as British prime minister and, following Germany's invasion of the Low Countries and northern France, British and Allied troops are evacuated from Dunkirk.

The US Pacific Fleet is moved from San Diego to Pearl Harbor, seen as a provocation by the Japanese.

Prehistoric paintings are uncovered in the Lascaux caves in France.

The Mortal Storm, Frank Borzage, USA

After Adolf Hitler rose to power, his government put pressure on Hollywood and the US government to curtail films critical of the Nazi regime. By the late 1930s, Warner Bros begins to rail against this policy. Other studios follow, among them MGM, which produces Frank Borzage's drama adapted from a novel written by British author Phyllis Bottome in 1937. She had first-hand experience of Nazi oppression and the film is forthright in its critique of the Nazis.

1940

PROPAGANDA

Cinema is a medium that reaches out to audiences en masse and possesses an extraordinary power to influence. It proved to be the most effective form of propaganda in the first half of the 20th century.

**LEFT. *Went the Day Well?*
(1942), Alberto Cavalcanti,
UK**
This Second World War
(1939–45) drama is a ruthlessly
efficient example of how
narrative cinema could be used
as propaganda, with its story of
a British village fighting an
incursion of Nazi troops.

One of the earliest examples of a
propaganda film was shot by J. Stuart
Blackton of the Vitagraph Company, in
1899. Just as William Randolph Hearst
and Joseph Pulitzer were waging a media
campaign around the Spanish-American
War (1898), *Tearing Down the Spanish
Flag* (1898) was a brief, single shot film of
a Spanish flag being replaced by the Stars
and Stripes. Blackton shot it in New
York and said: 'the people went wild'.

There were early experiments employing
film as a political tool in conflicts such
as the Boer War (1899–1902). Aristide
Demetriade's *The Independence of
Romania* (*Independenţa României*, 1912),
shot in collaboration with the Romanian
military, has claim to be the first feature
film made solely for propagandist purposes,
while D. W. Griffith's revisionist epic *The
Birth of a Nation* (1915) is recognized by
historians as a landmark of propagandist
cinema. Popular with audiences at the
time, the film's racist rhetoric rewrote
the United States' recent past and its
lauding of the Ku Klux Klan witnessed a
surge in the organization's popularity.

Cinema was employed as a tool during
the First World War (1914–18), but it
came into its own under the Soviet and
Nazi regimes. As a relatively new medium,
film was embraced as the perfect art form
of the revolutionary government of Vladimir
Lenin and a radical style of cinema
emerged. Even when interest in this kind
of cinema waned at the end of the 1920s
and was replaced by Socialist Realism
in the 1930s, the films produced still
evinced a strong ideological slant, praising
the communal spirit of Soviet society and
extolling the virtues of heroes who gave
their lives in the battle against capitalism.

Nazi Germany proved even more
effective. Joseph Goebbels, the Reich
Minister of Propaganda, was quick to
realize the power of the moving image.
Documentary was employed to emphasize
the scale of Adolf Hitler's vision for the Third
Reich, promoting Nazi culture and the
Aryan ideal. Leni Riefenstahl, once the star
of German Alpine films such as *The White
Hell of Piz Palü* (*Die weisse Hölle vom Piz
Palü*, 1929), had turned to directing with
a mountain adventure *The Blue Light* (*Das
blaue Licht*, 1932). Hitler was impressed
with it and commissioned her to film the
Nazi Party Congress, a huge gathering of
Hitler's supporters that had congregated
every year since 1923, but between 1933
and 1938 amassed in a stadium outside
Nuremberg. *Der Sieg des Glaubens* (*The
Victory of Faith*, 1934), an account of
the 1933 Congress, was a dry run for
what would become the much more
expansive *Triumph of the Will* (*Triumph
des Willens*, 1935). Riefenstahl followed it
with *Olympia* (1938), a two-part account
of the preparations for and events during
the 1936 Berlin Olympics, while Goebbels
turned to narrative cinema to further his
cause and to build hatred towards Jews
and any groups considered undesirable to
the Nazi regime.

By the time the Second World War
(1939–45) commenced, cinematic
propaganda had reached its peak, with
both sides of the conflict making use of the
medium to bolster morale, denigrate
the enemy and champion its own forces.
The Cold War (1947–91) employed
propaganda in more subtle ways – the
glut of US sci-fi movies of the 1950s
interpreted alien invasions as the perfect
allegory for paranoia over the creeping
influence of communism. The arrival of
television allowed propagandists to reach
into the family home. More recently, the
internet and social media has offered even
more reach and specificity than cinema
in influencing people.

1941–1942

A world at war.
While a Senate subcommittee is convened to determine whether Hollywood produced films to encourage US entry into the war, President Franklin D. Roosevelt's Lend-Lease Act enables him to send war materials, including ships, to friendly nations. He also allows the British Navy to repair and refuel its ships in the United States and announces that he is extending the US defence zone eastwards to Iceland and the western coast of Africa. Opposition to any support for Allied forces halts following the Japanese Navy's attack on Pearl Harbor. Germany begins conducting poison gas tests at Auschwitz, killing hundreds of Soviet prisoners of war. The Nazi occupying force in France bans the screening of English-language films. The final US film to play is *Mr Smith Goes to Washington* (1939), in which James Stewart's young and idealistic politician fights for the freedoms enshrined in a democracy.

The Maltese Falcon, John Huston, USA

This classic slice of hardboiled detective fiction, adapted from Dashiell Hammett's novel of 1930, cements Humphrey Bogart's cinematic tough-guy credentials and establishes the reputation of debut director John Huston. It is also one of the most iconic films from the classic period of film noir. Bogart's sleuth Sam Spade is hired by Mary Astor's client to investigate a disappearance, but matters soon become convoluted as various individuals are embroiled in the search for a priceless statuette.

Persecution of Jews across Europe continues, culminating in the mass execution of Kiev residents and their burial in the ravine known as Babi Yar.

The Japanese Navy launches a surprise attack on the US Fleet stationed at Pearl Harbor, bringing both countries into the Second World War.

Citizen Kane, Orson Welles, USA

Often cited by critics as the greatest film ever made, the debut of twenty-six-year-old wunderkind Orson Welles is a marvel of technological wizardry, narrative verve and directorial aplomb. Herman J. Mankiewicz's screenplay, inspired by newspaper magnates William Randolph Hearst and Joseph Pulitzer, sets up a mystery that explores the corrupting nature of power. Cinematographer Greg Toland made radical use of lighting and deep-focus techniques, the latter adding depth to a scene. The cast, comprised of members of Welles and producer John Houseman's Mercury Theatre company, provide strong support alongside Welles's central performance.

1941

Now Voyager, Irving Rapper, USA

There are star vehicles and then there are productions like *Now Voyager*, which gave Bette Davis one of her most iconic roles. She plays Charlotte Vale, a pathologically shy spinster dominated by and living in fear of her tyrannical mother. After being placed in the care of Claude Rains's psychiatrist, Charlotte rapidly gains confidence, even falling in love with Paul Henreid's unhappily married architect. Davis's transformation is one of the most dazzling moments in classical Hollywood cinema.

German SS official Reinhard Heydrich is fatally wounded in an assassination attempt in Prague. He was one of the architects of the Holocaust and the acting Reich-Protector of Bohemia and Moravia.

The Battle of Stalingrad begins, the largest confrontation of the Second World War, with an estimated two million casualties over a six-month period.

1942

1943–1944

Rays of hope. Frank Capra directs five of the seven *Why We Fight* (1942–45) propaganda films over the course of a year. The series is the most high-profile project by any film-maker working with the US armed forces. Other contributions include those by John Huston and John Ford, with the latter continuing his association with the military by making documentaries about US involvement in the Korean War (1950–53). There is a gradual tide of resistance in Nazi-occupied territories to the persecution of Jews, as well as a groundswell of opposition to Adolf Hitler's regime by German civilians, as evidenced by anti-Nazi slogans painted on walls in German cities. British actor and director Leslie Howard dies aboard a plane shot down by the Luftwaffe over the Bay of Biscay, off the coast of Portugal. An attempt to assassinate Hitler fails, but German forces are pulling back across occupied territories.

Obsession (*Ossessione*), Luchino Visconti, Italy

This crime drama presents a love affair between a married woman and a drifter. The fascist authorities had agreed to Luchino Visconti's adaptation of James M. Cain's novel *The Postman Always Rings Twice* (1934). Working in tandem with writers who would become key members of the Neorealist movement, Visconti presents a coruscating portrait of Italian working-class life. It incurs the wrath of the authorities, who destroy all copies of the film. However, Visconti is able to hide the film's negative.

The Allied invasion of Axis-controlled Europe begins with landings along the coast of Sicily.

Duke Ellington plays Carnegie Hall for the first time.

General Dwight D. Eisenhower is made supreme commander of the Allied invasion of Western Europe.

1943

The Man in Grey, Leslie Arliss, UK

In the early 1940s, Gainsborough Pictures produced a number of acclaimed contemporary dramas, such as *We Dive at Dawn* (1943). But beginning with *The Man in Grey* (1943), the studio was also responsible for a series of outrageous melodramas whose frequently surreal plots were of less concern than their swagger. Leslie Arliss's drama centres on the travails of Phyllis Calvert's Clarissa, whose relationship with Margaret Lockwood's treacherous friend and James Mason's rake of a husband threaten her sanity.

Canadian researcher Oswald Avery discovers that DNA is the substance responsible for heredity.

Allied forces commence the D-Day landings along the beaches of Normandy.

Ivan The Terrible (*Ivan Groznyy*), **Sergei Eisenstein, Soviet Union**

This is the first part of what Sergei Eisenstein envisioned would be a trilogy of the life of Ivan IV of Russia, whom Joseph Stalin admired. It portrays the ruler as a great man and national hero. Stalin signalled his approval. For *Ivan The Terrible, Part II: The Boyars' Plot* (*Ivan Groznyy. Skaz vtoroy: Boyarskiy zagovor*, 1946), Eisenstein hones in on the corrupting nature of unfettered power. Stalin was incensed, banned the film and called a halt to part three, all remains of which were destroyed shortly after Eisenstein's death in 1948.

1944

WAR

Combat has been a staple of cinema since its inception, but the glorification of war has been matched by the portrayal of its horrors, as film-makers increasingly chose to focus on the human cost of conflict.

The visceral power of cinema lends itself easily to the portrayal of conflict. But war films can also be a barometer of the times they were made in. If J. Stuart Blackton's *Tearing Down the Spanish Flag* was an act of jingoistic tokenism, produced the day after the United States declared war on Spain in 1898, films detailing the horrors of the First World War (1914–18) put paid to the notion of armed conflict as a noble pursuit.

Biblical and historical epics can benefit from the distance of time in allowing audiences the opportunity to enjoy the vicarious thrill of battle, but films detailing conflicts in the 20th century have offered mixed messages on the merits of war. Abel Gance's *J'accuse!* (1919) and Lewis Milestone's *All Quiet on the Western Front* (1930) portrayed the price paid in the trenches of the First World War and questioned the cost of victory. By contrast, William Wellman's *Wings* (1927) and Howard Hughes's *Hell's Angels* (1930) revelled in the action of aerial combat, while King Vidor's *The Big Parade* (1925) occupied the middle ground, neither glorifying the war nor offering a stance against combat, instead focusing on the human dramas that unfolded in its wake.

No other conflict has been as ubiquitous in cinema as the Second World War (1939–45). It is almost a genre unto itself. The majority of films produced treated it as a battle between right and wrong, or straightforward adventure cinema. But each film aimed to present a different perspective. *The Longest Day* (1962) offered an overview of the D-Day landings through the eyes of soldiers at different stages and levels of the operation. *A Bridge Too Far* (1977) was more focused on the failure of an ambitious military strategy further into the operation. *Saving Private Ryan* (1998) personalized the war into the search by a small unit across war-torn France for one soldier whose siblings have perished in combat. These films show how technology had progressed in the representation of conflict. But their account of war remains similar, in the way they grapple with the physical and mental impact of the conflict. Other films attempted to reach beyond the Manichean equation, in search of deeper meaning. Terrence Malick's *The Thin Red Line* (1998) and *A Hidden Life* (2019) play out as philosophical enquiries about the nature of war and its place in the world. Whereas Clint

Eastwood's Pacific conflict diptych of *Flags of Our Fathers* and *Letters From Iwo Jima* (both 2006) attempted a compassionate portrait of a brutal campaign from both sides.

War seen from the perspective of a child has been a frequent staple of the genre. There was Andrei Tarkovsky *Ivan's Childhood* (*Ivanovo detstvo*, 1962) and Jan Nemec's *Diamonds of the Night* (*Démanty noci*, 1964), as well as Isao Takahata's animated *Grave of the Fireflies* (*Hotaru no haka*, 1964) and Václav Marhoul's *The Painted Bird* (*Nabarvené ptáče*, 2019). Elem Klimov endured seven years of negotiations with state censors before finally gaining permission to make *Come and See* (*Idi i smotri*,1985) an account of the Nazi occupation of Belarus and the atrocities they committed there.

Recent wars, from Vietnam (1955–75) through to Afghanistan (2001–) and Iraq (2003–11) have run the gamut, from gung-ho actioners to critiques of the reasons for and impact of the conflicts. Some films, like *Apocalypse Now* (1979), edge towards the surreal. Others, such as *The Deer Hunter* (1978), evince enough ambiguity for critics to debate whether the films are pro- or anti-war.

1945-1946

The Second World War ends. Germany and then Japan crumble in the face of an Allied advance. Veit Harlan directs *Kolberg* (1945), one of the last films produced under the control of the Third Reich to boost German resistance. The war in Europe ends on 8 May 1945. Three months later, after the detonation of an atomic bomb over Hiroshima and Nagasaki, the Japanese government's surrender ends the war in the Pacific. Footage of the explosions signals the start of the atomic age. Other documentary footage, including the liberation of concentration camps, will be used as evidence in the trials of Nazi party members. William Wyler, who directed two documentaries during the conflict about the US Air Force, returns to Hollywood and directs *The Best Years of Our Lives* (1946), about civilian life for three returning servicemen. It wins the Oscar for Best Film.

Children of Paradise (*Les enfants du paradis*), Marcel Carné, France

During the German occupation of France, Marcel Carné was employed by the Vichy government, doing as much as he could to work against it. That included employing Jewish members of the film industry, such as set designer Alexandre Trauner who helped recreate 19th-century Paris for *Children of Paradise*. It is set in the theatrical world during the July Monarchy (1830–48). Arletty plays a courtesan desired by four men and the film is a celebration of life, love and freedom of expression at a time when the latter was repressed.

There is peace when Germany and Japan surrender unconditionally.

The United Nations Charter is signed by fifty nations.

1945

Brief Encounter, David Lean, UK

A tale of an encounter between two married
strangers on a train-station platform has come
to rank as one of cinema's great romantic
dramas. David Lean's fourth feature as
director, based on Noël Coward's play *Still Life*
(1936), offered audiences a portrait of British
life in the 1940s, balancing the desire the
characters feel for each other with the strict
mores of a reserved society. It is the barely
contained passions of two ordinary people,
unfolding in an everyday environment, that
make the film so compelling.

**Beauty and the Beast (*La belle et la bête*), Jean
Cocteau, France**

Jean Cocteau drew on the engravings of Gustav Doré for
his adaptation of 18th-century French author Jeanne-
Marie Leprince de Beaumont's tale of a prince transformed
into a beast and the girl who redeems him. He employed
a variety of special and visual effects to realize the Beast's
castle, whose state of disrepair reflects the torment of its
owner/prisoner. Cocteau embraces classical storytelling,
only breaking the fourth wall with the film's introduction,
as he asks of his audience a little 'childlike sympathy'.

Ho Chi Minh is
appointed President
of North Vietnam.

Juan Perón is elected
President of Argentina.

1946

1947–1948

Changing frontiers. The Marshall Plan presents an economic recovery strategy for a financially crippled Europe. In 1947, India achieves independence from Britain and the partitioning of India and Pakistan results in bloody clashes between Hindus, Sikhs and Muslims. The following year, the state of Israel is established, prompting a conflict between the fledgling state and the combined forces of Egypt, Iraq, Jordan and Syria. In Europe, the Cold War heats up. In the United States, paranoia over infiltration by Soviet forces creates heightened levels of hysteria. The House Un-American Activities Committee turns its attention to Hollywood, which some see as a hotbed of communist sympathies. The Supreme Court rules against vertical integration in United States v. Paramount Pictures. The decision, which breaks up the monopoly of studios controlling the production, distribution and exhibition of films precipitates the decline of the Hollywood studio system.

Black Narcissus, Michael Powell and Emeric Pressburger, UK
The Himalayas were brought to life in Michael Powell and Emeric Pressburger's third colour feature. Amazingly, the crew never left England to shoot the film. Instead, the back lot at Pinewood Studios and Leonardslee Gardens in West Sussex, with its exotic flora, gave Powell enough scope to recreate Nepal. Working with pioneering colour cinematographer Jack Cardiff, the palette of *Black Narcissus* – particularly the use of red – accentuates the illicit desires and sexual jealousy of a group of nuns.

The ship *Exodus* leaves France for Palestine, carrying 4,500 Jewish Holocaust survivors.

President Harry S. Truman creates the Central Intelligence Agency.

1947

Gentleman's Agreement, Elia Kazan, USA

Laura Z. Hobson's fictional account of institutionalized anti-Semitism is a cause célèbre when Fox studio head Daryl F. Zanuck green-lights the film adaptation. Some Jewish producers in Hollywood fear a backlash if the film is produced. But Zanuck pushes ahead, with director Elia Kazan at the helm and Gregory Peck – who accepted the role after Cary Grant turned it down – playing the journalist who pretends to be Jewish for an exposé on prejudice. The film would be one of the most successful of the year.

Mahatma Gandhi is assassinated by Hindu nationalist Nathuram Godse.

George Orwell writes *1984*.

The Berlin Blockade commences.

Hamlet, Laurence Olivier, UK

The only previous sound adaptation of *Hamlet* had been Sohrab Modi's Urdu-language production *Blood for Blood* (*Khoon Ka Khoon*, 1935). Laurence Olivier's version cuts a significant amount from the play to bring it in at just over 150 minutes, which annoys purists. But there is little doubting the actor-director's commitment. Olivier and his ensemble cast gathers praise, as does composer William Walton's rousing score. It is the only Shakespeare adaptation to win the Best Picture Oscar.

1948

ITALIAN NEOREALISM

The Italian Neorealist movement was formed during the Second World War and lasted less than a decade, but its influence was wide, inspiring other film movements around the world and generations of film-makers to come.

The roots of Italian Neorealism can be sourced to the group of left-leaning critics who contributed to the film journal *Cinema*. Vittorio Mussolini, son of Italian dictator Benito, edited it and so contributors were unable to discuss politics directly. Instead, their ire was directed at the bourgeois studio productions, known as 'white telephone' (*telefoni bianchi*) movies, which dominated film production. Critics included future film-makers Luchino Visconti and Giuseppe De Santis, as well as Cesare Zavattini, the main architect of Neorealism. They were soon joined by Roberto Rossellini, Vittorio De Sica, Federico Fellini and Alberto Lattuada.

The Neorealist movement was soon defined by a number of characteristics. The most important was the desire to move away from banal dramas of bourgeois life in favour of portraying the realities and hardships of Italy's poor and working class. To do so, film-makers would have to leave the confines of the studio and shoot on location. If the stories were to come out of the lives of the dispossessed, film-makers should try to feature real individuals rather than actors. However, for the most part the film-makers tended to cast skilled actors in major roles and surrounded them with non-professionals.

There is debate over which was the first Neorealist film. Some believe it is Visconti's *Obsession* (*Ossessione*, 1943), an adaptation of US crime novelist James M. Cain's *The Postman Always Rings Twice* (1934), with the action relocated from California to rural Italy. It follows Cain's plot, but Visconti infuses scenes with stark realism, capturing the gruelling drudgery of lives balanced on the edge of poverty. Others claim Rossellini's *Rome, Open City* (*Roma città aperta*, 1945) was the first. Rossellini had been approached to make documentaries about Don Giuseppe Morosini, the Roman priest accused of abetting the

resistance and executed by the Nazis in 1944, and the lives of child resistance members during the Nazi occupation. With screenwriters Sergio Amidei and Federico Fellini, the film eventually merged both in a narrative focusing on the last days of German control in the city and the resistance against them. In scrabbling for whatever film stock he could find, Rossellini's drama often resembles a newsreel documentary, giving the film an up-to-the-moment urgency. He would follow it with two more war-related films that fell under the banner of Neorealism: *Paisan* (*Paisà*, 1946) and *Germany, Year Zero* (*Germania anno zero*, 1948).

Other Neorealist film-makers sought to capture peasant and working-class life in post-war Italy. They include *Shoeshine* (*Sciuscià*, 1946), *The Earth Trembles* (*La terra trema*, 1948), *Bitter Rice* (*Riso amaro*, 1949) and *Bicycle Thieves* (*Ladri di biciclette*, 1948), arguably the most famous Neorealist film, which details a father's frantic search for his stolen bike. The film's climactic sequence, with Enzo Staiola's Bruno pleading for his father to be released by an angry mob, reaches a fever pitch of unbridled emotion.

The movement came to an end in the early 1950s, with some critics citing De Sica's *Umberto D.* (1952) as the final, pure example of Neorealism. By the 1950s, Italy was embarking on its economic miracle and it appeared audiences no longer wanted to see the suffering portrayed in these films. To Fellini, looking back from 1961: 'Neorealism is not about what you show, but how you show it. It's simply a way of looking at the world without preconceptions or prejudices.' The movement's influence is wide and can be seen in the work of film-makers as diverse as Satyajit Ray, Luis Buñuel, Ken Loach, Harmony Korine, Andrea Arnold, Jia Zhangke and Matteo Garrone.

1949–1950

The red threat. Ideological tensions in Asia heighten fears over the spread of communism in the West and its infiltration across all areas of society. Communist troops make significant ground in China and by early 1950 the international community recognizes the People's Republic of China. Shortly after, following the end of the blockade of Berlin, the declarations of nationhood by the Federal Republic of Germany and Democratic Republic of Germany will keep the once unified nation divided for forty years. The witch-hunt of suspected communists in the entertainment business reaches a critical point when the Hollywood Ten – writers and directors who refused to testify against their colleagues and peers before the House Un-American Activities Committee – begin their prison sentences. James Stewart embarks on an eight-film collaboration with director Anthony Mann on the Western *Winchester '73* (1950), with the actor signing a precedent-setting freelance contract that gives him a percentage of the film's profits.

Vinyl discs playing 45 rpm are introduced. They replace 78s, which have been in circulation since 1910.

The North Atlantic Treaty is signed by the United States and its European allies.

Arthur Miller's *Death of a Salesman* opens on Broadway.

○ ***Kind Hearts and Coronets*, Robert Hamer, UK**
Ealing Studios was already established as the home for a very British strain of comedy by the time Robert Hamer's pitch-black satire opened. It ranks among the studio's best films, pitching a class war between the disowned illegitimate son of an aristocratic family, played with rapier wit by Dennis Price, and the eight members of that family who are ahead of him in the line of succession to its fortune, all played by Alec Guinness. It is arguably the darkest of the Ealing comedies.

1949

La ronde, Max Ophüls, France

La Ronde retains the structure of Arthur Schnitzler's play Reigen (1897), presenting ten characters that engage in a series of liaisons, opening with a prostitute and soldier and, completing the circle, ending with a count and the same prostitute. Outside of this group, Anton Walbrook acts as Master of Ceremonies of this world, which causes outrage for its perceived immorality. Ophüls imbues the drama with such finesse and sophistication, it is impossible not to be seduced by his grown-up carousel.

Sunset Boulevard, Billy Wilder, USA

Billy Wilder's film, his last collaboration with co-writer Charles Bracket, is a withering portrait of Hollywood. Employing elements of film noir and profiting from the performances of silent era star Gloria Swanson and one of its most iconoclastic directors, Erich von Stroheim, Wilder's tale of the encounter between William Holden's struggling screenwriter and an ageing actress and her entourage is caustic in its examination of the cost of success in Tinseltown.

The Korean War begins.

Apartheid in South Africa intensifies with certain areas prohibited for non-whites under the Group Areas Act.

1950

1951–1952

Asian conflict.
The war in Korea escalates and divides public opinion, reflecting a shift away from national consensuses regarding military action that defined the previous decade. Disagreement on how to proceed in the Asian conflict results in President Harry S. Truman relieving the popular head of the UN forces General Douglas McArthur of his command, leading to a public outcry. Congress limits the terms a US President can take office to two. The US Constitution's First Amendment, upholding freedom of speech, is the centrepiece of the winning argument in Joseph Burstyn, Inc v. Wilson, which is an attempt to censor any motion-picture film that features 'sacrilegious' material. On television, CBS has a huge hit with *I Love Lucy*, becoming the most-watched television show for four of its six consecutive seasons.

US citizens **Ethel and Julius Rosenberg** receive the death penalty after being found guilty of conspiring to commit espionage and spying on behalf of the Soviet Union.

J. D. Salinger publishes the novel *Catcher in the Rye*.

Winston Churchill is re-elected as British Prime Minister.

The film journal *Cahiers du cinéma* is founded by a group of French critics and future film directors.

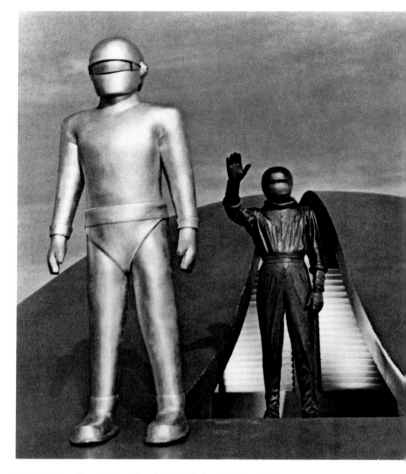

○ ***The Day the Earth Stood Still*, Robert Wise, USA**
The Cold War (1947–91) heightened levels of paranoia regarding Soviet infiltration of Europe and the United States, but also saw anxiety levels rise over the race to amass an arsenal of atomic weapons. These tensions provided the ideological underpinnings of a series of sci-fi movies churned out in the 1950s. Most were B-movie treats, but producer Julian Blaustein convinced Fox studio head Daryl F. Zanuck to green-light a sizeable production whose central theme is the danger that an arms race poses to the future of humanity. The result is one of the superior sci-fi dramas of the era.

1951

**The Life of Oharu (*Saikaku
ichidai onna*), Kenji
Mizoguchi, Japan**
Set during the 'floating world'
of urban Japan in the Edo
period (1603–1867) and told
in flashback by the eponymous
heroine, the film charts Oharu's
life through her encounters
with men who place little value
in women. Kenji Mizoguchi
witnessed his father's bullying
treatment of his mother and sister,
as well as his older sibling being
sold into geishadom. *The Life of
Oharu* represents his outrage
at such injustice.

John Cage's 4'33" is
premiered as part of
a recital series in
Woodstock, New York.

**A fog descends on
London** that will
eventually cause the
deaths of more than
5,000 people.

Charles Chaplin is
barred from re-entering
the United States after
travelling to London
for the premiere of his
film *Limelight*.

**Singin' in the Rain, Gene Kelly and
Stanley Donen, USA**
Singin' in the Rain is a joyous experience. A
hilarious and often ingenious lampooning of the
early days of sound in Hollywood productions,
the film showcases the studio star system at its
most effective: Debbie Reynolds shines as the
ingénue who gets a taste of the darker side of
showbusiness; Donald O'Connor and Jean Hagen
are fine comic support, and Cyd Charisse adds
glamour for the film's dance climax. All the while,
co-director and star Gene Kelly glides through the
film, embodying the consummate professional.

1952

FAMILY LIFE

Film-makers have employed the family dynamic as a way of exploring the full range of human emotions, while the way the family is presented is used to highlight cultural and generational difference.

Cinema has profited greatly from Russian writer Leo Tolstoy's maxim that 'every unhappy family is unhappy in its own way'. Drama in cinema has rarely been derived from the emotional journey of a family whose members are happy from the outset. A film's resolution may leave them with some sense of closure, if not complete happiness, but how they reach that point is where narratives are focused.

Family life has been a staple of cinema since its earliest years, and the fissures and conflict within the domestic environment have often been used to explore larger themes. The characters' troubles in two of the most ambitious US dramas of the silent era, Erich von Stroheim's *Greed* (1924)

and King Vidor's *The Crowd* (1928), result from the corrupting nature of unbridled capitalism. By contrast, Leo McCarey's moving drama *Make Way for Tomorrow* (1937) used one elderly couple's economic woes in the wake of the Great Depression as a device to allow them to see how selfish their children have become.

McCarey's film was the inspiration for Yasujirō Ozu's *Tokyo Story* (*Tōkyō monogatari*, 1953). By the time he made what many critics regard as his masterpiece, Ozu had become one of the most fastidious chroniclers of domestic life; his mostly static camera observing the strains between generations. Such a reserved approach was a contrast to Hollywood's depiction

of the family in the 1950s. Teenage rebellion provided the tension in Nicholas Ray's *Rebel Without a Cause* (1955), with James Dean's Jim Stark desperate to find meaning in his suburban life. Ray wanted his domestic dramas writ large, so filmed in CinemaScope. It magnified the angst Jim feels, while in *Bigger Than Life* (1956) Ray's use of the widescreen format blows up the paranoia and claustrophobia experienced by James Mason's small-town schoolteacher, whose world is turned upside down after he is prescribed behaviour-altering medication. Douglas Sirk was another Hollywood director to employ colour and scale in the service of exploring the family dynamic. If *Written on the Wind* (1956) presented a subversion of the 1950s American dream – a dream

fever companion to George Steven's tamer, but no less ambitious *Giant* (1956) – Sirk's *Imitation of Life* (1959) tackled the problems of racial prejudice in 'polite' middle-class US society.

Sirk's films may not have attracted critical acclaim at the time of their release, but they subsequently earned praise and have influenced a range of film-makers, from Rainer Werner Fassbinder to Todd Haynes, whose *Far From Heaven* (2002) is an understated homage to Sirk, albeit drawing out homoerotic themes that would never have been allowed on to the screen in the 1950s. Other film-makers noted for their focus on the family include Mike Leigh, whose portraits of British working-class life, from *Meantime* (1983) to *Another Year* (2010), present wry

examinations of class and social mobility. Ang Lee began his career with his 'father knows best' trilogy of *Pushing Hands* (*Tui shou*, 1991), *The Wedding Banquet* (*Xi yan*, 1993) and *Eat Drink Man Woman* (*Yin shi nan nu*, 1994), which reflects on the patriarchy in Asian families forced to change with the time. From there, he turned to 19th-century British family life (*Sense and Sensibility*, 1995) and the disintegration of the family in Richard Nixon's United States (*The Ice Storm*, 1997). Lee also directed *Brokeback Mountain* (2005), one of the many films that have engaged with sexuality in the family, which include *My Beautiful Laundrette* (1985) and *The Kids Are All Right* (2010), to *Moonlight* (2016), *God's Own Country* (2017) and *Boy Erased* (2018).

OPPOSITE. *Tokyo Story (Tōkyō monogatari*, 1953), **Yasujirō Ozu, Japan**
Director Yasujirō Ozu placed his camera at a low level – typically the height a person would sit on a tatami mat – and rarely moved it. What he captured were the subtlest gestures and moments of interaction between family members.

LEFT. *Bigger Than Life* **(1956), Nicholas Ray, USA**
An early portrait of prescription drug addiction and mental illness, *Bigger Than Life* also examines the corrosive nature of consumerism and the pressure to maintain the image of the perfect nuclear family in the United States during the Eisenhower era.

1953–1954

Conflicts and skirmishes. The death of Joseph Stalin and Dwight D. Eisenhower's ascending to the US presidency offer a glimmer of hope for peace, but ideological divisions around the world witness an increase in conflicts. Fidel Castro leads a force to attack the second largest military garrison in Cuba, but is defeated and imprisoned. As the French combat communist forces in Vietnam, Cambodia declares its independence from its colonialist European ruler. The Wilhelm scream, a sound effect recorded by actor Sheb Wooley first used in the Western *Distant Drums* (1951) gains its name from its use by a character in *The Charge at Feather River* (1953). It will eventually appear more than 400 times in film and television. The Academy Awards ceremony is broadcast for the first time on television.

Samuel Beckett's *Waiting for Godot* premieres in Paris.

Arthur Miller's *The Crucible*, an allegory for McCarthyism, opens on Broadway.

The CinemaScope widescreen format is launched with biblical epic *The Robe*.

Elizabeth II is crowned Queen of the United Kingdom.

○ *Gentleman Prefer Blondes*, Howard Hawks, USA
This film was Howard Hawks's only musical and a genre that seems at odds with his other work. Its dance numbers were mainly filmed by choreographer Jack Cole. However, the way that Marilyn Monroe and Jane Russell's characters manipulate the men around them is pure Hawks. His penchant for snappy dialogue delivered at speed allows the two stars to deliver charismatic and slyly knowing parodies of how Hollywood believes a woman is supposed to behave.

1953

**Summer with Monika
(Sommaren med Monika),
Ingmar Bergman, Sweden**
Summer with Monika established
Swedish film-maker and theatre
director Ingmar Bergman as a major
voice in world cinema. It was also
his first brush with moral groups, who
were outraged by the film's depiction
of nudity and sexuality. The drama
details an encounter between two
youths finding their way in the world.
Bergman captures the impetuousness
of youth with unbridled energy,
but also attempts to sidestep
conventional mores, recognizing
that the world is changing.

The first hydrogen bomb test
is carried out by the United
States across Bikini Atoll, in
the Marshall Islands.

Elvis Presley makes his radio
debut in Memphis, Tennessee
singing his first single 'That's
All Right'.

Joseph McCarthy is censured
by the US Senate.

Seven Samurai (Shichinin no samurai), Akira Kurosawa, Japan
Although it is one of the most famous samurai adventures, Akira Kurosawa's
epic does not play to the conventions of the *jidaigeki*, a drama set during
the Edo period (1603–1867). An admirer of John Ford, Kurosawa drew as
much from the Hollywood Western to forge his tale, but the kinetic drive
of the action and the way he filmed the close combat sequences would
themselves prove influential over subsequent film-makers, while the storyline
would form the basis of John Sturges's *The Magnificent Seven* (1960).

1954

1955–1956

A free rein. The Soviet Union and the United States claim that peace between their nations is possible, but covertly support opposing forces in countries around the world. By contrast, the cultural landscape is showing signs of shifting away from conservatism. *Blackboard Jungle* (1955), a film about teachers in an interracial inner-city school, features the first use of rock 'n' roll with Bill Haley and the Comets' 'Rock Around the Clock' on its soundtrack. United Artists revokes its membership of the Motion Picture Association of America over that body's refusal to grant the Otto Preminger drug-addiction drama *The Man with the Golden Arm* (1955) a Production Code Authority seal. The following year, the code relaxes its rules on the mention of abortion, drugs, kidnapping and prostitution in films. In London, the Free Cinema movement screens its first documentaries, a prelude to the working-class-oriented dramas that appear at the end of the 1950s.

Ordet, Carl Theodor Dreyer, Denmark

Religious faith dominates the Borgen family. Its head, Morten, remains pious even after the death of his wife. Shooting in his signature austere style, with a *mise-en-scène* that evokes 17th-century Dutch master Johannes Vermeer and late 19th-century Danish painter Vilhelm Hammershøi, Carl Theodor Dreyer's drama is a bleak but mesmerizing rumination on the nature of faith. The last-minute miracle divided audiences and critics alike, but it remains an extraordinary act of cinematic redemption.

The Warsaw Pact is formed, aligning countries allied to the Soviet Union and reinforcing the 'Iron Curtain' across Europe.

Alfred Hitchcock Presents debuts on US television.

Emmett Till, an African American teenager from Chicago is lynched while visiting Mississippi.

Civil-rights activist Rosa Parks is arrested in Montgomery, Alabama after refusing to give up her bus seat to a white man.

Pather Panchali, Satyajit Ray, India

Satyajit Ray encountered Bibhutibhushan Bandyopadhyay's novel *Pather Panchali* (*The Song of the Road*, 1929), when he was a graphic designer. He asked the author's widow for permission to adapt it. After funding problems were resolved – backers were unhappy with his refusal to include song and dance sequences – Ray's debut stands as a landmark in postcolonial Indian cinema. It is a key work of the Parallel Cinema movement – a Neorealist-inspired group of Bengali film-makers seeking an alternative to mainstream Hindi cinema.

1955

○ *The Searchers*, **John Ford, USA**
The tale of a man hell-bent on avenging the death
of family members at the hands of Comanche
outlaws and bringing his kidnapped niece home, *The
Searchers* is one of John Ford's most accomplished
Westerns. Shot in VistaVision, taking in the majesty of
Monument Valley, and with an atmospheric score by
Max Steiner that balances the film's epic moments
with the intimate domestic scenes, the film's darker
tone draws on the moral ambiguity displayed by John
Wayne's compromised protagonist Ethan Edwards.

Cecil B. DeMille's last film
The Ten Commandments,
a partial remake of his
1923 biblical epic, tops
the box office for the year.

**Soviet tanks and troops
invade** Hungary.

Screen idol Grace Kelly
marries Prince Rainier III
of Monaco and retires from
her screen career.

1956

FILM WAVES

Just as society changed in the years after the Second World War, so a new generation of film-makers not only challenged the role of cinema but questioned the way films were made and received.

The Italian Neorealists did not just change the way films had been made in their country, their influence created a ripple effect, inspiring waves of film movements around the world. Its impact was first felt in India with Parallel Cinema. Railing against the colourful spectaculars that dominated the country's film output, Ritwik Ghatak, Bimal Roy, Satyajit Ray, Tapan Sinha and Mrinal Sen sought to establish a movement whose work reflected the realities of life in their country.

A similar sentiment lay behind the Polish Film School and British New Wave. A brief moment of liberalism and relaxation in state censorship after the death of Stalinist Prime Minister Bolesław Bierut in 1956 saw a generation of film-makers that included Andrzej Wajda, Wojciech Has, Roman Polanski, Andrzej Munk and Tadeusz Konwicki examine the country's role in the Second World War (1939–45) and the Soviet rule that followed it. In Britain, a group of film-makers inspired by the 'kitchen sink' realism that had taken hold in the country's theatre produced films that sought to explore the lives of the working class. Their gritty portraits were leavened with humour, but sharp in the critique of class divisions.

The most important film movement to emerge was the French New Wave or *La Nouvelle Vague*. It evolved from a group of critics who wrote for the influential film journal *Cahiers du cinéma*, which questioned the value of contemporary French cinema, prizing instead Hollywood directors whose work had been dismissed as little more than genre entertainment. By the late 1950s,

the most prominent of these critics made short films, before progressing to a series of features that would challenge how films were made and employing techniques that went against the grain of mainstream film-making practices. The key members of the group were Jean-Luc Godard, François Truffaut, Éric Rohmer, Jacques Rivette and Claude Chabrol. They also included members of another group, the Left Bank or *Rive Gauche*, particularly Agnès Varda and Alain Resnais. If Truffaut's *The 400 Blows* (*Les quatre cents coups*, 1959) was a breath of fresh air when it premiered at the Cannes Film Festival, Godard's *Breathless* (*À bout de souffle*) was a whirlwind. It tore up the rule book of how films were made, from its playful narrative to the use of unconventional angles and inclusion of jump cuts – a cut in a continuous sequential shot – that disrupted a scene and made the audience aware of the film-making process.

The Japanese and Czech New Wave echoed the French New Wave's spirit of rebelliousness. In Japan, Nagisa Ōshima, Hiroshi Teshigahara and Shōhei Imamura led the charge in breaking down the rigidity of Japanese cinema and society. Czech film-makers, including Miloš Forman, Věra Chytilová, Jiří Menzel and Jan Němec used satire and absurdism to undermine the Communist regime, but often found their work subject to censorship. Brazil's Cinema Novo, particularly the films of Glauber Rocha, adopted a more radical stance. Like the films of Godard, they saw cinema as part of a revolutionary movement that envisaged a new society.

ABOVE. *Breathless* (*À bout de souffle*, 1960), Jean-Luc Godard, France
Shot with a handheld camera, featuring little lighting and jump cuts that disrupt scenes, Jean-Luc Godard's feature debut heralded a new era in cinema.

OPPOSITE. *Night and Fog in Japan* (*Nihon no yoru to kiri*, 1960), Nagisa Ōshima, Japan
The three films Nagisa Ōshima directed in 1960 – which included *Cruel Story of Youth* (*Seishun zankoku monogatari*) and *The Sun's Burial* (*Taiyō no hakaba*) – underpinned the director's emphasis on the gulf between Japan's generations.

1957–1958

The space race. The charge to gain the upper hand in military superiority between the West and East is escalated with the Soviet Union's foray into space, sparking fears of another global war. As the United States continues to experience difficulty in its attempts to send an unmanned rocket beyond the Earth's atmosphere, the Soviet Union launches Sputnik 1 on 4 October 1957. It orbits the planet for three weeks before gradually falling back to Earth. In 1958, President Dwight D. Eisenhower signs the National Aeronautics and Space Act, which establishes the National Aeronautics and Space Administration (NASA). The frenzy over this new front in the Cold War is reflected in the popularity of science fiction in comics, fiction and particularly film. These stories feature invaders from other worlds – often barely concealed allegories of the threat of the 'red peril' – or experiments gone awry, encapsulating fears of the atomic age.

Wild Strawberries (*Smultronstället*), Ingmar Bergman, Sweden

One of Ingmar Bergman's most admired films, it features acclaimed director and actor Victor Sjöström in his final role. He plays an ageing academic who travels with his estranged daughter-in-law to receive an honorary doctorate from his old university. En route, he ruminates on his past, assessing his life's worth. Bergman was inspired by a visit to his hometown of Uppsala and completed the screenplay during a two-month stay in a hospital.

The Suez Crisis results in the resignation of British Prime Minister Anthony Eden. He is replaced by Harold Macmillan.

Nine black students enter Little Rock High School in Arkansas under police protection but are removed in fear of mob violence.

1957

Ashes and Diamonds (*Popiól i diament*), Andrzej Wajda, Poland

Ashes and Diamonds completes Andrzej Wajda's war trilogy that begins with *A Generation* (*Pokolenie*, 1954) and continues with *Kanał* (1957). An adaptation of Jerzy Andrzejewski's novel of 1948, it unfolds at the end of the Second World War (1939–45), with a Home Army soldier ordered to assassinate a local communist leader. Wajda changed the novel's end, muddying its pro-communist stance, which was in keeping with the political climate. Lead actor Zbigniew Cybulskin dominates, exuding the rebellious charm of James Dean.

Mao Zedong announces the 'Great Leap Forward', his Second Five Year Plan for developing agriculture and industry.

Louis Malle's *Lift to the Scaffold* (*Ascenseur pour l'échafaud*) presages the arrival of the French New Wave.

Vertigo, Alfred Hitchcock, USA

Alfred Hitchcock's study in obsession and desire stars James Stewart as Scottie, an ex-cop with a fear of heights. Hitchcock employs a panoply of visual effects, including the expressive use of colour filters, to accentuate Scottie's psychological state. Hitchcock transformed Stewart's screen persona to achieve one of his most committed performances. *Vertigo* was a highpoint in Hitchcock's collaborations with composer Bernard Herrmann and graphic designer Saul Bass, who designed the film's poster and credit sequence.

1958

1959–1960

Out with the old. After the success of his rebel army and departure of Fulgencio Batista, Fidel Castro arrives in Havana in January 1960. A month later, he is made prime minister and begins dispersing foreign and privately owned land among the rural peasant class, as well as nationalizing industry. President Dwight D. Eisenhower recognizes the new government but when Castro visits his neighbour in April he is only met by Vice President Richard Nixon. At the same time, the 'peoples' war' to resist foreign control and unite Vietnam that Ho Chi Minh declares in March 1959, sees an escalation in early 1960 that continues throughout the decade. The spread of film waves in national cinemas globally reflects the tension in the political arena. Some movements appear more concerned with challenging film language, but by the end of the decade they are transformed through political action, as a new generation rebels against the legacy of imperialism.

Pickpocket, Robert Bresson, France

Robert Bresson's three films in the 1950s embraced a minimalist aesthetic that sought a psychological and spiritual understanding of their protagonists. Following his *Diary of a Country Priest* (*Journal d'un curé de campagne*, 1951) and *A Man Escaped* (*Un condamné à mort s'est échappé ou Le vent souffle où il veut*, 1956), *Pickpocket* details the day-to-day experiences of a small-time con. Less interested in the conventions of plot, Bresson draws us into Michel's world, which fluctuates between euphoria – the thrill of stealing – and fear that he will eventually be caught.

'Kind of Blue', Miles Davis's groundbreaking jazz album is released.

Ben-Hur is the most expensive film ever made and goes on to win a record eleven Academy Awards

1959

La dolce vita, Federico Fellini, Italy

Federico Fellini's *La dolce vita* is a rambunctious carnival of excess, detailing the wild side of Rome's celebrity world. Seen through the eyes of Marcello Mastroianni's journalist, this *beau monde's* existence is an extended party. Opening with the now-famous prologue, featuring a helicopter carrying a statue of Christ over the Italian capital, the film presents seven episodes – along with an intermezzo and epilogue – that unfold over the course of a week, as Marcello searches for love and meaning in his life.

The 400 Blows (Les quatre cents coups), François Truffaut, France

Director François Truffaut's *The 400 Blows* was the clarion call of the French New Wave. His semi-autobiographical portrait of an adolescent boy whose parents who do not understand him, it follows Antoine Doinel on a series of adventures on the streets of Paris. Seen from his perspective, as he plays hooky and embarks on a series of pranks that result in his being sent to a juvenile home on the coast, Truffaut refuses to sentimentalize his character or the world around him.

South African police fire on unarmed protesters demonstrating against apartheid at the black township of Sharpeville, and kill sixty-nine people.

John F. Kennedy beats Richard Nixon to become the 35th President of the United States.

1960

4
—

BREAKING
BARRIERS

From 1960, cinema around the world underwent a tectonic shift. Like-minded directors began to coalesce into movements that expressed a desire for a change. The increasing popularity of what would be known as art-house cinema, as well as the changing characteristics of popular genres, led to the most radical transformation of cinema since the arrival of sound.

These changes were mostly attributed to a younger generation challenging traditions that no longer chimed with the times. But many established directors also embraced the opportunities of more relaxed restrictions on what was permissible on the screen, as a sixty-year-old Alfred Hitchcock showed with *Psycho* (1960). His 47th feature as director since his 1925 debut, *Psycho* was one of Hitchcock's most radical films. A director who had worked at the heart of Hollywood's studio system for two decades, he broke away to take a chance on a low-budget, black and white thriller that played with the conventions of narrative, upped the ante in terms of sexuality and violence, and introduced the wider world to the slasher genre. The risk paid off. Hitchcock's Midas-touch for self-promotion (after five years introducing the *Alfred Hitchcock Presents* television series, he was both a household name and face) and his belief that audiences were ready for something more risqué made the film an unqualified success.

Hitchcock was not alone. In late 1960, Robert Wise began working with choreographer Jerome Robbins to bring the smash Broadway success *West Side Story* (1961) to the screen. Updating William Shakespeare's *Romeo and Juliet* (1597) to modern-day New York, the film's producers chose Wise – who started out as an editor in Hollywood in the 1930s – because he had proven himself a capable director of tough urban dramas. The resulting film was a world away from the musicals produced in the 1940s and 1950s, as evidenced in the film's opening. Designer Saul Bass created a changing spectrum of colours, which are punctuated by a graphic featuring static vertical lines – as abstract, if less urgent, than the credits he produced for *Psycho* – that turn out to be the buildings of lower Manhattan. Following it is a series of aerial shots that take viewers over docks, a network of roadways and parks, as well as the United Nations, Empire State building and Yankee Stadium. They are followed by images of tenement blocks – a world away from the settings of earlier New York musicals such as *On the Town* (1949). As Wise's camera reaches ground level, the actors dancing reminds viewers that they are watching a musical, but the locations are mostly gritty, run-down and all too real. *West Side Story* is the bridge between the sophisticated Manhattan comedies, romances and thrillers of old and subsequent portraits of a neglected city that provide the backdrop to *Midnight Cowboy* (1969), *The French Connection* and *Shaft* (both 1971).

Many of the films by film-makers keen to challenge cinematic traditions were premiered at film festivals, which grew in importance as the decade progressed. Venice, the oldest film festival, was created in 1932. Its main prize, the Golden Lion, was introduced in 1949. In 1951, it was awarded to Akira Kurosawa's *Rashomon* (*Rashōmon*, 1950), a key moment in the recognition of Japanese cinema on the international stage. The Cannes Film Festival followed in 1938. Its major prize, arguably the most important international film festival prize, is the Palme d'Or (Golden Palm). The Berlin Film Festival was created in 1951 and with its Golden Bear award, it rounds off the top three international festivals that dominated the film calendar during this era. The 'Big Five' festivals today still include these festivals, but also Toronto and Sundance, which were founded in 1976 and 1978. Of these festivals, Cannes would become the world leader in serious

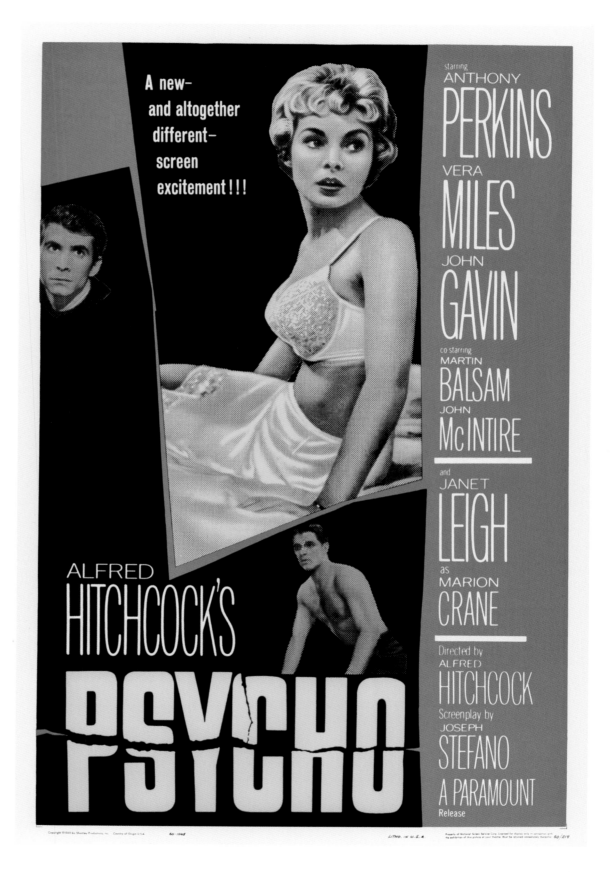

RIGHT. *Psycho* (1960), Alfred Hitchcock, USA

Alfred Hitchcock's slasher is a landmark in horror cinema. It was promoted by an innovative marketing campaign, dispatched its star almost an hour in and pushed the level of violence in a mainstream film.

cinema. If its image throughout much of the 1950s was one of glamour, bringing the world's stars to the French Riviera, it had also begun a move towards signalling cinema's cultural importance. The creation of the Critics' and Special Jury Prizes were aimed at widening the scope of the festival and rewarding more challenging films, and 1960 was a breakthrough year for the event. Novelist Georges Simenon was president of the jury that divided the top prizes between Federico Fellini's *La dolce vita* (1960), which was awarded the Palme d'Or and Michelangelo Antonioni's *L'avventura* (1960), which shared the Jury Prize with Kon Ichikawa's *Odd Obsession* (*Kagi*, 1959). Fellini's film was the popular choice, while Antonioni's received a more polarized reaction. Although critics and the jury members found much to admire in Antonioni's critique of bourgeois society, some audience members at the premiere booed the film, a reaction that has since become a regular feature of Cannes. But what Fellini and Antonioni's films represented was a growing interest in cinema beyond mainstream entertainment. Both went on to enjoy commercial success and their directors were positioned at the vanguard of a new era in cinema, which challenged the way audiences consumed film and how they viewed the world through it.

Earlier in 1960, Jean-Luc Godard received the Silver Bear at the Berlin Film Festival for *Breathless* (*À bout de souffle*, 1960). A radical departure from the conventions of classical film-making style, Godard's feature debut defined the French New Wave. The film movement was joined by the Japanese and Czech New Waves, Brazil's Cinema Novo, Argentina's Grupo Cine Liberación, New German Cinema and the Yugoslav Black Wave.

Film movements were key to film-makers' effectiveness in bringing on change in the medium. But each film-maker eventually broke away to seek their own path. Godard's would become – and remain – one of the most unique. From key New Wave entries such as *Vivre a vie* (1962), *Le mépris* (1963), *Bande à part* (1964) and *Pierrot le fou* (1965), he moved into radical politics in the late 1960s and early 1970s with the Dziga Vertov Group, and thereafter continued to produce polemical and uncompromising works across film and video.

Other film-makers during this period forged distinctive paths that would expand the possibilities of cinema and further prove its importance as a serious art form. Ingmar Bergman produced the majority of his most vital work during this period. After completing his loose trilogy that explored the nature and limits of faith, comprising *Through a Glass Darkly* (*Såsom i en spegel*, 1961), *Winter Light* (*Nattvardsgästerna*) and *The Silence* (*Tystnaden*, both 1963), he embarked on what has come to be regarded as his most radical work, *Persona* (1966). A drama between two women, one who has stopped speaking and the other present to help cure her, all set on the island of Fårö where Bergman lived, *Persona* unsettles as the actors peel away the layers of their characters' psyches and the film examines the notion of identity. Bergman would continue to mine a rich vein of drama with *Shame* (*Skammen*, 1968), *The Passion of Anna* (*En passion*, 1969), *Cries and Whispers* (*Viskningar och rop*, 1972) and *Scenes from a Marriage* (*Scener ur ett äktenskap*, 1974). In the same period, Luis Buñuel produced most of his greatest work. After creating *An Andalusian Dog* (*Un chien andalou*, 1929) with Salvador Dalí and the controversial *L'âge d'or* (1930), Buñuel led a peripatetic life for a decade, leaving Spain when General Francisco Franco's fascists came to power and travelling wherever work took him across the United States, before settling in Mexico, just as the country's cinema was enjoying a golden age in popularity. His account of dispossessed youth in Mexico City *The Young and the Damned* (*Los olvidados*, 1950) won him the

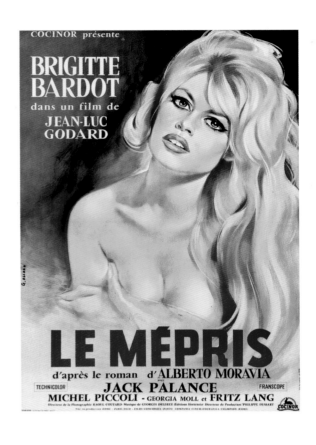

ABOVE. *Le mépris* (1963), Jean-Luc Godard, France
With Raoul Coutard's rapturous imagery and Georges Delerue's plaintive score, Jean-Luc Godard's deconstruction of the movie business is one of the key films of the French New Wave.

ABOVE RIGHT. *L'avventura* (1960), Michelangelo Antonioni, Italy

Few film-makers have represented the ennui of their characters as perfectly as Michelangelo Antonioni's breakthrough film, one of a wave of 1960s' films that rewrote the grammar of cinema.

RIGHT. *Persona* (1966), Ingmar Bergman, Sweden

Director Ingmar Bergman's portrait of the relationship between an actor who has seemingly lost the power of speech and the nurse looking after her, is one of the pinnacles of art-house cinema.

Best Director award at the Cannes Film Festival, which he would return to in 1961, taking the top prize for *Viridiana*, a scathing portrait of religious hypocrisy. That film launched a run of piercing satires of the church, state and bourgeoisie that included *Belle de jour* (1967), *The Discreet Charm of the Bourgeoisie* (*Le charme discret de la bourgeoisie*, 1974) and his final film *That Obscure Object of Desire* (*Cet obscur objet du désir*, 1977).

The work of these individual film-makers, whose thematic concerns ran the gamut from national identity and the coercive nature of power to explorations of sexuality and the politics of gender, helped establish what would become known as art-house cinema. But visionary directors also existed within the margins of mainstream cinema. Hollywood's golden age was populated by directors whose work existed in the commercial sphere, but when viewed as a whole they featured thematic concerns that led to critics regarding them as 'auteurs' – film-makers with a cohesive vision that is evident across all their work. In the 1960s, such traits could be found in a number of directors working in commercial Italian cinema. Both Mario Bava and Sergio Leone began their careers as directors for hire, but their contribution to two genres would have a lasting impact.

Bava had been working in the Italian film industry since the late 1930s. By the late 1940s, he was an experienced cinematographer and was gaining valuable knowledge in the nascent area of special effects. His early work was dominated by comedies, with the occasional historical and sword and sandal drama. But it was his debut as sole director, the horror *Black Sunday* (*La maschera del demonio*, 1960), that helped define his subsequent work. Bava brought a level of visual style to the genre that shaped the development of the *giallo* (a murder mystery or horror thriller named after the crime-mystery pulp novels whose covers mostly featured a yellow background, hence its title) as it developed into the 1970s. Though he would often shift gear and tackle other genres, it is films like *The Whip and the Body* (*La frusta e il corpo*, 1963), *Blood and Black Lace* (*6 donne per l'assassino*, 1964), *Kill, Baby... Kill* (*Operazione paura*, 1966) and *A Bay of Blood* (*Ecologia del delitto*, 1971) for which he is best known.

Bava had directed a Spaghetti Western, *Roy Colt & Winchester Jack* (1970), late in his career. But the genre was Leone's, who created it and whose small but hugely significant body of work dominated it. Like Bava, Leone's early career saw him assisting on sword and sandal epics, most notably alongside William Wyler on *Ben-Hur* (1959), before replacing director Mario Bonnard on *The Last Days of Pompeii* (*Gli ultimi giorni di Pompei*, 1959) and striking out on his own with *The Colossus of Rhodes* (*Il colosso di Rodi*, 1961). However, it was with his 'Dollar' trilogy that Leone cemented his reputation. It also introduced Clint Eastwood, who replaced John Wayne as a contemporary Western icon, whose moral ambiguity better reflected the times. *A Fistful of Dollars* (*Per un pugno di dollari*, 1964) highlighted Leone's penchant for cutting between long shots and extreme close-ups, which reached its apotheosis in the extended three-way shootout climax of *The Good, the Bad and the Ugly* (*Il buono, il brutto, il cattivo*, 1966). That film also highlighted the successful relationship between Leone and his composer Ennio Morricone, who would continue to score for him, on the more political *Once Upon a Time in the West* (*C'era una volta il West*, 1968) and *A Fistful of Dynamite* (*Giù la testa*, 1971), as well as the director's single entry into the gangster genre, *Once Upon a Time in America* (1984).

Leone's vision of the West played out on a grand scale and was a variation on the epic that had been a popular element of cinema since the 1910s. But like David Lean's *Lawrence of Arabia* (1962) and Sergey Bondarchuk's nearly seven-hour-long adaptation of Leo Tolstoy's *War and Peace* (*Voyna i mir*, 1966), Leone understood the necessity of balancing scale with intimacy. It was also an element that made *Spartacus* (1960) one of the most successful Hollywood epics. Stanley Kubrick took over from Anthony Mann early in the production and brought psychological rigour to his account of the slave uprising. The film-maker had already employed a similar tactic to his acclaimed First World War (1914–18) drama *Paths of Glory* (1957) and would prove a singular presence on the landscape of Cold War films with his chilling but relentlessly funny *Dr Strangelove or: How I Learned to Stop Worrying and Love the Bomb* (1964). Such was the uniqueness of Kubrick's place that he stands alone from genres, movements and comparisons with other directors. His *2001: A Space Odyssey* (1968) is a singular achievement that profits from its ambiguity, while *Barry Lyndon* (1975) once again found Kubrick engaging with cinema that unfolds across a vast canvas. The latter hones in even more on the intimate, achieved through the stately movement of his camera and innovative use of candlelight as the sole light source for interior scenes.

A number of genres enjoyed spectacular moments of success during this period. None more so than the disaster movie. Films detailing some great calamity, from the destruction of cities to the sinking of ships such as the RMS *Titanic* – a popular subject in cinema, from *In Night and Ice* (*In Nacht und Eis*, 1912) and *A Night to Remember* (1958) through to James Cameron's Oscar-winner of 1997 – had been popular. But the glut of films that emerged in the 1970s, the genre's golden age, employed a successful format. Featuring a large cast of stars, whose initial interactions in the drama played out somewhere between the debonair shenanigans of *Grand Hotel* (1932) and a daytime soap, audiences' suspense – and pleasure – was gained from watching them dispatched, one by one, as the disaster that engulfed them grew in intensity. Popularity increased following the success of *Airport* (1970), the first in a series of airline disaster narratives whose originality waned with each entry. *The Poseidon Adventure* (1972) gave the genre one of its creative and commercial highs. It was produced by Irwin Allen, who became known as the king of the disaster movie and would achieve the era's greatest success with his subsequent film *The Towering Inferno* (1974), as well as its nadir with *The Swarm* (1978). *Earthquake* (1974) was the third great disaster success of the decade, while other titles proved less popular and the genre as a whole was subject to parodies such as *The Big Bus* (1976) and *Airplane!* (1980).

Martial-arts films had been popular in Asian cinema since Zhang Shichuan's epic, 27-hour-long Chinese film serial *Burning of the Red Lotus Monastery* (*Huo shao hong lian si*, 1928). The modern martial-arts film emerged to resounding success in the 1960s. The Shaw Brothers' film-production company and the siblings who ran it, Runje, Runme and Runde, raised the bar on the genre transforming it into a vast and prolific industry. They oversaw films that ran from the high-art acrobatics of King Hu's *Come Drink with Me* (*Da zui xia*, 1966), *Dragon Gate Inn* (*Long men kezhan*, 1967) and *A Touch of Zen* (*Xia nü*, 1971) to the more commercially minded *The 36th Chamber of Shaolin* (*Shao Lin san shi liu fang*, 1978). The cinema

OPPOSITE. *2001: A Space Odyssey* **(1968), Stanley Kubrick, USA/UK**
Stanley Kubrick's visionary journey into space offers up a cinema that poses more questions than it answers as it probes the nature of existence.

RIGHT. *The Poseidon Adventure* **(1972), Ronald Neame, USA**
The disaster genre reached its pinnacle in the 1970s, as evinced by Ronald Neame's maritime adventure, in which a small group of passengers and crew aboard an overturned liner struggle to survive.

found its first superstar in Bruce Lee, in a series of films that prioritized kinetic action scenes over narrative logic. The vacuum that was left by his death in 1973 at the age of thirty-two was filled by Jackie Chan, whose blend of athleticism and high-jinks comedy outlasted martial-arts cinema's popularity, which waned from the late 1970s.

Blaxploitation embraced martial-arts cinema, most notably *Black Belt Jones* (1974), with Jim Kelly who starred opposite Lee in *Enter the Dragon* (1973). But blaxploitation was not so much a genre as an attempt to create a cinema that featured a representation of African American characters and culture that did not kowtow to mainstream stereotypes. Melvin Van Peebles's *Sweet Sweetback's Baadasssss Song* and photographer Gordon Parks's *Shaft* (both 1971) are early entries and were followed by a range of films that spanned the 1970s. Their quality varied and opinions on whether they resisted or reinforced African American stereotypes remain divided. But they created some of the earliest female action heroes in Pam Grier and Tamara Dobson. Such was their popularity among mainstream audiences that the James Bond adventure *Live and Let Die* (1973) drew heavily from them.

This era saw nations and cultures that had recently won independence reject the white-dominated narratives of colonial rule. Third Cinema, a movement that began in Latin America, soon spread out across the world. Directors keen to hear their voices heard responded to the call of Argentine film-makers Fernando Solanas and Octavio Getino in their 'Toward a Third Cinema' manifesto, which stressed that the greatest struggle was 'the most gigantic cultural, scientific, and artistic manifestation of our time, the great possibility of constructing a liberated personality with each people as the starting point – in a word, the

decolonization of culture'. A powerful cinema in Africa was visible through the work of Ousmane Sembène (Senegal), Med Hondo (Mauritania), Mohammed Lakhdar-Hamina (Algeria), Omar Khlifi (Tunisia), Moustapha Alassane and Oumarou Ganda (Niger), Dia Moukouri (Cameroon), Ibrahim Mallassy (Sudan) and Benoît Ramampy (Madagascar).

Cinema during this period shifted between the sublime and the shocking. At one end, cinema presented an opportunity to reflect on the past. Theo Angelopoulos employed long and complex takes in his exploration of history and time, most notably in *The Travelling Players* (*O thiasos*, 1975), his study of mid-20th-century Greece. By contrast, Sergei Parajanov created a rich *mise-en-scène* with a cinema constructed of tableaux that did not so much attempt to capture the culture that formed the bedrock of his influences – spanning Russian, Georgian and Armenian traditions – but witnessed a singular vision employing the medium to forge his own view of the world. There had never been anything quite like *Shadow of Forgotten Ancestors* (*Tini zabutykh predkiv*, 1965) or *The Colour of Pomegranates* (*Sayat Nova*, 1969).

Parajanov cited Russian film-maker Andrei Tarkovsky's feature debut as a significant influence over his decision to make films. *Ivan's Childhood* (*Ivanovo detstvo*, 1962) presented a child's view of the Second World War (1939–45) from a perspective that was so artfully composed – the director used the term 'poetic logic' – it stood apart from most other dramas dealing with the conflict. However, the film was a project that had been hoisted on to Tarkovsky and he regarded it more as his 'qualifying examination' to be a film-maker. His next feature *Andrei Rublev* (*Andrey Rublev*, 1966) fully realized his cinematic vision. A portrait of the 15th-century Russian icon painter,

ABOVE LEFT. *Mirror (Zerkalo, 1975)*, **Andrei Tarkovsky, Russia**
Blurring dreams and memories, with his father's poetry scattered throughout, Andrei Tarkovsky's fourth feature conflates personal and national histories to create a deeply personal form of cinema.

LEFT. *Salò, or the 120 Days of Sodom (Salò o le 120 giornate di Sodoma, 1975)*, **Pier Paolo Pasolini, Italy**
This was Pier Paolo Pasolini's final film. Inspired by the writings of the Marquis de Sade, Dante Alighieri, Friedrich Nietzsche and Marcel Proust, it presented a shocking portrait of unbridled power, whose graphic imagery and violent tone has divided audiences and critics.

ABOVE. *Raging Bull* (1980),
Martin Scorsese, USA
Director Martin Scorsese and
screenwriter Paul Schrader's
searing portrait of masculinity
and self-destruction featured a
transformative performance by
Robert De Niro as real-life boxer
Jake LaMotta.

Tarkovsky's film explores his subject's development as an artist, influenced by and productive in spite of the tumultuous events he lived through. In *Solaris* (*Solyaris*, 1972), an adaptation of Polish writer Stanislav Lem's novel of 1961, Tarkovsky transports audiences to the outer reaches of space. Fragments from memories become part of characters' waking lives, reminding them that they cannot escape the life they have created. Whereas in *Mirror* (*Zerkalo*, 1975), existence blurs with memory and dreams to create a film that is close to a poem. He returned to science fiction with *Stalker* (1979), working with brothers Arkadiy and Boris Strugatskiy on an adaptation of their novel *Roadside Picnic* (*Piknik na obochine*, 1972). A haunting, visually dazzling film, it bolstered the film-maker's reputation as one of the singular artists of the medium.

In the same year that Tarkovsky produced *Mirror*, another poet, Pier Paolo Pasolini, completed *Salò, or the 120 Days of Sodom* (*Salò o le 120 giornate di Sodoma*). The Italian film-maker had courted controversy before with his work, most notably *Pigsty* (*Porcile*, 1969). But in detailing four corrupt Italian libertines' abuse of a group of kidnapped teenagers during the German occupation of Italy in the latter stages of the Second World War, Pasolini's final film was shocking. Combining stories of acts carried out in the Italian Social Republic with an adaptation of the Marquis de Sade's *The 120 Days of Sodom* (*Les 120 Journées de Sodome*, 1785), Pasolini's drama was the continuation of a series of films that confronted societal and cultural taboos. The year before, Yugoslavian film-maker Dušan Makavejev's *Sweet Movie* (1974) featured unsimulated sex acts, coprophilia, emetophilia and implied child molestation. Before that, audiences had witnessed extreme acts of sex and violence in Sam Peckinpah's *Straw Dogs*, Ken Russell's *The Devils*, Kubrick's *A Clockwork Orange* (all 1971), Wes Craven's *Last House on the Left*, Bernardo Bertolucci's *Last Tango in Paris* (*Ultimo tango a Parigi*) and Gerard Damiano's *Deep Throat* (all 1972). Opposition to Makavejev's film was led by moral and religious groups who expressed concern over cinema's corrupting influence. Similar concerns would become magnified with the use of videocassettes in the 1980s.

The creative freedom many directors enjoyed during this period became limited in the 1980s, a confluence of the shifting social and political landscape, as well as economic factors. The crises that unfolded across the West from the mid 1970s made film production difficult in many countries. Meanwhile, in Hollywood the studios were transforming. Some were merged into larger global media conglomerates where creative voices were stifled in the race to bolster box-office returns. The success of blockbusters such as *Jaws* (1975) and *Star Wars* (1977) highlighted how lucrative this kind of cinema could be. But focus on them came at the expense of riskier ventures. Author Peter Biskind's celebrated account of the era between the end of the studio system and the new corporate Hollywood took as its title two films that bookended this time. *Easy Riders, Raging Bulls* (1998) witnesses a moment when a group of talented directors and writers, supported by understanding producers and an army of gifted practitioners, drew on the world's cinema to create a kind of film-making that was fearless and challenging. Dennis Hopper and Peter Fonda's trans-American travelogue could be seen as a celebration of that culture, which was undermined by the myopic vision of big business. Martin Scorsese's *Raging Bull* (1980) was one of the last gasps of total creative freedom from this group. A new generation emerged that attempted to work around the straitjacketing of studio control, sometimes with success. But as the 1980s progressed, the landscape that produced such extraordinary cinema in the 1960s and 1970s was gone.

1961–1962

Rising tensions. Three months after John F. Kennedy is sworn in as the 35th US President, an anti-Castro force attempts to invade Cuba at the Bay of Pigs. The mission fails and the next eighteen months see an escalation in tension between the United States and the alliance of Cuba and the Soviet Union, culminating in the Cuban Missile Crisis. Tensions are also stretched by Kennedy's visit to Berlin in July 1961, just a month before a wall is constructed that will divide the city for three decades. Preparations for the construction of the Berlin Wall prevented Billy Wilder filming a scene from his madcap Cold War satire *One, Two, Three* (1961) at the Brandenburg Gate. Instead, it is constructed on a sound stage. A darker vision of international tensions is presented the following year in John Frankenheimer's *The Manchurian Candidate*.

Last Year in Marienbad (*L'année dernière à Marienbad*), Alain Resnais, France

A member of the *Rive Gauche* (Left Bank) movement of artists, writers and film-makers, Alain Resnais had already impressed with the documentary short *Night and Fog* (*Nuit et brouillard*, 1956) and his feature debut *Hiroshima mon amour* (1959) by the time he released this enigmatic study of memory, space and time. It is playful and dreamlike, yet serious in its study of what Resnais described as 'the complexity of thought'.

The Beatles perform for the first time at Liverpool's The Cavern Club.

Joseph Heller publishes *Catch-22*.

The trial of Adolf Eichmann begins in Jerusalem.

1961

Cleo from 5 to 7 (Cléo de 5 à 7), Agnès Varda, France

Unfolding over a two-hour period as Cléo (Corinne Marchand) awaits the results of a medical test, Agnès Varda's sophomore feature is a pensive study in existentialism. A gifted photographer and member of the Left Bank group, Varda's *La Pointe-Courte* (1955) presaged the arrival of the French New Wave. With *Cléo*, she established herself as one of French cinema's most important voices, confronting attitudes to women and the myopia of patriarchy, as well as engaging with the Algerian conflict, which was dividing French society.

The Exterminating Angel (El ángel exterminador), Luis Buñuel, Mexico/Spain

Members of Mexico City's ruling elite attend a dinner party. They soon discover that they are trapped in one of the rooms. Unable to leave, they quickly descend into savagery. After attracting the ire of the Catholic Church for his perceived blasphemy with *Viridiana* (1961), Luis Buñuel took aim at bourgeois hypocrisy and latterly the Church with his scathing and surreal satire. Buñuel would return to a similar theme with *The Discreet Charm of the Bourgeoisie* (*Le charme discret de la bourgeoisie*, 1972).

In Berlin, former U-2 pilot Francis Gary Powers is exchanged for the Soviet spy, Rudolf Abel, which eventually becomes the subject of Steven Spielberg's *Bridge of Spies* (2015).

Screen icon Marilyn Monroe is found dead in her home in Brentwood, California, having overdosed from barbiturates. She was thirty-six years old.

1962

1963–1964

The world on film. The importance of international film festivals reflects the appetite of audiences for new cinematic experiences from around the world. If Japanese cinema became popular in the 1950s, so the profile of other national cinemas and their film-makers grows. Ingmar Bergman, whose *Summer with Monika* (*Sommaren med Monika*, 1953) established his reputation, is a regular presence on art-house screens, while Italy boasts an embarrassment of cinematic riches. Vittorio De Sica represents the old guard, while Federico Fellini and Michelangelo Antonioni cement their brand of modernism, with the latter's *Red Desert* (*Il deserto rosso*, 1964) pushing his style further with the striking use of colour. If Luchino Visconti's *The Leopard* (*Il gattopardo*, 1963) represents cinema at its most opulent, Pier Paolo Pasolini's *The Gospel According to Matthew* (*Il vangelo secondo Matteo*, 1964) strips the medium to its barest essentials. Italian mainstream cinema enters its most fruitful period, with baroque horror and the Spaghetti Western.

8 ½, Federico Fellini, Italy

Accurately named, as film-maker Federico Fellini had to date directed six features, contributed to two portmanteau films and co-directed his debut with Alberto Lattuada, 8 ½ was a portrait of an artist in a state of crisis. As played by regular collaborator Marcello Mastroianni, Guido Anselmi is a gifted film-maker at the height of his powers, whose chaotic personal life collides with the madness of the film industry and sends him spiralling into a funk of self-doubt and stifled creativity. Hugely influential, the film saw Fellini at the height of his powers.

John F. Kennedy is assassinated on a visit to Dallas, Texas.

The first multiplex cinema opens in the Ward Parkway Shopping Center in Kansas City, Missouri.

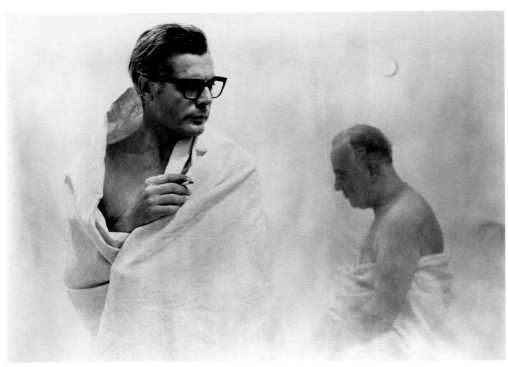

1963

**The Umbrellas of Cherbourg (Les parapluies de Cherbourg),
Jacques Demy, France**

Director Jacques Demy embraces the classical Hollywood musical but grounds it in the story of everyday life on the French coast. Featuring continuous music with the dialogue sung rather than spoken, and enlivened by the director's inventive use of colour, *The Umbrellas of Cherbourg* is a sweetly romantic tale of young love impacted by the real world. It gave Catherine Deneuve her breakthrough role.

In South Africa, Nelson Mandela and seven others are sentenced to life imprisonment and sent to Robben Island prison.

One Potato, Two Potato is the first film to feature an interracial marriage.

Sidney Poitier becomes the first African American man to win an Oscar, for his performance in the drama *Lilies of the Field* (1963).

**Dr Strangelove or: How I Learned to Stop Worrying and Love the Bomb,
Stanley Kubrick, UK/USA**

This blistering satire savages the rush by the military and political elite to gain the upper hand in the Cold War (1947–91). Stanley Kubrick's film is divided between the War Room, where the US president attempts to assure his Soviet counterpart that he has no aggressive intentions; a US air base where an unhinged brigadier general has launched a nuclear offensive; and a bomber that has lost contact with the world as it delivers its payload to the USSR. It is bleak, uncompromising and hilarious.

1964

REVOLUTIONARY CINEMA

Politics and cinema collided in the 1960s. Cinema continued to play a significant role in seismic social, cultural and political changes that unfolded well into the 1970s.

The 1968 edition of the Cannes Film Festival was a defining moment for cinema. Just as a number of European countries were experiencing increasing unrest, the festival was forced to close following film-makers' calls for solidarity with the wave of protests. As the festival began, student demonstrations in Paris had spread to factories around the country. Some film-makers on the jury expressed concern that the festival was out of touch with the real world. As the

screening of Carlos Saura's psychological thriller *Peppermint Frappé* (1967) was about to begin, the film-maker and his lead actor Geraldine Chaplin, along with François Truffaut and Jean-Luc Godard, stormed the stage to prevent the screen's curtains from opening. Uproar ensued and the following day, the festival was cancelled.

The closure of Cannes was a gesture of support for the students and workers, but cinema around the world had been sowing

the seeds of dissent since the early 1960s. In Britain, moving on from the 'kitchen sink' realism that offered up the angst-driven working-class anti-heroes of films like *This Sporting Life* (1963), Lindsay Anderson directed *If....* (1968). Inspired by Jean Vigo's *Zéro de conduite* (1933), the film chronicled a public-school pupil's rebellion against the establishment. Likewise, in Japan the young film-makers that comprised the country's new wave were immediately linked to a turbulent

OPPOSITE. *Black God, White Devil* (*Deus e o Diabo na Terra do Sol*, 1964), Glauber Rocha, Brazil
Glauber Rocha's *sertão* (backcountry) Western, made when he was twenty-five years old, drew on the visual style of Neorealism but exuded a surrealist edge in critiquing the exploitation of the poor.

LEFT. *The Girls* (*Flickorna*, 1968), Mai Zetterling, Sweden
This landmark in feminist cinema finds three actors who are performing in a touring production of Aristophanes' *Lysistrata* (411 BC) discuss how women's roles in society have changed little.

political scene, which culminated in the assassination of Japan Socialist Party leader Inejiro Asanuma by a right-wing student in 1960. Nagisa Ōshima's *Night and Fog in Japan* (*Nihon no yoru to kiri*, 1960) was banned as a result, which the director criticized as a politically motivated act.

In Europe, films such as *The Battle of Algiers* (*La battaglia di Algeri*, 1966) and *Man on Horseback* (*Michael Kohlhaas – Der Rebell*, 1969) stoked the fires of anti-colonialism and class conflict, while Greek director Costa-Gavras's *Z* (1969) and Francesco Rosi's *Hands Over the City* (*Le mani sulla città*, 1963), *The Mattei Affair* (*Il caso Mattei*, 1972) and *Illustrious Corpses* (*Cadaveri eccellenti*, 1976) were damning indictments of institutionalized corruption and state-sanctioned terror. Jean-Luc Godard, who had broken away

from the French New Wave by the late 1960s, even forewent his name on a series of films that appeared under the banner of the Dziga Vertov Group. Produced between 1968 and 1972, and including *Wind From the East* (*Le vent d'est*, 1970) and *Tout va bien* (1972), they employed Brechtian alienation techniques and espoused Marxist principles in their rejection of Western values.

The most radical engagement between politics and cinema at this time were the films made in Latin America. Nelson Pereira dos Santos's *Barren Lives* (*Vidas Secas*, 1963), Ruy Guerra with *The Guns* (*Os Fuzis*, 1964) and Glauber Rocha's *Black God, White Devil* (*Deus e o Diabo na Terra do Sol*, 1964) led the way for Brazil's Cinema Novo. In Cuba, Tomás Gutiérrez Alea's *Memories of Underdevelopment*

(*Memorias del subdesarrollo*, 1968) was hailed as a cinematic expression of the Cuban Revolution (1953–59). Argentine directors Octavio Getino and Fernando E. Solanas's documentary *The Hour of the Furnaces* (*La hora de los hornos*, 1968) represented the forces opposed to colonialism, capitalist exploitation and the money-making structure of the Hollywood system that defined Third Cinema films. Ranging from Ousmane Sembène and Djibril Diop Mambéty in Senegal, Med Hondo in Mauritania, Raoul Peck in Haiti, Sara Gómez and Alea in Cuba, Heiny Srour in Lebanon and Paul Leduc in Mexico, these film-makers rejected the principles of Hollywood (First Cinema) and the European art-house film (Second Cinema) in favour of a new way of film-making that railed against imperialism.

1965–1966

New world order. The fallout of the tensions between the East and West gradually works its way into popular culture. Novelists such as Ian Fleming, John Le Carré and Len Deighton not only grapple with the complexities of espionage, but touch on the possibilities of technological advances and a new world order controlled by those with access to destructive weapons that are both more portable and deadly than ever before. Film adaptations soon ensue. The success of the James Bond series, particularly *From Russia with Love* (1963) and *Goldfinger* (1964), are followed in 1965 by *Thunderball, The Ipcress File* – the first entry in the Harry Palmer trilogy starring Michael Caine – and the Le Carré adaptation *The Spy Who Came in from the Cold*. The Harold Pinter scripted *The Quiller Memorandum*, the spy spoof *Our Man Flint* (both 1966) and another Le Carré adaptation, *The Deadly Affair* (1967), follow.

Daisies (*Sedmikrásky*), Věra Chytilová, Czechoslovakia

Two young girls (Jitka Cerhová and Ivana Karbanová), both named Marie, embark on a series of adventures after deciding they want to behave badly. There is no logic to their actions in the series of loosely connected, often wildly funny episodes. Dedicated to 'those who get upset only over a stomped-upon bed of lettuce', Věra Chytilová's absurdist satire, an anarchic yet formally daring critique of patriarchy, remains a landmark of the Czech New Wave.

The Sound of Music beats *Gone with the Wind* (1939) to become the most successful film at the box office.

Bob Dylan goes electric at the Newport Folk Festival, Rhode Island.

Malcolm X is assassinated while giving a speech in New York.

Alabama State Troopers attack 525 civil rights demonstrators in Selma, Alabama as they attempt to march to the state capitol in Montgomery.

1965

The Battle of Algiers (La battaglia di Algeri), Gillo Pontecorvo, Italy/Algeria

Reconstructing the events that unfolded in Algiers between November 1954 and December 1957, Gillo Pontecorvo's film employs fictional realism to recount the efforts of Ali La Pointe, the Algerian revolutionary fighter and guerrilla leader of the National Liberation Front, to repel French colonial rule. Pontecorvo avoids any romantic portrayal of the rebels by depicting the atrocity of acts committed by both sides. The film's effectiveness in detailing guerrilla activity resulted in the Pentagon screening the film in 2003 for commanders operating in Iraq.

The Round-Up (Szegénylegények), Miklós Jancsó, Hungary

Bookended by *My Way Home* (*Így jöttem*, 1965) and *The Red and the White* (*Csillagosok, katonák*, 1967), Miklós Jancsó's celebrated trilogy focuses on the futility of conflict. It takes place in 19th-century Hungary after a quelled uprising, with members of the Austro-Hungarian army hunting down rebel factions. Actors and animals are choreographed with geometric precision across the sparse landscape, Jancsó's framing accentuating the inhumanity of war.

The US military presence in Vietnam increases substantially.

1966

1967–1968

To space and beyond. In 1961, both the Soviet Union and the United States successfully sent a man into space, and President John F. Kennedy announced his intention to support a programme to send a man to the moon. The Space Race moved up a gear and with it the public's fascination regarding the possibility of a manned lunar mission. If science fiction in 1950s' cinema was populated by films whose allegorical undertow exploited fears of Cold War (1947–91) tensions and the threat of a nuclear apocalypse, a strand of films in the 1960s speculates hopefully on the possibilities of space travel. As the Apollo missions edge closer to their goal, the films produced range from astronauts-on-a-mission dramas such as Robert Altman's *Countdown* (1967) and John Sturges's *Marooned* (1969), to Roger Vadim's psychedelic romp *Barbarella* and the era-defining *Planet of the Apes* and *2001: A Space Odyssey* (all 1968).

Bonnie and Clyde, Arthur Penn, USA

A landmark in presaging a new era in Hollywood film-making, this film is based on the real-life exploits of 1930s' bank robbers Bonnie Parker and Clyde Barrow. Writers Robert Benton and David Newman originally envisaged Jean-Luc Godard directing their screenplay. Arthur Penn eventually came on board and drew together disparate styles, from Keystone Cops-era slapstick to the French New Wave, to create a thrilling portrait of an outlaw gang whose anti-establishment image chimed perfectly with the times.

The Six-Day War, between Israel and the neighbouring states of Egypt (then the United Arab Republic), Jordan, Iraq, Lebanon and Syria, is fought between 5 and 10 June.

The Jungle Book, the last animated feature supervised and overseen personally by Walt Disney before his death in December 1966, is released.

1967

Playtime, Jacques Tati, France

This is the third of four outings for Jacques Tati's singular comic character Monsieur Hulot who first appeared in *Les vacances de Monsieur Hulot* (1953) followed by *Mon oncle* (1958) and *Trafic* (1971). It finds Hulot wandering through a sterile world. If his screen persona echoes Chaplin's journeyman tramp, *Playtime* is very much Tati's *Modern Times* (1936), the film's six sequences presenting an automated world lacking in warmth. It is a *tour de force* of production design – a small city was built for it – while Tati's comic set pieces are skilfully choreographed.

If...., Lindsay Anderson, UK

Malcolm McDowell became the face of rebellion in the late 1960s thanks to his debut in Lindsay Anderson's unsparing satire of English public-school life. He plays Mick Travis, a senior pupil whose antipathy towards the stifling formality and severe discipline of the school leads to his armed insurrection. The film encapsulates the spirit of May 1968 and the student demonstrations across Europe. Anderson and McDowell returned to Travis for two further satires, *O Lucky Man!* (1973) and *Britannia Hospital* (1982).

Martin Luther King Jr is assassinated in Memphis, Tennessee in April.

Robert F. Kennedy is fatally shot in Los Angeles, two months later.

Following the Prague Spring liberal reforms introduced by Alexander Dubček, more than half a million Warsaw Pact troops invade Czechoslovakia to restore authoritarian rule.

1968

MODERN HORROR

The horror film has been an unsettling presence in cinema since the emergence of German Expressionism. In the 1930s, Universal embraced it with a series of monsters and ghouls, while cinemas around the world found unique ways to unsettle audiences. Then in 1960, a series of films redefined the parameters of the genre, preparing the way for more visceral journeys into the dark.

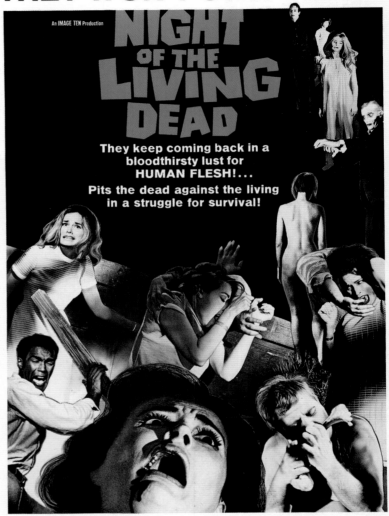

In April 1960, Michael Powell's *Peeping Tom* was released. A far cry from the romantic films he had created with Emeric Pressberger in the 1940s and 1950s, this portrait of a professional photographer and serial killer who uses his camera to simultaneously film and murder his victims was universally reviled by critics and audiences. A different fate lay

in store for Alfred Hitchcock's *Psycho*, which came out five months later. His take on the slasher thriller, with its shock dispatching of the main protagonist after an hour, was a sensation. It had been a risk for Hitchcock, who had stepped away from his pattern of colourful prestige studio productions to fund this small-scale but ruthlessly effective

thriller. By this point, French audiences had already been unsettled by George Franju's chilling *Eyes Without a Face* (*Les yeux sans visage*), about a plastic surgeon dispatching young women in Paris in order to restore the face of his daughter, who was disfigured in an automobile accident. Then, in August, Mario Bava's *Black Sunday* (*La maschera del* demonio) was released. It marked the inception of a genre of Italian horror films known as *giallo*. With these films, a new kind of horror was unleashed on audiences.

Roger Corman was another key factor in the development of horror in the 1960s. His brand of low-budget genre film-making turned a healthy profit, offering a viable avenue of business for small studios and independent film-makers. But films like his Edgar Allen Poe series also displayed a certain flair that placed them above most other US horror films of the era.

George A. Romero's *Night of the Living Dead* (1968) was a landmark in modern horror. It introduced the world to the flesh-eating zombie, which Romero followed with five sequels between 1978 and 2009. It also highlighted the genre's potential for social or political allegory, which was taken up by Wes Craven with his disturbing and graphic *The Last House on the Left* (1972) and by Tobe Hooper with *The Texas Chainsaw Massacre* (1974). They were joined by *Halloween* (1978) director John Carpenter as film-makers producing effective horror films on a small budget, a stark contrast to more sizeable studio productions of the era such as *The Exorcist* (1973), *Carrie* and *The Omen* (both 1976).

Meanwhile, Italian horror in the hands of directors such as Dario Argento and Lucio Fulci had shifted gear to become more operatic and explicit.

The availability of home video from the late 1970s saw an explosion in low-budget horror, while *Alien* (1979), *Friday the 13th* (1980) and *A Nightmare on Elm Street* (1984) took the slasher film in different directions, from outer space to teenagers' nightmares, and spawned multiple sequels. Jonathan Demme's *The Silence of the Lambs* (1991) saw horror embraced by the mainstream, becoming only the third film to win the top five accolades at the Academy Awards. Mainstream audiences were also quick to embrace Craven's postmodern makeover of the slasher genre with *Scream* (1996), a trick repeated by *The Cabin in the Woods* (2011). But that latter film stands in contrast to much post-9/11 horror, which has ranged from the popularity of Japanese and Korean horror to the 'torture porn' of the *Saw* (2003–) and *Hostel* (2005–11) series, low-budget paranormal thrillers and original horror tales such as *The Babadook*, *It Follows*, *A Girl Walks Home Alone at Night* (all 2014), *The Witch* (2015), *The Untamed* (*La región salvaje*, 2016), *Get Out* (2017) and *Midsommar* (2019).

OPPOSITE. *Night of the Living Dead* **(1968), George A. Romero, USA**
Released as opposition to the Vietnam conflict was increasing in the United States, George A. Romero's low-budget shocker encapsulated a state of unease. It was unusual for featuring a black actor in a lead role. It became a runaway success.

BELOW. *Suspiria* **(1977), Dario Argento, Italy**
Horror meets the art film in Dario Argento's much-admired tale of a supernatural conspiracy at a prestigious dance school. Narrative logic takes a back seat to a series of set-ups that are as inspired as they are gruesome.

1969–1970

Sense of despair. The Summer of Love of 1967, in which a generation of revellers who believed they could change the world descended on San Francisco, is a distant memory as the 1960s comes to a close. Richard Nixon's administration has all but declared war on the US counterculture, while student opposition to the situation in Vietnam and Cambodia increases. Woodstock music festival brings generations together in August 1969. But four months later, violence dominates the Altamont Free Concert in California. Documentaries record both events. Whereas Michael Wadleigh's *Woodstock* (1970) focuses on the music, David and Albert Maysles's *Gimme Shelter* (1970) evinces a despairing tone that reflects the sea change across US society as a new decade begins. The dark mood culminates in the Ohio National Guard opening fire on unarmed demonstrators at Kent State University on 4 May 1970, killing four students.

Easy Rider, Dennis Hopper, USA

Peter Fonda and Dennis Hopper's characters were named after Wyatt Earp and Billy the Kid, underpinning Fonda's vision of *Easy Rider* as a modern-day Western. The story was co-written by Fonda, Hopper and novelist Terry Southern, but much of it was improvised, while the drugs taken were real. The film became a counterculture sensation and heralded a new generation in US film-making. But it was also a bleak commentary on the fissures that divided US society.

Apollo 11's *Eagle* landing craft touches down on the moon and footage of Neil Armstrong stepping on to its surface, the first film shot on another celestial body, are relayed around the world.

The Stonewall riots in New York mark the start of the LGBTQI-rights movement in the United States.

1969

Kes, Ken Loach, UK

Adapted from Barry Hines's novel about a physically abused fifteen-year-old who finds respite from his life when he encounters and looks after a kestrel, Ken Loach's affecting drama has come to define his socially conscious cinema. Like so many of Loach's films, *Kes* not only presents a moving tale of hardship but highlights the economic impoverishment that communities in the mining towns in the north of England were forced to endure at the end of the 1960s.

Midnight Cowboy (1969) becomes the first X-rated film to win a Best Picture Academy Award.

The Nuclear Non-Proliferation Treaty comes into effect, with more countries party to it than any other arms limitation and disarmament agreement.

The Conformist, Bernardo Bertolucci, Italy

Bernardo Bertolucci's adaptation of Alberto Moravia's novel is a visual *tour de force* that examines one man's collusion with a brutal political regime in his desire to conform and be seen as normal. But his lack of any moral, ethical or political foundation finds him willing to betray those closest to him to ensure his survival. Shot by Vittorio Storaro, the film's expressionistic imagery would heavily influence the work of the New Hollywood film-makers of the 1970s.

1970

1971–1972

Tackling taboos. Just as societal norms shifted throughout the 1960s, leading to a relaxation in attitudes regarding issues thought to be taboo, so film-makers in the early 1970s push the envelope in what is permissible on the screen. Yugoslav film-maker Dušan Makavejev confounds and outrages the establishment with his *W. R.: Mysteries of the Organism* (*W. R. - Misterije organizma*, 1971), which conflates the psychoanalytic theories of Wilhelm Reich with communist politics and sexuality. At the same time, horror reaches new levels with the graphic depiction of violence in Mario Bava's *giallo A Bay of Blood* (*Ecologia del delitto*, 1971), while Wes Craven's *The Last House of the Left* (1972) and Sam Peckinpah's *Straw Dogs* (1971) ground their brutal acts of violence in everyday life. The latter features a scene of rape that attracts as much outrage as the content of Stanley Kubrick's controversial *A Clockwork Orange* (1971), while Bernardo Bertolucci's *Last Tango in Paris* (*Ultimo tango a Parigi*) and Gerard Damiano's *Deep Throat* (both 1972) present frank portraits of sexuality.

The mob wanted Harlem back. They got Shaft... up to here.

SHAFT

SHAFT's his name. SHAFT's his game.

METRO-GOLDWYN-MAYER Presents "SHAFT" Starring RICHARD ROUNDTREE · Co-Starring MOSES GUNN · Screenplay by ERNEST TIDYMAN and JOHN D. F. BLACK · Based upon the novel by ERNEST TIDYMAN · Music by ISAAC HAYES · Produced by JOEL FREEMAN · Directed by GORDON PARKS · METROCOLOR

The French Connection, William Friedkin, USA

Loosely based on a real-life drugs operation and employing a style that owes more to documentary than the traditions of conventional crime drama, William Friedkin's breakthrough film helped define the New Hollywood style. Gene Hackman's Oscar-winning portrayal of anti-hero detective Jimmy 'Popeye' Doyle drives the narrative, alongside Friedkin's kinetic direction, capturing the tawdriness of early 1970s' New York and producing one of cinema's most thrilling car chases. It also won Academy Awards for Best Film, Best Director, Best Film Editing and Ernest Tidyman's adapted screenplay.

Shaft, Gordon Parks, USA

An early example of blaxploitation cinema, Richard Roundtree plays the eponymous private detective employed by a Harlem crime boss to rescue his kidnapped daughter from Italian mobsters. Although critics subsequently questioned claims that Gordon Parks's crime drama was a trailblazer in the representation of African Americans on the screen, Isaac Hayes's music would remain hugely influential. He became the first African American to win an Academy Award in a non-acting category for the film's iconic theme song.

The New York Times publishes the *Pentagon Papers* detailing US political and military involvement in Vietnam.

US President Richard **Nixon** declares a war on drugs.

The world's first permanent **IMAX** movie theatre opens in Toronto.

1971

Aguirre, the Wrath of God (Aguirre, der Zorn Gottes), Werner Herzog, Germany
Among the group of directors that represent New German Cinema, none were as ambitious in their vision as Werner Herzog. His breakthrough film was the first of five collaborations with lead actor Klaus Kinski. Their fiery relationship is the stuff of legend and both excelled with *Aguirre, the Wrath of God*. Kinski convinced as a soldier with delusions of grandeur who is destroyed by greed, while Herzog eschewed the more tasteful conventions of period drama, presenting the conquistadores' search for El Dorado as a journey into hell.

Five White House operatives are arrested for burglarizing the offices of the Democratic National Committee at the Watergate complex in Washington, D.C.

Eleven Israeli athletes at the 1972 Summer Olympics in Munich are murdered after eight members of the Palestinian militant group Black September invade the Olympic Village.

1972

LEFT. *Taxi Driver* (1976), **Martin Scorsese, USA**
If Travis Bickle's journey was inspired by a dark period writer Paul Schrader experienced in his twenties, it was fully realized by Martin's Scorsese's virtuoso direction and Robert De Niro's committed performance.

BELOW. *The Godfather* (1972), **Francis Ford Coppola, USA**
Like *Chinatown* (1974), *The Godfather* took the conventions of the classical Hollywood style and infused them with an edginess that was reflected in the work of this new generation of film-makers.

NEW HOLLYWOOD

The Hollywood Antitrust Case of 1948, which led to studios losing their monopoly of the production, distribution and exhibition of films, undermined their power over a global industry they had dominated for decades. However, a rapidly changing US society, which found the studios out of touch with their audience, was the key factor that sealed their fate.

The Motion Picture Production Code, whose strict moral guidelines seemed old fashioned in the 1960s, was finally scrapped in 1968. The new films that challenged it were made by directors who had either been waiting to break free from the shackles of an outdated system, or were the first generation to attend film school. These film-makers were also inspired by the visionary films coming out of Europe, which aimed for a new language of expression in cinema. As the 1960s progressed, the role of the producer was eclipsed by the rise of the director as the leading creative force.

John Cassavetes, with his independently produced *Shadows* (1958), a landmark for its representation of race as well as a cornerstone in film production outside the Hollywood system, offered inspiration to this new generation. But it was an attack from within that transformed Hollywood. In 1967, Warren Beatty produced and starred in *Bonnie and Clyde* directed by Arthur Penn. The film's representation of violence and ambiguous sexuality unsettled Warner Bros head Jack L. Warner, who was just holding on to his studio.

However, *Bonnie and Clyde*'s eventual success proved that there was an audience for a new vision of the United States past and present. Like Francis Ford Coppola's

subsequent *The Godfather* (1972), Roman Polanski's *Chinatown* (1974) and films by directors such as Sydney Pollack and Sidney Lumet, *Bonnie and Clyde* played a magpie role, taking what still thrilled audiences from classical Hollywood while investing it with an urgency prevalent in more contemporary film-making styles. The death of the film's eponymous anti-heroes, shredded in a hail of bullets that are delivered in slow motion, would be taken further in the climax of Sam Peckinpah's *The Wild Bunch* (1969). That film's standoff between its motley gang of ageing outlaws and the Mexican army could be viewed as the allegorical death of the classical Western.

The success of Dennis Hopper and Peter Fonda's *Easy Rider* (1969), with its focus on countercultural life and a bleak denouement underpinning the vast gulf between two kinds of America, cemented the need for new visions and film-makers willing to buck conventions. Mike Nichols followed *The Graduate* (1967), his striking portrait of youthful rebellion, with an ambitious adaptation of Joseph Heller's novel *Catch-22* (1970) and the sexually frank *Carnal Knowledge* (1971).

Nichols's former comedy partner Elaine May directed two subversive satires with *A New Leaf* (1971) and *The Heartbreak Kid*

(1972), while Barbara Loden made a striking directorial debut with the hard-hitting drama of a housewife turned robber, *Wanda* (1970).

As Steven Spielberg and George Lucas were honing their instincts for a new kind of mainstream fare, which would draw on the nascent visual-effects industry, Martin Scorsese and Coppola were focused on crime. Coppola's *The Godfather* and *The Godfather: Part II* (1974) were sprawling underworld epics, while *The Conversation* (1974), shot between the two, was a claustrophobic chamber piece that chimed with a nation rapt by the Watergate scandal of 1972 to 1974. Scorsese's *Mean Streets* (1973) and *Taxi Driver* (1976) established him as the most exciting and cine-literate film-maker of his generation. Robert Altman was the most industrious film-maker of the time, his films from *M*A*S*H* (1970) to *A Wedding* (1978) offering a deconstruction of almost every major genre from Hollywood's golden age.

The success of this era was not to last. By the early 1980s, producers began to take control in Hollywood and the breadth of originality on display in the 1970s would become subservient to an industry more focused than ever on box-office returns. But the influence of this era can be found in work by later generations of film-makers.

1973–1974

Emerging cinema. With the collapse of colonial governments, African culture comes into focus internationally, drawing on the continent's distant and recent past, as well as its present. By the early 1970s, Senegal already boasts two established film-makers in Ousmane Sembène and Djibril Diop Mambéty. An acclaimed writer whose French-language fiction debut *The Black Docker* (*Le Docker Noir,* 1956) charts the plight of an African labourer working on Marseilles's docks and battling racism, Sembène turned to film with his short *Borom Sarret* (1963), produced his feature debut *Black Girl* (*La noire de...*) in 1966 and followed it with the acclaimed *Mandabi* (1968) and *Emitaï* (1971). Following his earlier, frank portraits of life in Senegal's capital Dakar, *City of Contrasts* (*Contras' city*, 1968) and *Badou Boy* (1970), Mambéty's *Journey of the Hyena* (*Touki Bouki*, 1973) is awarded the International Critics Award at Cannes Film Festival. It is one of the most influential postcolonial African films, presenting a complex depiction of youth in Senegal.

La grande bouffe, Marco Ferreri, Italy/France
Excess, of food, sex and eventually death, drives Marco Ferreri's portrait of four middle-aged men who gather for a weekend of gluttony, with moments of debauchery thrown in for good measure. However, the men, played by four icons of European cinema – Marcello Mastroianni, Michel Piccoli, Philippe Noiret, Ugo Tognazzi – are not driven by desire so much as disgust and Ferreri's excessive dose of absurdism plays out as a satire of the bourgeois class whose appetites know no bounds.

US involvement in the Vietnam War ends with the signing of the Paris Peace Accords.

An Arab oil embargo against countries that support Israel triggers an energy crisis.

Film star and martial artist Bruce Lee dies of cerebral edema in Hong Kong, six days before his final film *Enter the Dragon* is released.

1973

**The Spirit of the Beehive
(El espíritu de la colmena),
Victor Erice, Spain**

By any standards, Victor Erice's
five-decade career has produced
a slim body of work. Alongside
eleven shorts, a collaboration
with Abbas Kiarostami in 2016
and his documentary *The Quince
Tree Sun* (*El sol del membrillo,*
1992), the Spanish film-maker
has made just two narrative
features. His first, *Spirit of the
Beehive*, is frequently cited as
the greatest of all Spanish films,
and weaves together cinema and
reality in the mind of a young
girl. It is a magical, rapturously
shot drama and one of the finest
films made about childhood.

**Fear Eats the Soul (Angst essen Seele auf),
Rainer Werner Fassbinder, Germany**

Shot in less than two weeks, between his work on
Martha and *Effi Briest* (*Fontane Effi Briest*, both
1974), Rainer Werner Fassbinder's depiction of an
interracial, cross-generational relationship between
Brigitte Mira's West German cleaner and El Hedi ben
Salem's migrant Moroccan worker was meant to be
little more than an exercise for the film-maker. It is
seen as one of the writer-director's most vital films. An
homage to Douglas Sirk, replete with dramatic shifts
in tone and plot surprises, its black humour eventually
gives way to a moving portrait of loneliness.

Stephen King publishes
his first novel *Carrie*.

**US President Richard
Nixon** announces his
resignation on 8 August.

1974

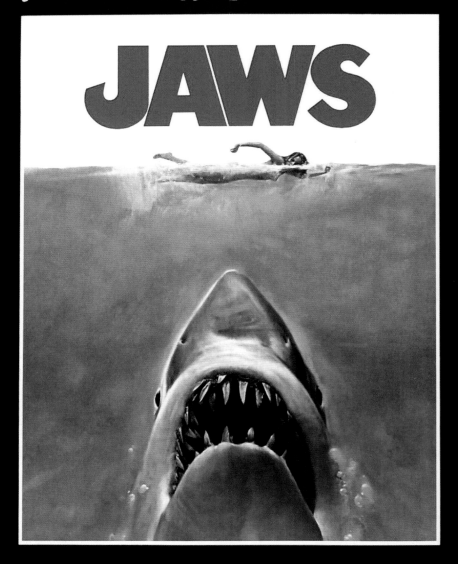

The terrifying motion picture from the terrifying No. 1 best seller.

JAWS

ROY SCHEIDER · **ROBERT SHAW** · **RICHARD DREYFUSS**

JAWS

Co-starring LORRAINE GARY · MURRAY HAMILTON · A ZANUCK/BROWN PRODUCTION
Screenplay by PETER BENCHLEY and CARL GOTTLIEB · Based on the novel by PETER BENCHLEY · Music by JOHN WILLIAMS
Directed by STEVEN SPIELBERG · Produced by RICHARD D. ZANUCK and DAVID BROWN · A UNIVERSAL PICTURE ·
TECHNICOLOR® PANAVISION® **PG** PARENTAL GUIDANCE SUGGESTED SOME MATERIAL MAY NOT BE SUITABLE FOR PRE-TEENAGERS ORIGINAL SOUNDTRACK AVAILABLE ON MCA RECORDS & TAPES ...MAY BE TOO INTENSE FOR YOUNGER CHILDREN

LEFT. *Jaws* (1975), Steven Spielberg, USA
The first modern blockbuster built on the success of Peter Benchley's bestselling novel with an effective and intensive marketing campaign that appealed to the widest possible audience.

OPPOSITE. *Batman* (1989), Tim Burton, USA
For months prior to its debut, all people saw of Tim Burton's superhero adaptation was the Batman logo. More than a blockbuster release, it was billed as the cinematic event of the year.

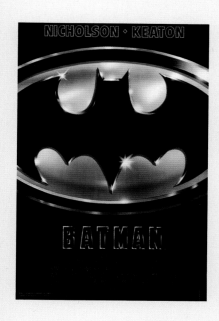

THE BLOCKBUSTER

If viewed as thrilling cinema that appeals to a mass audience, blockbuster cinema has been a constant on screens, from the first epics by Enrico Guazzoni and Giovanni Pastrone through to the adventures of James Bond and Alfred Hitchcock's *North by Northwest* (1959). But the blockbuster era began in the mid 1970s with the arrival of a shark and an epic space saga.

The word 'blockbuster' initially appeared in the press to describe a form of aerial bomb used by the British Royal Air Force in the Second World War (1939–45) that was capable of levelling a large building or entire street. It was first employed for a film in 1943, to advertise the US propaganda drama *Bombardier*: 'The block-buster of all action-thrill-service shows!' But it became more common in the wake of Steven Spielberg's thriller *Jaws* (1975).

Early audience test screenings, an industry tool for gauging the potential commercial success of a film that was first used by US actor Harold Lloyd in the 1920s, hinted at *Jaws'* box-office potential. In response, Universal embarked on an unprecedented marketing campaign and decided to release the film wide for its opening weekend. The only films previously released widely on their opening weekend were ones that were not expected to attract critical acclaim and so aimed to make the most amount of money as quickly as possible. The *James Bond* (1953–) series was a rare exception to this rule. These two factors, mass publicity and a wide release strategy, became the staple of a blockbuster release. It worked for *Jaws*, with Spielberg's

film breaking box-office records globally. But those figures were soon dwarfed by the success of George Lucas's *Star Wars* (1977).

Star Wars was initially seen as a trickier investment. Science-fiction films were not a huge attraction at the time and Lucas's film had gone significantly over budget. The initial release was modest. However, the audience reaction was immediate and ecstatic. Studio 20th Century Fox quickly increased the number of screens showing the film in order to accommodate the demand. Where it progressed from *Jaws* was in its ancillary revenue streams. *Star Wars* was not just a film, it was a sensation. To profit from it, a vast swathe of merchandise, from caps and T-shirts to dolls and models, were produced. The film was also an example of an entertainment with four-quadrant appeal: it attracted both males and females under and over the age of twenty-five. This became a significant determinant for future blockbusters

In the 1980s, blockbuster production was streamlined. Studios no longer took a chance on whether a film would become a hit – with escalating costs, there was too much at stake with 'tent-pole' releases, as blockbusters became known. They did not necessarily

have to be an extravagant space epic, but these films needed to possess a high-concept idea – a plot that could be encapsulated in an easily communicated premise. Studios also dedicated certain 'windows', dates or periods in the year that were most optimal for a blockbuster release. It might coincide with a national holiday or school break. Release dates could be booked by a studio years in advance, heightening audience expectations of an upcoming film but also warning other studios to steer clear of that opening weekend with any of their blockbuster releases. Over time, the counterprogramming of films aimed at audiences unlikely to be interested in blockbuster releases also became a feature of release schedules.

In the 21st century, blockbusters are mostly comprised of sequels or franchise spin-offs, from successful fiction series or comic-book adaptations to fairground rides or bestselling toys. Some critics bemoan the loss of original stories and studios' over-reliance on expensive productions. With more blockbusters, the release window for them occupies a greater part of the year. However, the growing influence of streaming services might change the role of the blockbuster in the future.

1975–1976

States of unease. Events around the Watergate scandal that led to President Richard Nixon's impeachment and eventual resignation, and perhaps exacerbated by his being pardoned by Gerald Ford within a year of assuming office, magnify suspicions of deep state conspiracies. Since the escalation of the Cold War (1947–91) in the early 1960s and doubts surrounding Lee Harvey Oswald's guilt in the assassination of John F. Kennedy in 1963, conspiracy theories are on the rise. If John Frankenheimer's *The Manchurian Candidate* (1962) perfectly encapsulates these concerns and his *Seconds* (1966) raises doubts about identity within the countercultural world. Alan J. Pakula's trilogy of *Klute* (1971), *The Parallax View* (1974) and *All the President's Men* (1976), as well as Sydney Pollack's *Three Days of the Condor* (1975) and Peter Hyams's *Capricorn One* (1977), all suggest a rot at the heart of the US establishment. They are not alone: Francesco Rosi's *Illustrious Corpses* (*Cadaveri eccellenti*, 1976) offers a critique of institutionalized corruption in his native Italy.

Pier Paolo Pasolini is murdered.

Spain's dictator, Francisco Franco, dies at the age of eighty-two.

Stanley Kubrick's *Barry Lyndon* is the first film to be shot entirely using natural candlelight.

Home videotape systems (VCRs) are released in Japan by Sony (Betamax) and a year later by Matsushita (VHS).

Saigon falls to the North Vietnamese, bringing the Vietnam War to a close and ending years of US presence in South Vietnam.

○ *Nashville*, **Robert Altman, USA**
Robert Altman's most expansive ensemble film since *M*A*S*H* (1970) presents a musical portrait of the capital of US country music, from the stars and their entourage to the new arrivals with aspirations of success. It also plays out as a satire of the country as a whole, at the midpoint of a divisive decade in which the political, cultural and moral intransigence between generations has rarely been greater. The film-maker's signature use of sound, never solely focusing on the main action in a scene, is at its most effective.

1975

Delphine Seyrig

JEANNE DIELMAN
23, quai du Commerce
1080 Bruxelles

Un film de Chantal Akerman
avec Jan Decorte, Henri Storck, Jacques Doniol-Valcroze, Yves Bical. Images de Babette Mangolte
COPRODUCTION PARADISE FILMS · UNITÉ TROIS · DIFFUSION MONDIALE ARTCO FILMS GENÈVE

Jeanne Dielman, 23 quai du Commerce, 1080 Bruxelles, Chantal Ackerman, Belgium

Chantal Ackerman's second narrative feature unfolds over three days and primarily details the domestic activities of Delphine Seyrig's single mother. Her routine also involves earning money as a sex worker to provide for her and her son. But gradually, that routine begins to unravel, which presages her act of violence on the third day. Ackerman's measured drama rigorously examines gender roles in society and features work such as washing and cooking that is usually left out of films. It is a key entry in avant-garde and feminist cinema.

Kings of the Road (*Im Lauf der Zeit*), Wim Wenders, Germany

Wim Wenders's three-hour travelogue is third in a loose trilogy of road movies after *Alice in the Cities* (*Alice in den Städten*, 1974) and *The Wrong Move* (*Falsche Bewegung*, 1975). It focuses on the terse friendship that develops between a movie-projector engineer travelling along the border with East Germany and a depressed intellectual he encounters just as the young man half-heartedly attempts suicide. Evocatively shot in black and white, the film plays out as a barometer of the German national psyche.

The Steadicam is first used in Hal Ashby's *Bound for Glory*. Audiences first see its use in *Marathon Man*, which is released two months earlier.

1976

BOLLYWOOD

Representing the Indian Hindi-language film industry
based in Mumbai, whose domestic audience is vast
enough to support its sizeable yearly output, Bollywood
is the byword for a certain kind of cinema. Yet its
history embraces a wider spectrum of films that date to
its golden age in the 1950s and resurgence in the 1970s.

OPPOSITE. *Ashoka the Great* (*Asoka*, 2001), Santosh Sivan, India
An epic adventure with echoes of earlier films such as *Mughal-E-Azam* (1960), Santosh Sivan's film, along with Ashutosh Gowariker's *Lagaan: Once Upon a Time in India* (2001) highlighted the global potential of this new era of Hindi cinema.

RIGHT. *Sholay* (1975), Ramesh Sippy, India
The ultimate Masala film blended the conventions of the Indian dacoit bandit film with elements of Spaghetti Western and samurai adventures.

A portmanteau of 'Bombay' (now Mumbai) and 'Hollywood', it is unclear who came up with the term 'Bollywood', but it gained traction in the 1970s. It followed Tollywood, the name for Bengali cinema, which was based in the Kolkata neighbourhood of Tollygunge. (Telugu cinema has been given the same label.) To some, these terms are derogatory as they imply the industries are inferior to their US counterpart.

Prior to the partition of India in 1947, the Bombay film industry had counterparts in Kolkata and Lahore, now part of Pakistan. But as production centralized around the west coast city, directors, actors, writers and technicians who had been working in Hindustani cinema across the country gravitated there. The fifteen years after the country's independence became known as the golden age of Hindi cinema. It saw the release of films that have become key works in its history. They attempted to balance entertainment with social concerns. Among the early landmark films are Raj Kapoor's *Awaara* (1951), Mehboob Khan's *The Savage Princess* (*Aan,* 1952), Guru Dutt's *Pyaasa* (1957) and K. Asif's *Mughal-E-Azam* (1960).

Kapoor's crime drama features him as a tramp that directly references Charles Chaplin's earlier screen incarnation. (Along with Dilip Kumar, Kapoor was one of the first major stars of Bollywood cinema.) It played in competition at the Cannes Film Festival and became a success in China and the Soviet Union, where it was seen by more than sixty-four million viewers. Khan's *The Savage Princess*, the first Indian film to be made in Technicolor, was a lustrous romantic adventure that became the highest-grossing Indian film at home and overseas. Dutt was also the star of *Pyaasa*, playing a poet struggling to be known in post-independence India and a benevolent prostitute who attempts to help him. Although Asif's romantic epic *Mughal-E-Azam* took fifteen years to make, it remained the country's most successful film until the mid 1970s. Khan's *Mother India* (1957) also played a key role during this period. One of the most expensive films of the era, it was the first Indian film to be nominated for an Academy Award.

The two components these films shared were the incorporation of song and dance numbers into their narratives and the promotion of stars. It is what distinguishes the films

from the country's Parallel Cinema, which emerged in the mid 1950s. These elements were key to Bollywood's resurgence in the 1970s, after more than a decade of creative and commercial stagnancy. The screenwriting team of Salim-Javed (Salim Khan and Javed Akhtar) is credited with this resurgence this reversal in fortunes, penning a series of exciting crime thrillers that also launched the career of Bollywood superstar Amitabh Bachchan. He starred in their *Procession of Memories* (*Yaadon Ki Baaraat*, 1973), *The Wall* (*Deewaar*) and *Sholay* (both 1975), which defined the Masala film as a hybrid of several popular genres. Plot was secondary to star performances, original musical numbers and a high quotient of thrills.

Another stagnant period followed in the 1980s, but Bollywood returned with renewed vigour in the 1990s. New Bollywood has vastly improved its technical and production quality in order to stave off domestic competition from Hollywood. But its own market stretches far beyond its borders and into the vast Indian diaspora. It remains dominated by a roster of stars whose fame travels far beyond the screen.

1977–1978

Vietnam revisited. The Vietnam conflict ended on 30 April 1975 with the Viet Cong's arrival in Saigon. Unlike the Second World War (1939–45), cinematic representations of it emerge slowly. There had been documentaries, such as the French portmanteau film *Far From Vietnam* (*Loin du Vietnam*, 1967) and two portraits of life in the military, *A Face of War* (1968) and *In the Year of the Pig* (1968). There was also the John Wayne vehicle *The Green Berets* (1968). But the late 1970s sees the appearance of films that acknowledge the psychological impact of the conflict. *Rolling Thunder* (1977), *Big Wednesday* and the Oscar-winning *Coming Home* (both 1978) offer different perspectives on veterans returning to civilian life. Michael Cimino's *The Deer Hunter* (1978) contrasts a brutal – and controversial – portrayal of the conflict with the civilian lives of three friends before and after it. The film ends ambiguously with a scene whose meaning continues to be debated.

Apple Computer is incorporated.

Elvis Presley dies at his home, Graceland, in Memphis, Tennessee.

Charles Chaplin dies at his home in Switzerland.

Magnetic Video is the first company to sell pre-recorded videos of feature-length films.

Annie Hall, Woody Allen, USA

Diane Keaton's charismatic Oscar-winning turn, her fourth role opposite Woody Allen and third in a film directed by him, anchors his study of one man's attempts to understand what went wrong in his relationship with his eponymous ex. *Annie Hall* is a shift away from the madcap, screwball style of comedy that Allen had previously produced, in favour of a nuanced, but no less funny, portrait of modern relationships. It is one of his most beloved films and set the template for countless sophisticated romantic comedies.

1977

Eraserhead, David Lynch, USA
One of the films that began the trend for late-night screening programmes, which became known as Midnight Movies, in the mid 1970s, David Lynch's experimental feature debut remains a singular work on the landscape of US film. A nightmarish portrait of a young man left to care for a deformed baby in a strange, otherworldly environment, it took Lynch three years to gain the funding to complete the film. He spent another year working on its complex, layered sound design, an element that has played a key role in all his subsequent work.

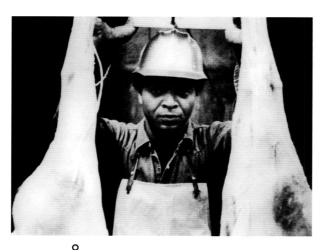

Killer of Sheep, Charles Burnett, USA
Charles Burnett drew on Italian Neorealism for his compassionate portrait of an African American family living in the Los Angeles' neighbourhood of Watts. Comprising a series of episodes from the life of a slaughterhouse employee, played by Henry G. Sanders, the film encapsulates the socio-economic hardships of being black in the United States. Burnett also wanted the film to be a history of African American music, the most poignant example of which is Paul Robeson's rendition of 'The House I Live In' (1947), which accompanies scenes of children playing together.

Cardinal Karol Wojtyla becomes Pope John Paul II, the 264th pontiff and the first Polish pope.

Dallas debuts on US television.

1978

1979–1980

End of an era. For twenty years, cinema around the world seemed to thrive on responding to the times. But the landscape for daring, groundbreaking cinema appears to be diminishing. In Italy, a national cinema that was once such a vital presence on the world stage, enters a period of stagnation, save for the work of a few key film-makers. The United Kingdom and Germany follow suit. Even in the United States the outlook seems grave. Many will point to the commercial disaster of Michael Cimino's *Heaven's Gate* (1980) as the final nail in the coffin of a Hollywood dominated by the director. But the popularity of blockbuster films, a new generation of commercially-minded producers and the acquisition of studios by business conglomerates control what people watch and the way they watch it throughout the 1980s.

My Brilliant Career, Gillian Armstrong, Australia

The sole female film-maker most prominently associated with the Australian New Wave, Gillian Armstrong's feature debut attracted international acclaim for its portrait of a young woman in the 19th century who chooses to forge her own path in the world. As Armstrong noted: 'I wanted to make the statement that the heroine is a full woman who can develop her talents and have a career. I didn't want to reinforce the old stereotypes that a woman who has a career only does so only because she can't get a man.'

Screen legend John Wayne dies in Los Angeles.

The China Syndrome, a film about a fictional nuclear plant that narrowly avoids a nuclear meltdown, opens twelve days before an actual partial nuclear reactor core melt-down occurs at the Three Mile Island nuclear facility in Pennsylvania.

1979

Apocalypse Now, Francis Ford Coppola, USA

Updating Joseph Conrad's *Heart of Darkness* (1899) from the Congo to Vietnam, Francis Ford Coppola's fever dream of a war film finds Martin Sheen's Captain Benjamin L. Willard journeying deep into enemy territory in order to dispatch a colonel who has gone both AWOL and insane. Unlike previous films about Vietnam, which grappled with its politics, Coppola emphasizes the surreal nature and horror of war. He is aided by advances in sound technology and the ingenuity of Vittorio Storaro's cinematography.

Cannibal Holocaust, Ruggero Deodato, Italy

This is one of the earliest films to employ the found-footage narrative format that was used for *The Blair Witch Project* (1999) and subsequent horror films. Ruggero Deodato recounts the experiences of a group of film-makers who go missing in the Amazon rainforest. Controversy followed the film wherever it opened because of its graphic and realistic violence, and actual harm caused to animals. Deodato defended his film, claiming somewhat spuriously that it was an attempt to grapple with the ethics of journalism.

Alfred Hitchcock dies.

John Lennon is shot and killed by Mark David Chapman outside his home in New York.

The Trial of the Gang of Four begins in China.

Former film star Ronald Reagan wins the US presidential election.

1980

5
___

ART V.
COMMERCE

At 12.01 a.m. on 1 August 1981, Russell Mulcahy's music video for the hit of 'Video Killed the Radio Star' (1978) welcomed the world to MTV. It was the perfect opening track for a channel that posed another threat to cinema through its appeal to one of the film industry's key demographics: the teenager. As far as it was concerned, the song may as well have been called 'video killed the movie theatre'.

By the early 1980s, video and home entertainment was as great a challenge to cinema as the one the industry faced in the 1950s with the television. But video technology was not just competition, it stole from cinema. The popularity of film rentals saw nefarious elements finding ways to illegally copy recent releases for home viewing. The window between a cinema and home-entertainment release was wide enough for profit to be made by pirates recording new films. When studios realised the need for increased security, the quality of these versions diminished, but they remained in circulation.

The emergence of smaller production companies specializing in straight-to-video films also posed a threat. If a film could be made on a small enough budget, it was almost guaranteed to make a profit. Horror in particular benefited from this new avenue. From audiences' perspective, the cost was significantly cheaper than the price of a cinema ticket. For anyone not too bothered about quality or the pleasure of watching a film on a big screen, it was an irresistible option.

Of course, video was not all bad. It offered a secondary market to studios, where they could profit from second viewings or an audience who had not seen the film in the cinema. There were also the films that had experienced a lacklustre performance in the cinema but enjoyed a more profitable second life on video. *Blade Runner* (1982) was shunned by audiences on its first release, but attracted a cult following that would see its stock rise and result in various versions being released over the course of the next three decades. Another action adventure, George Miller's *Mad Max 2* (1981), retitled *The Road Warrior* in the United States, which was a modest hit on first release, became immensely successful following its video release.

If video was seen as a threat to cinema in some countries, in others it resulted in an explosion in film production. By the late 1970s, many African countries were gradually establishing their own national cinemas. Video technology increased the speed of the transformation. Nigeria was one of the first countries to enjoy an independent cinema, but from the 1980s it became a major hub for low-budget, straight-to-video film production. So much so that it earned the moniker 'Nollywood'. If the quality of the films was questionable, their popularity was not.

The landscape of cinema in the United States changed in the 1980s. The commercial disaster of Michael Cimino's *Heaven's Gate* (1980), which contributed to the financial woes of United Artists, is seen as a major factor in ending the era when film-making mavericks controlled the studios. Instead, a new generation embraced the outsider status of independent film-making, recapturing the spirit of John Cassavetes, the godfather of US independent film. His *Shadows* (1959) and subsequent career offered a road map for how independent cinema could flourish in the United States.

In the late 1970s and early 1980s, the No Wave cinema movement in New York inspired a group of film-makers to create works that existed far outside the mainstream. The most notable writer-director to emerge from this period was Jim Jarmusch, who followed his low-key debut *Permanent Vacation* (1980) with the acclaimed character-driven comedy-dramas *Stranger Than Paradise* (1984) and *Down by Law* (1986). Jarmusch's success came just as the profile of

TOP. *Down by Law* **(1986), Jim Jarmusch, USA**
Tom Waits, John Lurie and Roberto Benigni play three escapees from a New Orleans jail cell in Jim Jarmusch's third feature, which cemented his position as one of the key US independent film-makers of the 1980s.

ABOVE. *Daughters of the Dust* **(1991), Julie Dash, USA**
The first feature by an African American woman to be distributed theatrically in the United States, and one of the few to feature Gullah dialogue, *Daughters of the Dust* took almost two decades to produce.

the Sundance Film Festival was growing. Founded in 1978 as the Utah/US Film Festival, its name was changed to the Sundance Film Festival in 1984. Sundance soon become a driving force in championing films produced on a low to medium budget. Along with Miramax, the powerhouse company whose reputation was built on recognizing the best home-grown talent, the profile of independent US cinema began to flourish. By the early 1990s, the American Indie was a brand unto itself, representing an array of films, from Steven Soderbergh's *Sex, Lies, and Videotape* (1989) and Julie Dash's *Daughters of the Dust* (1991) to Allison Anders's *Gas Food Lodging*, Quentin Tarantino's *Reservoir Dogs* (both 1992) and Kevin Smith's *Clerks* (1994). Although artistry and independent expression were key, one of the best examples of its commercial potential was proven by the success of *The Blair Witch Project* (1999) following its sensational debut at Sundance. A film that originally cost in the tens of thousands of dollars– its quality bolstered by a few hundred thousand spent in post-production – it went on to earn $250 million at the global box office. This era also saw the emergence of New Queer Cinema, which led to a rise in the number of mainstream LGBT (more recently defined as LGBTQI+) films.

The success of the blockbuster in the 1970s sealed the future for US studio production. As the 1980s dawned, studios moved away from low-key, character-driven films in favour of an increased focus on major tentpole titles whose immense production costs were added to by expensive marketing campaigns and whose commercial success depended on each film's appeal to the widest demographic. The resulting high-concept movies came to define Hollywood in the 1980s. These films were mostly based on a concept that could be easily conveyed in one sentence. (The thriller *Snakes on a Plane* (2006) went one further by making the concept the title of the film.) In marketing terms, it has been referred to as 'the look, the hook and the book': the visual element that draws an audience in; the story that keeps them watching; and the potential of an ancillary market, from books and toys to food or clothing tie-ins. These films offered audiences something familiar yet fresh enough for them not to feel cheated. The idea is satirized in the opening sequence of Robert Altman's Hollywood-set *The Player* (1992), when two screenwriters pitching their idea to a studio executive describe it as '*Out of Africa* meets *Pretty Woman*'.

A key factor in the appeal of these films was the manufacturing of stars far removed from everyday life: supermen capable of outrageous feats. Sylvester Stallone and Arnold Schwarzenegger became the poster boys for this new kind of hero, whose prowess was echoed down into the lower budget vehicles for action stars Chuck Norris, Jean-Claude Van Damme, Dolph Lundgren and subsequent other high-octane performers. Later in the decade, their mantle was challenged by the blue-collar heroics of Bruce Willis and Mel Gibson in the *Die Hard* (1988–2013) and *Lethal Weapon* (1987–1998) series, but these films still kept to the simple equation of the high-concept movie.

The era also saw an increase in female action stars. Not that they had not previously existed. Pam Grier and Tamara Dobson became stars through the blaxploitation films *Coffy* and *Cleopatra Jones* (both 1973). Before them, Cheng Pei-pei made a strong impression in Hong Kong director King Hu's exhilarating martial-arts actioner *Come Drink*

LEFT. *Terminator 2: Judgment Day* (1992), James Cameron, USA

The sequel to James Cameron's low-budget sci-fi thriller of 1984 became a showcase for the advances in visual effects and computer-generated technology, particularly in the creation of the shapeshifting T-1000 cyborg.

with Me (*Da zui xia*, 1966), while in Japan Meiko Kaji made for a ruthless and vengeful killer in the *Lady Snowblood* (*Shurayukihime*, 1973–74) series. Sigourney Weaver and Linda Hamilton brought the female action hero into mainstream Hollywood. The transformation of Ellen Ripley in *Alien* (1979) and Sarah Connor in *The Terminator* (1984) found them taking control in the films' final scenes. But their return in *Aliens* (1986) and *Terminator 2: Judgment Day* (1992) saw them embrace a more sinewy look and embrace a tougher role, which became a model for future Hollywood female action characters such as Charly Baltimore in *The Long Kiss Goodnight* (1996), Beatrix Kiddo in the *Kill Bill* (2003–04) series, Mallory Kane in *Haywire* (2011) and Imperator Furiosa in *Mad Max: Fury Road* (2015).

Terminator 2: Judgment Day is also notable for its landmark visual effects. The development of computer-generated imagery (CGI) had come a long way since 2D computer animation was employed by Michael Crichton for his sci-fi film Western *Westworld* (1973). *Star Wars* (1977) proved a landmark in what could be achieved, while George Lucas's founding of Industrial Light and Magic in 1975 to create the effects needed for his space adventure significantly expanded their potential. The thriller *Looker* (1981) included the first CGI human character. After further advances with two more *Star Wars* films in 1980 and 1983, *The Last Starfighter* (1984) not only became the first sci-fi adventure to solely feature CGI spaceships, it also marked a first in the use of CGI-integrated objects within a scene. The next year, *Young Sherlock Holmes* featured the first photorealistic CGI character, a stained-glass knight.

The next major chapter in the development of visual effects was driven by James Cameron. His aquatic sci-fi thriller *The Abyss* (1989) integrated a constantly morphing, watery alien presence within the human environment of a deep-sea station. But the advancements Cameron achieved with *Terminator 2* were extraordinary. Robert Patrick's T-1000 cyborg passes through cell bars, mutates into various characters and objects, transforms at one point from a linoleum floor into a security guard and in the film's climax, pieces itself back together from a pool of molten metal. Cameron delayed making the film in

order to wait on the technology becoming available for the effects he required, which finally constitute just five minutes of the film. He had to delay production on *Titanic* (1997) and *Avatar* (2009) for the same reasons. The gains he achieved with *Terminator 2* were reflected in the visual effects featured in *Jurassic Park* (1993), *Independence Day* (1996) and countless other blockbusters. They were employed on a smaller scale with films where the use of a visual effect was either more economic for a production or safer for a crew.

Animation also profited from advances in technology. Mainstream animated entertainment in the United States entered a creative nadir in the 1960s, which lasted until the late 1980s. Disney, in particular, suffered. Its low point came with *The Black Cauldron* (1985), an expensive commercial film whose failure threatened future animation production at the studio. By contrast, animation in small European production houses increased throughout the same period. It included the visionaries Karel Zeman, Jan Švankmajer and Yuri Norstein, whose *Tale of Tales* (*Skazka skazok*, 1979) is often cited as the greatest animated film ever made.

In Japan, anime became popular during the same period. Studio Ghibli was founded in 1985, which would grow in stature to rank alongside a revitalized Disney as one of the most important animation studios. That rebirth began with the launch of the newly titled Walt Disney Feature Animation department in 1985. It was run by Roy E. Disney (Walt's nephew) and over the course of the next decade it not only reversed the studio's fortunes, it ushered in a renaissance in animated features, first with *The Little Mermaid* (1989) and then *The Rescuers Down Under* (1990), *Beauty and the Beast* (1991), *Aladdin* (1992) and *The Lion King* (1994). The films introduced computer technology alongside traditional cell-painted animation, most notably in the ballroom sequence of *Beauty and the Beast*. At the same time, Disney became more involved with Pixar, whose entirely computer-generated animation was less competition than a contrast to Disney's traditional output. It culminated in the release of the first fully computer-generated animated feature *Toy Story* (1995). Pixar is like Studio Ghibli in that it produces consistently high-quality output.

RIGHT. *Toy Story* (1995),
John Lasseter, USA
Pixar's first feature set the
template for the studio's
regular output, combining
colourful CGI with witty,
intelligent and emotionally
complex screenwriting.

The studio's visual imagination is also matched by its strength in storytelling, rarely faltering in its balance of intelligence and wit with emotional heft.

While Disney spent much of the 1970s and 1980s in the doldrums, Steven Spielberg saw his stock rise meteorically. He began directing for a studio aged just twenty-one. By the time he reached the age of thirty, his second feature *Jaws* (1975) had become a global success. He continued to entertain for another decade, before shifting into more serious drama with *The Colour Purple* (1985) and *Empire of the Sun* (1987). In 1993, he directed *Schindler's List* and *Jurassic Park*. The former was celebrated for its account of the Holocaust and won seven Academy Awards including Best Director and Best Film, and the latter became the third Spielberg film to break global box-office records. Such was his position in the industry that in 1994, in partnership with former Disney executive Jeffrey Katzenberg and music mogul David Geffen, Spielberg set up DreamWorks SKG, the first time in decades a major live-action and animation studio had been established in Hollywood.

Beyond studios in Hollywood or any other part of the globe, independent voices continued to appear. The 1960s explosion of film movements saw their influence filter down to later generations of film-makers seeking their own voice as storytellers and visual stylists. The Australian New Wave, which emerged in the early 1970s and included directors Peter Weir, Fred Schepisi, Gillian Armstrong, George Miller and Bruce Beresford, continued to hold sway into the 1980s until many of the directors started spreading out internationally. In France, the *Cinéma du look* offered a portrait of ennui among the country's disenfranchised youth. A different youth culture would be represented a decade later in Matthieu Kassovitz's incendiary *La haine* (1995), a powerful portrait of race, racism and economic inequality in Paris, whose impact echoed the reaction by audiences in the United States to Spike Lee's comedy-drama *Do the Right Thing* (1989).

There were new waves in Hong Kong and Taiwan. The former was represented by Ann Hui, Tsui Hark, John Woo and Patrick Tam, followed by a second wave comprising Stanley Kwan, Mabel Cheung, Peter Chan, Fruit Chan and Wong Kar-wai. If Hong Kong cinema from the 1980s and 1990s appeared to be dominated by action, Kwan's *Rouge* (*Yim ji kau*, 1987) and *Center Stage* (*Ruan Ling Yu*, 1991) explored period melodrama with nuance, while Wong brought elegance and sophistication with his internationally acclaimed *In the Mood for Love* (*Fa yeung nin wah*, 2000). Taiwan's cinema also experienced two waves in the 1980s and 1990s. the first was best represented by the films of Hou Hsiao-hsien and Edward Yang, while the second saw Tsai Ming-liang and Ang Lee achieve critical acclaim, with Lee going on to enjoy significant success with his international productions. There was also a radical shift in Chinese cinema over the same period, as the country's arts landscape recovered from the Cultural Revolution (1966–76) and brutal rule of the Gang of Four. In the late 1990s, Danish film-makers Lars von Trier and Thomas Vinterberg launched the Dogme 95 movement with their films *The Idiots* (*Idioterne*) and *Festen* (both 1998).

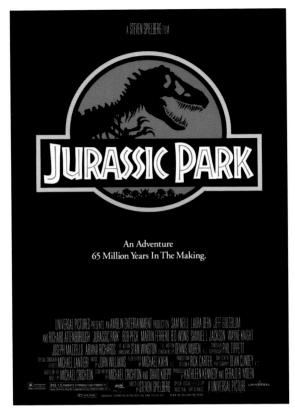

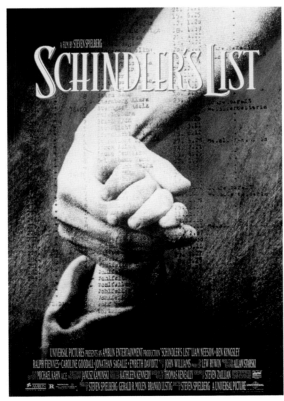

OPPOSITE. *Jurassic Park* and *Schindler's List* (both 1993), Steven Spielberg, USA
In the same year, Steven Spielberg directed his third global box-office record-breaking success with *Jurassic Park* and one of his most acclaimed dramas with the Oscar-winning *Schindler's List*.

ABOVE. *La haine* (1995), Matthieu Kassovitz, France
The Paris of Matthieu Kassovitz's sophomore feature is riven with class and racial conflict as it chronicles twenty-four hours in the lives of three disenfranchised youths, becoming one of the most controversial French films of the 1990s.

RIGHT. *The Idiots* (*Idioterne*, 1998), Lars von Trier, Denmark
Lars von Trier's playful satire of bourgeois values embraces the rules of the Dogme 95 manifesto he co-created, which polarized both critics and audiences.

1981–1982

Surface is everything. Overviews of 1980s cinema will note an emphasis on style over substance. Paul Schrader turns it to his advantage with razor-sharp effectiveness in *American Gigolo* (1980), his portrait of vacuous lifestyles in Los Angeles. MTV embodies that notion when it begins airing in August 1981. But it is most clearly pronounced in the work of a loose movement in French cinema that in 1989 film critic Raphaël Bassan coined '*Cinéma du look*'. The films focus on alienated youth, doomed love and deep mistrust of the establishment. They are hyper-stylized, deeply embedded in pop culture and exude effortless cool. Yet the surface appeal is also an act of rebellion, a symbol of opposition to the French government of François Mitterrand, who is seen to be out of touch with the country's younger generation. The movement is represented by Jean-Jacques Beineix, Leos Carax and Luc Besson, with the films *Diva* (1981), *Boy Meets Girl* (1984), *Subway* (1985), *The Night Is Young* (*Mauvais Sang*) and *Betty Blue* (*37°2 le matin*, both 1986).

Diva, Jean-Jacques Beineix, France

A young postman, an opera fanatic, illicitly records a soprano who only ever performs live. He also comes into possession of a recording that incriminates a high-ranking police officer. He is pursued for both transgressions and seeks refuge in various Paris hideaways. Jean-Jacques Beineix's thriller marked a shift away from the realism that had dominated much of French cinema in the 1970s, creating an ultra-stylish thriller and the first film associated with *Cinéma du look*, for which the image was everything.

The Space Shuttle *Columbia* is the first Earth-to-orbit spacecraft to leave the planet's atmosphere, returning two days later.

The attempted **assassination** of President Ronald Reagan by John W. Hinckley Jr is linked to Martin Scorsese's *Taxi Driver* (1976).

1981

Man of Iron (*Czlowiek z zelaza*), Andrzej Wajda, Poland

The second part of a cinematic diptych that began with *Man of Marble* (*Czlowiek z marmuru*, 1977), which detailed the facade of socialist myth-making, *Man of Iron* presents an account of the rise of Solidarity, the labour movement that grew out of Poland's Gdańsk Shipyard. It focuses on the man who heads a powerful union, a fictional version of Solidarity leader Lech Wałęsa. The film wins the Palme d'Or at Cannes, but its strident take on recent events sees it banned by Polish authorities.

Blade Runner, Ridley Scott, USA

One of the first films to embrace the cyberpunk subgenre, meshing visions of the future with older technology to create a postmodern bricolage of a city, *Blade Runner* has become a highly influential film. Based on Philip K. Dick's *Do Androids Dream of Electric Sheep?* (1968), Ridley Scott's stylish thriller was a commercial failure, but became a cult classic via home video, spawning a sequel and countless imitations, as well as generating the trend for multiple versions, or 'director's cuts', of a film.

Steven Spielberg's *E. T. the Extra-Terrestrial* tops the year's global box office and will go on to become the most successful film of the decade.

The Lebanon War begins.

Canada gains official independence from the United Kingdom.

1982

1983–1984

The battle of formats. The popularity of home entertainment impacts cinemas. A battle over video formats edges towards a conclusion. In 1975, Sony made the Betamax format available to consumers. A year later, JVC introduced the VHS. Betamax is superior in sound and image quality, but the tapes and the machines that play them are more expensive. However, the tipping point in favour of VHS is length. Sony initially limits its tapes to 60 minutes, whereas the earliest VHS tape can record – and play – up to two hours' worth of material. This is eventually extended to four hours. Sony catches up, but by the early 1980s VHS machines have cornered the consumer market. However, the danger for studios with home video and the various formats that follow it is not just the loss of box-office revenues but the added threat of piracy.

The Ballad of Narayama (Narayama bushikō), Shōhei Imamura, Japan

Shōhei Imamura won the first of two Palme d'Or awards at Cannes for his adaptation of Shichirō Fukazawa's debut novel of 1956. His second was for *The Eel* (*Unagi*, 1997). In a remote village, when someone reaches seventy years old, they have to make their way to a mountaintop to die, no matter the state of their health. Imamura's film focuses on one woman as she approaches her end, detailing her life over the course of her last year. In doing so, the film reflects on what it means to be human.

Return of the Jedi, the third instalment in the *Star Wars* saga, becomes the first film to utilize THX sound system technology.

The television premiere of *The Day After*, which details the impact of a nuclear conflict on families living in Kansas and Missouri, is watched by more than one hundred million US viewers.

Argentina becomes a democracy after decades of military rule and is followed throughout the decade by Uruguay, Brazil and Chile.

1983

○ *Blood Simple*, **Joel and Ethan Coen, USA**
One of the finest examples of neo-noir announced the arrival of two film-makers whose subsequent films skilfully play with genre conventions, albeit shot through with a skewed worldview and pitch-black humour. The Coens' debut is a ruthlessly effective and visually stylish thriller set in rural Texas. It begins with a tryst between a young couple, follows the response of the woman's husband on finding out about her infidelity and the actions of a murderous private detective he hires to kill the lovers.

○ *El Norte*, **Gregory Nava, USA/UK**
Two siblings, Rosa and Enrique, flee for their lives from a Guatemalan village and make their way to the United States. Gregory Nava's powerful drama is divided into three sections, chronicling the impoverished existence of an exploited indigenous population before charting the perilous journey through Mexico and life in the United States. The film remains all too relevant, asking viewers to consider the reasons why people have to risk their lives crossing borders to seek out a new and safer life.

1984

ABOVE. *Born in Flames* (1983), Lizzie Borden, USA
Lizzie Borden's documentary-style sci-fi drama examines gender, race and class in the United States, resulting in one of the most radical landmark feminist films of the 1980s.

LEFT. *The German Sisters* (*Die bleierne Zeit*, 1981), Margarethe von Trotta, Germany
Margarethe von Trotta creates an incendiary mix of gender and politics in this portrait of two siblings, one a journalist who campaigns for women's right to abortion and the other a member of the Red Army Faction.

FEMINIST FILM

Feminist cinema became an increasing presence with the emergence of Second Wave Feminism in the 1970s and an increased academic interest in examining the way patriarchy has informed film production and reception. Subsequent studies have expanded to encompass sexuality, identity and race, just as new generations of film-makers have fought for increased diversity in making films.

A feminist perspective on cinema covers a wide range but one of the pivotal works remains Laura Mulvey's essay *Visual Pleasure and Narrative Cinema* (1973), which established the notion of the male gaze, subsequently borne out in her film *Riddles of the Sphinx* (1977). Other examples of feminist film stretch back as far as the pioneering early work of Alice Guy-Blaché and Lois Weber, as well as such experimental film-makers Germaine Dulac and Maya Deren.

Agnès Varda emerged out of the French New Wave as its sole prominent female voice, articulating the way society stereotypes women. The Czech New Wave's Věra Chytilová probed the role of women in society. Her debut *Something Different* (*O necem jiném*, 1963) compared the life of a gymnast with an overworked and underappreciated housewife and mother. But it was her celebrated second feature *Daisies* (*Sedmikrásky,* 1966) that coalesced her thoughts on gender and society. Likewise, Chantal Ackerman's films, dominated by *Jeanne Dielman, 23 quai du Commerce, 1080 Bruxelles* (1975), highlight gender inequality. Ackerman was later joined by film-makers such as Catherine Breillat, whose *A Real Young Girl* (*Une vraie jeune fille*, 1976), *Romance* (1999) and *Fat Girl* (*À ma soeur!*, 2001) have attracted controversy for their frankness in exploring sexuality.

In the United States, Barbara Loden's *Wanda* (1970) is a landmark in the representation of working-class women. In the same way that Barbara Kopple's *Harlan County USA* (1976) reviewed the role of women in a series of crippling Kentucky miners' strikes, Loden's film is a raw portrait of a character – whom she also plays – whose status as an outsider in society lies in her unwillingness to conform to patriarchal precepts of what is expected of a woman. A similar theme is explored in subsequent films such as Susan Seidelman's *Desperately Seeking Susan* (1985), Allison Anders's *Gas, Food, Lodging* (1992) and Kelly Reichardt's *Certain Women* (2016).

The proliferation of academic and popular writing that defined the Second Wave Feminism, from the 1960s through to the early 1980s, had a profound impact on films that surveyed ingrained attitudes to women. In Marleen Gorris's unsettling *A Question of Silence* (*De stilte rond Christine M.*, 1982), three women who have had to endure the jibes and condescension of men channel their rage into the seemingly random killing of a shopkeeper. The resulting trial, overseen by men, fails to understand the symbolic importance of their actions. A trenchant exploration of patriarchy and misogyny is central to Margarethe von Trotta's *The German Sisters* (*Die bleierne Zeit*, 1981) and Monika Treut's *Female Misbehaviour* (1992). Sally Potter's *The Gold Diggers* (1983) and Lizzie Borden's *Born in Flames* (1983) played with genre conventions, while elsewhere films such as Claire Denis's *Chocolat* (1988) and Gurinda Chadha's *Bend It Like Beckham* (2002) sought a perspective that examined life through the prism of gender and race.

Since 1990, there has also been a shift in the representation of women or a challenge to what has been perceived as the traditional role of women around the world, ranging across the spectrum of cultures and religions. They range from an examination of life for two generations of women living in a prince's palace in Moufida Tlatli's *The Silences of the Palace* (*Samt el qusur*, 1994) to Deepa Mehta's *Fire* (1996), which focuses on the growing intimacy between two women trapped in loveless marriages. Elsewhere, Zeresenay Mehari's *Difret* (2014) tells the true story of a young Ethiopian girl abducted for marriage.

At the same time, Kimberly Pierce's *Boys Don't Cry* (1999) and Lucía Puenzo's *XXY* (2007) represent films from around the world that highlight transgender issues. Just as the language of cinema has shifted to include a more diverse array of life stories, so films show how societies are revising opinions and attitudes within gender and identity debates.

1985–1986

Portraits of youth. John Hughes did not invent the teen movie, but in 1980s US cinema he is its resident auteur. As a writer and occasional director, he defines white working- and middle-class life with his films *Sixteen Candles* (1984), *The Breakfast Club*, *Weird Science* (1985), *Pretty in Pink*, *Ferris Bueller's Day Off* (both 1986) and *Some Kind of Wonderful* (1987). *The Breakfast Club* explores the archetypes of school life, with five characters forced to spend a Saturday in detention. The actors playing them are referred to as the 'Brat Pack', a grouping that also includes the cast members of *The Outsiders* (1983) and *St Elmo's Fire* (1985). The pre-teen experience is better represented by the Stephen King adaptation *Stand by Me* (1986), while an edgier portrait of youth is evinced in *River's Edge* (1986). An equally troubled portrait of youth is present in the landmark British film *My Beautiful Laundrette*, while in France Agnès Varda chronicles one young woman's fate as she attempts to live outside society in *Vagabond* (*Sans toit ni loi*, both 1985).

Ran, Akira Kurosawa, Japan
Akira Kurosawa planned *Ran* in the early 1970s, but as he was developing the story of the 16th-century feudal lord Mōri Motonari, he segued into making *Dersu Uzala* (1975) and *Kagemusha* (1980). His return to the project saw him influenced by William Shakespeare's *King Lear* (1608). His third adaptation of the playwright's work, after his nod to *Macbeth* (1623) in *Throne of Blood* (*Kumonosu-jō*, 1957) and *Hamlet* (1603) in *The Bad Sleep Well* (*Warui yatsu hodo yoku nemuru*, 1960), it is one of his most expansive, visually dazzling and well-received films.

The Ethiopian famine, which has ravaged the country for two years, leaves more than one million dead and millions more displaced.

Mikhail Gorbachev becomes leader of the Soviet Union and initiates reforms as part of his programme of *glasnost* (openness) and *perestroika* (restructuring).

1985

Blue Velvet, David Lynch, USA

The Saturday Evening Post illustrator Norman Rockwell's vision of small-town America is turned on its head in David Lynch's disturbing portrait of criminality lurking beneath the veneer of respectable middle-class society. Employing the iconography of the American Dream in its opening sequence, Lynch sends his naive protagonist Jeffrey Beaumont hurtling into the subterranean vortex ruled over by Dennis Hopper's psychopath in order to save Isabella Rossellini's chanteuse. Quite unlike any other US film of the 1980s, it established Lynch as the era's pre-eminent auteur.

Space Shuttle *Challenger* breaks apart 73 seconds after lift-off, killing all seven crew members aboard on its tenth flight.

The No. 4 reactor explodes in the Chernobyl Nuclear Power Plant in the Ukraine and becomes the worst-ever nuclear disaster.

President Ferdinand Marcos ends twenty years of brutal rule of the Philippines when he is replaced by Corazon Aquino.

Caravaggio, Derek Jarman, UK

One of the UK's most distinctive film-makers and artists, Derek Jarman challenged the realist trend in British cinema and his representation of homosexuality provoked a strong reaction from the establishment. His most expansive work – and the result of seven years of struggle to gain funding – *Caravaggio* is a rapturous biographical portrait that employs visual anachronisms just as the painter did in his work. It featured the debut of Tilda Swinton, who would continue to work with Jarman until his death in 1994.

1987-1988

An animated world. Walt Disney Feature Animation hit its creative nadir when *The Black Cauldron* (1985) proved a critical and commercial failure. The company reorganizes its animation division and would return to its former position with *The Little Mermaid* (1989) and *Beauty and the Beast* (1991). In the meantime, Universal Pictures and Steven Spielberg's Amblin Entertainment release *An American Tail* (1986) and *The Land Before Time* (1988). However, the most exciting animation is produced far from Hollywood. After dazzling shorts that blended live action with stop-motion, Jan Švankmajer produces his first feature with *Alice* (*Neco z Alenky*, 1988) an inventive take on Lewis Carroll's *Alice's Adventures in Wonderland* (1865). In Japan, audience passion for anime achieves new heights with Katsuhiro Otomo's *Akira* (1988) and animation house Studio Ghibli rockets to success in 1988 with *Grave of the Fireflies* (*Hotaru no haka*) and *My Neighbour Totoro* (*Tonari no Totoro*).

Malian **Souleymane Cissé** is the first black African film-maker to compete at the Cannes Film Festival with his drama *Brightness* (*Yeelen*).

Black Monday sees shares on the Dow Jones stock-market index dive on 19 October, sending a ripple effect through the world's financial markets.

○ *A Short Film About Killing* (*Krótki film o zabijaniu*), **Krysztof Kiewślowski, Poland**

Expanding one of the episodes from his *Dekalog* (1988–90) television series – each presenting a contemporary interpretation of one of the Ten Commandments – Krysztof Kiewślowski details the senseless killing of a taxi driver, the murderer's trial and then his ruthlessly efficient execution. Although the film was controversial in equating state-sanctioned punishment with a violent crime, it was seen as instrumental in ending the death penalty in Poland.

1987

Women on the Verge of a Nervous Breakdown (Mujeres al borde de un ataque de nervios),
Pedro Almodóvar, Spain

The Spanish film-maker's international breakthrough witnessed a marked development in his career. Pedro Almodóvar's seventh feature, a comedy-tinged melodrama detailing the way women are let down by men and how they vent their anger, dazzles with its visual style – bold use of contrasting colours and inventive camera angles – and liberally borrows from other sources, from Jean Cocteau's play *The Human Voice* (*La voix humaine*, 1930) to classical Hollywood.

○ *Who Framed Roger Rabbit*, Robert Zemeckis, USA

Robert Zemeckis enjoyed success with *Romancing the Stone* (1984) and its playful subversion of 1930s' serial adventures, and the clash of past and present in *Back to the Future* (1985). For *Who Framed Roger Rabbit*, he seamlessly merged state-of-the-art animation with live action in this tale of a missing cartoon character that draws heavily on the tropes of classic film noir. Jeffrey Price and Peter S. Seaman's screenplay is as dazzling as the visual effects, which find Bob Hoskins's sleuth having to deal with the wacky world of Toontown.

Tin Toy, Pixar's 5-minute short, is the first computer animation to win an Academy Award.

The Iraq-Iran War ends after eight years with no change to the border between the countries and the loss of almost one million lives.

1988

CHINA'S GENERATIONS

The cinema of mainland China attracted international attention with the emergence of its Fifth Generation in the mid 1980s. The Sixth Generation, a stark contrast in style and outlook, followed a decade later. The contrast between the two reflects the way the country's cinema has developed since it emerged from the silent era.

Referred to as 'Western shadow play' or 'electric shadows', and initially dominated by films from the West, Chinese cinema entered a golden age in the 1930s. Mirroring a growing progressive political movement in the country, films such as *Street Angel* (*Ma lu tian shi*, 1937), *The Goddess* (*Shen nu,* 1934) and *New Women* (*Xin nu xing*, 1935) sought to forge a vision of Chinese society that would benefit all. The Japanese invasion in 1937 stalled the film industry for almost a decade, but better days returned in the late 1940s with Chusheng Cai and Junli Zheng's epic *The Spring River Flows East* (*Yi jiang chun shui xiang dong liu*, 1947) and Fei Mu's intimate love triangle drama *Spring in a Small Town* (*Xiao cheng zhi chun*, 1948).

Mao Zedong's rise to power changed the course of every aspect of Chinese life, including cinema. Propaganda dominated and output diminished. The Hundred Flowers Campaign of 1956 led to a loosening of state censorship and saw another generation emerge. Xie Jin's *The Red Detachment of Women* (*Hong se niang zi jun*, 1961) remains one of the best examples of films from this period, imbuing the communist struggle with a fable-like quality. But the Cultural Revolution (1966–76) put a stop to almost all film production and exhibition. It was only in the years after

OPPOSITE. *Xiao Wu* (1998), Jia Zhangke, China
The international breakthrough for the Sixth Generation, *Xiao Wu* tackled hypocrisy and corruption endemic in the Chinese establishment, which Jia Zhangke would explore further in films such as *A Touch of Sin* (*Tian zhu ding*, 2013).

LEFT. *Red Sorghum* (*Hong gao liang*, 1987), Zhang Yimou, China
In his directorial debut, which starred Gong Li in her first screen role, Zhang Yimou produced an expressionistic portrait of lust and revenge that raised the profile of mainland Chinese cinema on the world stage.

the overthrow of the Gang of Four political faction in 1976 that the third generation of film-makers re-emerged. Xie had success with his dramas *Legend of Tianyun Mountain* (*Tian yun shan chuan qi*, 1980), *The Herdsman* (*Mu Ma Ren*, 1982) and *Hibiscus Town* (*Fu rong zhen*, 1986), alongside other directors such as Cheng Yin with *The Xi'an Incident* (*Xi'an shi bian*, 1981) and Ling Zifeng with *Rickshaw Boy* (*Luo tuo Xiang Zi*, 1982). Most of these films shied away from social critique or confronting the country's political ideology.

In the 1980s, the work of three generations of directors intersected. As the third generation were returning, a fourth generation emerged. Among those who won acclaim were Zhang Zheng and Huang Jianzhong with *Little Flower* (*Xiao Hua*, 1979) and Quimin Wang with *At Middle Age* (*Ren dao zhong nian*, 1982).

Their influences drew on international cinema while reflecting on the clash between China's recent past and its present.

The Fifth Generation presented a radical break with the past. Most of the film-makers were the first graduates from the Beijing Film Academy since the end of the Cultural Revolution. Their arrival was marked by the release of Zhang Junzhao's *One and Eight* (*Yi ge he ba ge*, 1983) and Chen Kaige's *Yellow Earth* (*Huang tu di*, 1984). The most noted films were set in the past and employed symbolism and colour in their veiled critiques of society. Tian Zhuangzhuang followed with *On the Hunting Ground* (*Lie chang zha sha*, 1985) and *The Horse Thief* (*Dao ma zei*, 1986), while cinematographer Zhang Yimou turned director with *Red Sorghum* (*Hong gao liang*, 1987), which he followed

with international successes including *Ju Dou* (1990) and *Raise the Red Lantern* (*Da hong deng long gao gao gua*, 1991).

The Sixth Generation could not have been more different to their predecessors. Emerging from the turbulence that led to the Tiananmen Square demonstrations of 1989, these films were not state funded. They were shot on small budgets with handheld cameras and evinced an edgy documentary feel, which reflected a younger generation's exasperation with Chinese society. Wang Xiaoshuai's *The Days* (*Dongchun de rizi*, 1993) and Zhang Yuan's *Beijing Bastards* (*Bei Jing za zhong*, 1993) led the way and were followed by Jia Zhangke's *Xiao Wu* (1998), Wang Quan'an's *Lunar Eclipse* (*Yue shi*, 1999), He Jianjun's *Postman* (*Youchai*, 1995) and Li Yang's *Blind Shaft* (*Mang jing*, 2003).

1989–1990

Fall of communism. Mikhail Gorbachev's policy of openness sees the first live, uncensored coverage of the Soviet legislature's deliberations, leading to limited democratic elections in the spring of 1989. The spirit of democracy ripples through the Soviet Union and the satellite countries that make up the Eastern Bloc. Poland takes advantage of the shift in the Kremlin and Politburo, which leads to the removal of the communist government in the summer. The soft revolutions continue in Hungary, Bulgaria, Czechoslovakia and East Germany, where the wall dividing East and West Berlin, is opened in early November and crowds tear it down soon after. Romania's Nicolae Ceaușescu's brutal rule comes to an end early in December. The Soviet Union is dissolved in December 1991.

Do the Right Thing, Spike Lee, USA

Spike Lee's third feature chronicles the racial discord in one Brooklyn neighbourhood over the course of the hottest day of the year, culminating in the death of a young African American at the hands of the police and a riot that destroys a pizzeria. Lee's film was always going to be incendiary but the climate it opened in made it the locus for debates about the state of racial integration in the United States. The film appears no less stylish, provocative or relevant in the 21st century.

Iran's Ayatollah Khomeini declares a fatwa on novelist Salman Rushdie for his novel *The Satanic Verses* (1988).

British engineer Tim Berners-Lee invents the World Wide Web. He writes the first web browser a year later.

Sex, Lies, and Videotape, Steven Soderbergh, USA

Sex, Lies, and Videotape is a smart and articulate portrait of four characters' intersecting lives, confronting their personal, professional and sexual frustrations. It proved influential in the development of the nascent US independent film scene. At twenty-six years old, Steven Soderbergh was the youngest sole recipient of the Palme d'Or at the Cannes Film Festival. He has since balanced a mainstream Hollywood career with more low-key films, such as *Schizopolis* (1996) and *High Flying Bird* (2018), which have allowed him to experiment.

1989

○ *Close-Up (Nema-ye Nazdik)*, Abbas Kiarostami, Iran

In Tehran in the late 1980s, Hossain Sabzian, a fan of Mohsen Makhmalbaf's films, was arrested for impersonating the director. Abbas Kiarostami read about the story and was granted access to the court trial. He then gained permission to recreate the events with the actual people playing themselves. What emerges is a fascinating docudrama that explores the blurred line between reality and fiction. Although dismissed domestically, the film's positive international reception was a key moment for Kiarostami and contemporary Iranian cinema.

Nelson Mandela is released from prison in South Africa.

Iraq invades Kuwait, which results in the Gulf War and increased tensions between Saddam Hussein's regime and the United States that culminates in the Iraq War in 2003.

1990

1991–1992

Oscars upsets. Hollywood's annual celebration of its industry, the Academy Awards, has always grappled with the relationship between commerce and art. It generally rewards films with a message or prestige productions. *The Silence of the Lambs* (1991) proves an exception. It is not only the first horror film – and one whose roots lies in exploitation and slasher thrillers – to win Best Picture, it is only the third film after *It Happened One Night* (1934) and *One Flew Over the Cuckoo's Nest* (1975) to win the top five Oscars for film, director, screenplay (original or adapted) and the two lead acting categories. That the film is released in January 1991, outside the awards season window, shows how unexpected the victory is. In the same period, the Academy overlooks two Hollywood-set comedy-dramas, the Coen brothers' *Barton Fink* (1991), which is awarded the Palme d'Or at the Cannes Film Festival, and Robert Altman's *The Player* (1992), arguably the sharpest satire on the industry since Billy Wilder's *Sunset Boulevard* (1950).

The Adjuster, Atom Egoyan, Canada

The protagonist of Atom Egoyan's fourth feature is an insurance adjuster whose dedication to his clients goes far beyond the remit of his job. The film was inspired by the fire that destroyed the director's parents' house in 1989 and explores the line between personal and public life. It makes fine use of locations – particularly a half-completed house – to underpin the emotional vacuum in the adjuster's life and marked the emergence on the international stage of one of the most distinctive film-makers of the 1990s.

Disney's *Beauty and the Beast* (1991) is the first fully animated feature film to be nominated for a Best Picture Academy Award.

John Singleton is the first African American film-maker and youngest director to be nominated for a Best Director Academy Award for the twenty-four-year-old's *Boyz n the Hood* (1991).

Amateur video footage captures the beating of African American Rodney King by white Los Angeles Police Department officers in one of the first public uses of the medium. The officers' acquittal in 1992 sparks the Los Angeles Riots.

1991

Thelma & Louise, Ridley Scott, USA

Callie Khouri's Academy Award-winning screenplay tells the story of two women whose road trip is derailed by an attempted assault. They go on the run, committing robberies and evading the law, before deciding their fate in a climax that presents a gendered spin on the myth-making of *Butch Cassidy and the Sundance Kid* (1969). The film was controversial at the time for its negative portrayal of almost every male character. It has since been acknowledged as a timely critique of patriarchy and one of the most successful female buddy films.

The European Union is formed under the Maastricht Treaty.

The Earth Summit is held in Rio de Janeiro, in which several countries commit to protect the environment, signing the Convention on Biological Diversity.

Hard Boiled (Lat sau san taam), John Woo, Hong Kong

John Woo had established himself as the master of the Hong Kong action film by the early 1990s. *A Better Tomorrow* (*Ying hung boon sik*, 1986) cemented his reputation, while *The Killer* (*Dip huet seung hung*, 1989) refined his style. The excess of the bullet ballets in *Hard Boiled*, from the opening set piece in a teahouse to the climax in a hospital, saw Woo gain Hollywood's attention, culminating in the giddy *Face/Off* (1997). But it is this thriller that catches him at his most kinetic.

1992

NEW QUEER CINEMA

The term 'New Queer Cinema' was introduced to represent a group of mostly independent films made in the early 1990s whose overriding concerns were the representation of gay, lesbian, bisexual and transgender lives. It also heralded a major turning point, when films exploring LGBTQI+ life shifted from the periphery of cinema towards the mainstream.

The cultural critic who coined the term 'New Queer Cinema', B. Ruby Rich, highlighted a panoply of films that questioned, challenged or celebrated the way sexuality and gender were treated in society. Their complexity resisted promoting queerness solely in terms of positive images. Moreover, Rich noted, these films 'were great precisely because of the ways in which they were gay... Their queerness was no more arbitrary than their aesthetics, no more than their individual preoccupations with interrogating history... The queer present negotiates with the past, knowing full well that the future is at stake'.

This loose grouping emerged in the wake of growing academic interest in queer theory in the 1980s. The word 'queer' was reappropriated by academics and artists from its previously negative connotation. Queer cinema existed long before, from the films of Jean Cocteau, Jean Genet and Kenneth Anger, through the work of Andy Warhol, to Rainer Werner Fassbinder and Derek Jarman. The 1980s saw some inroads made by directors edging towards the mainstream, such as Donna Deitch's *Desert Hearts* (1985), Bill Sherwood's *Parting Glances* (1986) and James Ivory's *Maurice* (1987). But Rich's article, which appeared in a 1992 issue of the British film journal *Sight & Sound* and

subsequently developed in New York's *The Village Voice*, made it clear that a cultural shift was underway.

One of the first films to appear was Jennie Livingstone's documentary *Paris Is Burning* (1991), which captured the thrill and energy of New York's vogue and drag-ball culture. Premiering alongside it at the 1991 edition of the Sundance Film Festival – which like the nascent independent cinema scene of the 1980s was the locus of many New Queer Cinema films – was Todd Haynes's *Poison*. Winner of the festival's Grand Jury Prize, Haynes's drama wove together three narratives: a faux documentary about a boy in an abusive household who one day flies away; a Jean Genet-inspired gay prison tale, and an AIDS allegory modelled on a 1950s' sci-fi B-movie.

Isaac Julien's *Young Soul Rebels*, which focused on race, youth and sexuality in late 1970s Britain, premiered at the 1991 Cannes Film Festival, while later in the year, Jarman unveiled his adaptation of Christopher Marlowe's play *Edward II* (1594). It emphasized the monarch's relationship with Piers Gaveston, which had sometimes been downplayed. The film screened at the Venice and Toronto film festivals, alongside Christopher Münch's *The Hours and Times*, which imagined a relationship taking place

between John Lennon and The Beatles' manager Brian Epstein. Also screening at the Toronto festival was Gus Van Sant's *My Own Private Idaho*, which starred River Phoenix and Keanu Reeves. Their involvement in the film saw its profile rise significantly and it has since come to be regarded as one of the landmark LGBTQI+ films of the 1990s.

As *The Silence of the Lambs* (1991) and *Basic Instinct* (1992), prompted debate about trans, lesbian and bisexual representation in mainstream cinema, Sundance offered equally provocative portraits of queer criminal life with Tom Kalin's rapturous black and white period drama *Swoon* (1992) and Gregg Araki's visceral road movie *The Living End* (1992). If this period was initially dominated by gay stories, lesbian-themed dramas such as Rose Troche's *Go Fish* (1994), Cheryl Dunye's *The Watermelon Woman* (1996) and Lisa Cholodenko's *High Art* (1998) soon followed. The subsequent success of *Brokeback Mountain* (2005), *The Kids Are All Right* (2010), *Blue Is the Warmest Colour* (*La vie d'Adèle*, 2013), *Tangerine* (2015), *Disobedience* (2017) and *Portrait of a Lady on Fire* (*Portrait de la jeune fille en feu*, 2019) is evidence of how LGBTQI+ stories have started to become part of the fabric of mainstream cinema and culture.

OPPOSITE. *The Kids Are All Right* **(2010), Lisa Cholodenko, USA**
The Kids Are All Right was one of the first mainstream films to show a same-sex family. Lisa Cholodenko introduces a straight male character as the outsider and destructive influence on 21st-century nuclear family life.

RIGHT. *My Own Private Idaho* **(1991), Gus Van Sant, USA**
Gus Van Sant's portrait of two street hustlers is loosely based on William Shakespeare's plays *Henry IV, Part 1* (c. 1597), *Henry IV, Part 2* (1596–99) and *Henry V* (c. 1599).

1993–1994

The information superhighway. For most of humanity's history, non-verbal forms of communication and information have relied on the availability of materials such as stone, wood, paper, charcoal, chalk and ink. Tim Berners-Lee changes that in 1989 with the invention of the World Wide Web. Originally intended to aid information sharing among scientists around the world, information is identified via Uniform Resource Locators (URLs) and can be accessed via the internet. Further development unfolds over the subsequent three years before the software for the World Wide Web is made available to the public on 30 April 1993. Its use as a tool for film production, distribution and exhibition is some way off, but shortly after it becomes universal the internet hosts a film site created by British engineer Col Needham called the Internet Movie Database (IMDb). It develops into the most expansive resource for information on global cinema and television.

The North Tower of the World Trade Center in New York survives after a failed attempt to bomb it.

The Oslo Accords sees Israeli Prime Minister Yitzhak Rabin and leader of the Palestine Liberation Organization Yasser Arafat agree to the Israeli-Palestinian peace process.

○ *The Piano*, **Jane Campion, New Zealand/Australia/France**
Jane Campion's atmospheric 19th-century drama tells the story of a psychologically mute woman who arrives in New Zealand with her brutish husband and young daughter. She then has an affair with a retired sailor who has embraced Maori culture. Like the film-maker's previous work, *The Piano* posits the story from a feminist perspective. Campion became the first and only woman to win Cannes Film Festival's top prize, the Palme d'Or, for the film.

1993

Chungking Express, Wong Kar-wai, Hong Kong

Wong Kar-wai perfected his visually rapturous, non-linear approach to cinema when he made *Chungking Express*, his international breakthrough, during a short break from his more taxing *wuxia* (martial hero) epic *Ashes of Time* (1994). A tale of two doomed love affairs, set within the bustling heart of Hong Kong, Kar-wai inventively plays with slow and fast motion to accentuate the passage of time in his study of longing and loss.

Pulp Fiction, Quentin Tarantino, USA

Quentin Tarantino's second feature, for which he won the Palme d'Or and an Academy Award for Original Screenplay – shared with co-writer Roger Avary – not only confirmed the promise of his *Reservoir Dogs* (1992), it established him as the most influential US film-maker of his generation. Assimilating a landscape of western popular culture and employing an intricate and cleverly constructed non-linear narrative, Tarantino creates an homage to and reinvention of Hollywood genres and crime fiction, embracing their iconography as it assumes its own iconic status.

The Provisional Irish Republican Army and the British government make a truce and start political negotiations, marking the beginning of the end of the violent Troubles.

The Rwandan genocide unfolds over three months, during which more than half a million people are killed.

1994

1995–1996

Censoring cinema. As the medium reaches its 100th anniversary, the debate over the representation of graphic imagery on the screen once again rears its head. In 1992, three controversial films were released: *Reservoir Dogs*, *Bad Lieutenant* and *Man Bites Dog* (*C'est arrivé près de chez vous*), all of which feature sequences of extreme violence. The latter two films also feature scenes of sexual violence. The debate became more heated following the release in late 1994 – and worldwide distribution in 1995 – of Oliver Stone's *Natural Born Killers*. It is followed by Kathryn Bigelow's equally divisive *Strange Days*, while photographer Larry Clark adds fuel to the fire of censorship campaigners with *Kids* (both 1995), a portrait of teen life that focuses on underage sex. A year later, Canadian director David Cronenberg attracts further ire at the Cannes Film Festival with his uncompromising adaptation of J. G. Ballard's *Crash* (1973). All the films are eventually released, albeit accompanied by tabloid furore over their perceived immorality and corrupting influence.

Secrets & Lies, Mike Leigh, UK

Mike Leigh spent three decades dramatizing working- and middle-class British lives before he was awarded the Palme d'Or – alongside Brenda Blethyn's Best Actress win – at the Cannes Film Festival for the most expansive of his contemporary-set films. Interested in exploring issues around adoption, Leigh focuses on Marianne Jean-Baptiste's middle-class black woman who discovers her real mother is Blethyn's white working-class mother. The film typifies Leigh's balance of heightened drama, humour and humanism.

Pixar's *Toy Story* becomes the first fully computer-generated animated feature.

The Nuclear Non-Proliferation Treaty is extended indefinitely on 11 May.

1995

Breaking the Waves, Lars von Trier, Denmark/UK

The controversial Danish director's English-language debut details the descent into madness of a young woman from a strict religious community after her marriage to an oil-rig worker who is subsequently paralyzed in an accident. The intensity of Emily Watson's performance and Robby Müller's intimate camerawork marked a shift from Von Trier's previous focus on male protagonists and more austere formalism. It is one of his most admired films and presaged the later features made under the aegis of the Dogme 95 manifesto.

The Taliban seizes control of Afghanistan.

DVDs become available, gradually phasing out the inferior videocassette.

Fire, Deepa Mehta, India

The film is adapted from Ismat Chughtai's story *The Quilt* (*Lihaaf,* 1942) and is the first instalment of Deepa Mehta's 'Elements' trilogy, being followed by *Earth* (1998) and *Water* (2005). *Fire* focuses on two sisters-in-law whose bonding over their loveless marriages soon transforms into intimacy between them. The film was praised for its focus on the plight of women in a society where their lives are often deemed subservient to men. It is a landmark in Indian LGBTQI+ cinema.

1996

IRAN'S FILM WAVES

Iranian cinema attracted international attention from the late 1980s with its chronicles of everyday life, developing into explorations of the line between fiction and reality. In contrast to certain portrayals of the country as a radicalized state, Iranian film-makers have proven a vital and diverse cinematic presence.

The first Iranian silent feature *Abi and Rabi* (*Abi va Rabi*) was completed in 1930, and was followed by the country's first sound film *The Lor Girl* (*Dokhtar-e Lor*, 1933). It was not until the early 1960s that Iran began to produce films on a significant scale. As its mainstream cinema grew, feeding audience's appetite for melodramas, *luti* (tough guy) films and a hybrid of genres that became known as Filmfarsi, an alternative cinema began to emerge. It developed at the same time as a golden age in Iranian literature and social changes that transformed the country.

With its echoes of Italian Neorealism Forugh Farrokhzad's *The House Is Black* (*Khaneh siah ast*, 1963) is seen as the precursor of a new strand in Iranian film,

treating the medium as a serious art form. A compassionate portrait of life in a community populated by those afflicted with leprosy, it blends unflinching documentary footage with voiceover readings from the Qur'an, Old Testament and Farrokhzad's own poetry. Hajir Dariush's *Serpent's Skin* (*Jeld-e maar*, 1964) followed it. An adaptation of D. H. Lawrence's *Lady Chatterley's Lover* (1928) whose realism and focus on the psychology of its characters contrasted with mainstream entertainments, Dariush's drama is regarded as the first Iranian New Wave film. It was followed by Davoud Mollapour's *Madam Ahou's Husband* (*Shohar-e Ahu khanom*, 1968), a landmark in the representation of women in Iranian film, and Masoud Kimiai's polished *luti*,

Gheisar (1969). But it was Dariush Mehrjui's second feature *The Cow* (*Gaav,* 1969) that attracted the most attention, after its screening at the Venice Film Festival. It established a style that inspired a new generation of film-makers. These included Bahram Beizai with *Downpour* (*Ragbar*, 1971), Sohrab Shahid Saless with *A Simple Event* (*Yek Etefagh sadeh*, 1973) and Abbas Kiarostami with *The Traveller* (*Mossafer*, 1974). Kiarostami is also important for overseeing the creation of the film-making department at the Institute for Intellectual Development of Children and Young Adults in Tehran.

The upheaval of the revolution in 1979 saw hundreds of cinemas destroyed. To ensure films maintained the moral standards

demanded by the Khomeini regime, stricter censorship was introduced. A second wave of Iranian film-makers, who emerged in the aftermath of the revolution, still made films that drew on elements of Neorealism. Their work also had a poetic quality and featured narratives whose opacity enabled subtle critiques of Iranian society to be included. The most prominent film-makers in the 1980s included Nasser Taqvai with *Captain Khorshid* (*Nakhoda Khorshid*, 1986) and Beizai, whose *Bashu, the Little Stranger* (*Bashu, gharibeye koochak*, 1985) was voted the greatest Iranian film by a group of the country's critics and film-makers in 1999. Films that focused on women such as Pouran Derakhshandeh's *Little Bird of Happiness* (*Parandeyeh koochake*

khoshbakhti, 1988) and Tahmineh Milani's *The Legend of a Sigh* (*Afsane-ye-ah*, 1991) were notable for the absence of the male gaze.

Many films avoided censorship by channelling their themes through stories about children. Such is the case with Kiarostami's *Where Is the Friend's House?* (*Khane-ye doust kodjast?*, 1987), the first part of his celebrated 'Koker' trilogy. Like his drama *Close-Up* (*Nema-ye Nazdik*, 1990), they introduced a more self-reflexive kind of cinema that influenced films such as Samira Makhmalbaf's *The Apple* (*Sib*, 1998). It is also present in the work of Jafah Panahi and Mohammad Rasoulof, which has earned them censure by Iranian authorities, leading to criminal charges and imprisonment or house arrest.

OPPOSITE. *The Apple* (*Sib*, 1998), Samira Makhmalbaf, Iran
The film tells the true story of two siblings locked away for years by their grandparents. Samira Makhmalbaf has the real people play themselves as she details the girls' encounters with the outside world.

ABOVE. *The Cow* (*Gaav*, 1969), Dariush Mehrjui, Iran
With its striking evocation of rural life, Dariush Mehrjui's deceptively simple tale of a cow's disappearance and its owner's subsequent descent into some kind of madness employs metaphor to powerful effect.

1997–1998

Dogme 95. On 13 March 1995, at *'Le cinéma vers son deuxième siècle'* (Cinema towards its second century) conference in Paris, Danish film-makers Lars von Trier and Thomas Vinterberg announce the Dogme movement and unveils its manifesto. The ten rules, referred to as the 'Vow of Chastity', require a film to be shot on location; all props used must come from that location; sound must only be that produced in tandem with the image; the camera must be handheld and the film shot in colour, with all optical work forbidden; genres are unacceptable and films must feature no superficial action; the period must be the present; the film format must be Academy 35 mm, and the director must not be credited. Regarded by some critics as a gimmick typical of Von Trier's playfulness, the movement nevertheless inspires directors to take up the gauntlet. Thirty-five Dogme 95 films are shot between 1998 and 2004, beginning with Vinterberg's *Festen* and Von Trier's *The Idiots* (*Idioterne*, both 1998).

Hana-bi, Takeshi Kitano, Japan

Takeshi Kitano first gained international recognition as Sergeant Hara in Nagisa Ōshima's *Merry Christmas Mr Lawrence* (1983), but by the time he received the Golden Lion for *Hana-bi* at the Venice Film Festival, he had built a career as a formidable director. His seventh feature continues the crime theme of his previous *Violent Cop (Sono otoko, kyōbō ni tsuki*, 1989), *Boiling Point (3-4 x jûgatsu*, 1990) and magisterial *Sonatine* (1993) but infuses it with an emotional reach and artistry that elevates the film far beyond the trappings of genre cinema.

Tony Blair is voted Prime Minister of the first Labour government in Britain in almost two decades.

Diana, Princess of Wales is killed in a car accident in Paris.

James Cameron's *Titanic* is the first film to cost more than $200 million to make and is the first to gross more than $1 billion at the global box office.

1997

○ *Funny Games*, **Michael Haneke, Austria**
Michael Haneke is one of the most provocative critics
of the mediated image and had previously explored
the relationship between screen violence and its real
counterpart in *Benny's Video* (1992). He went further with
Funny Games detailing the terror inflicted on a holidaying
family by two teenage boys. The film's violence unfolds off-
screen, but its impact is no less shocking as Haneke asks
viewers why such 'entertainment' is culturally acceptable.

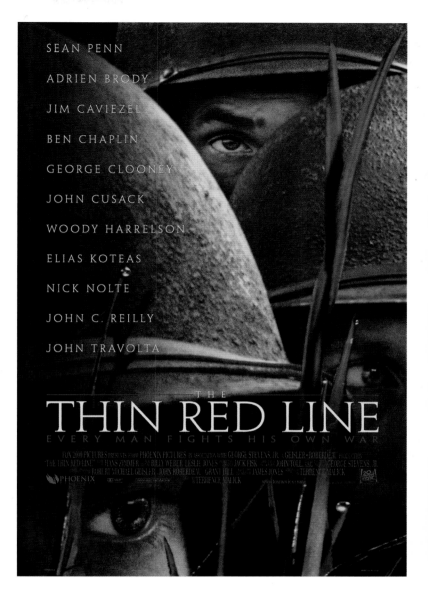

SEAN PENN
ADRIEN BRODY
JIM CAVIEZEL
BEN CHAPLIN
GEORGE CLOONEY
JOHN CUSACK
WOODY HARRELSON
ELIAS KOTEAS
NICK NOLTE
JOHN C. REILLY
JOHN TRAVOLTA

THE
THIN RED LINE
EVERY MAN FIGHTS HIS OWN WAR

Google is established
by Stanford University
PhD candidates Larry
Page and Sergey Brin.

Osama bin Laden
publishes a fatwa,
declaring jihad
against 'Jews
and Crusaders'.

○ *The Thin Red Line*, **Terrence Malick, USA**
Released in the same year as *Saving Private Ryan*, Terrence Malick's
adaptation of James Jones's novel of 1962, based on the author's
experiences as a soldier fighting in the Guadalcanal campaign in the
Second World War (1939–45), could not be more different to Steven
Spielberg's visceral and kinetic D-Day drama. Malick's film opens with
the line: 'What's this war in the heart of nature ?' He engages with
conflict on a philosophical level, employing multiple voiceovers to
express soldiers' thoughts and to explore the nature of war.

1998

1999-2000

Digital cinema. As the new millennium approaches, cinema once again finds itself in a transformative moment. Digital technology has been developing since the late 1970s. In 1996, *Rainbow* becomes the first film to be shot in high-definition video and to employ digital post-production techniques. It is followed by *The Last Broadcast* (1998), which is shot and edited using consumer-level digital equipment. However, George Lucas's *Star Wars* (1977–2019) prequel *The Phantom Menace* (1999) not only becomes the first major film to be shot featuring sequences captured by high-definition digital cameras, it is the first major film to be exhibited – in a limited number of cinemas – digitally. Lucas's second film in the trilogy, *Attack of the Clones* (2002), is entirely filmed in digital. The primary advantage to film-makers and the studios or production companies financing them is cost – production and distribution are drastically cheaper. However, the battle over the aesthetics of film versus digital continues.

All About My Mother (*Todo sobre mi madre*), Pedro Almodóvar, Spain
Securing Pedro Almodóvar's position as one of contemporary cinema's pre-eminent film-makers, *All About My Mother* details the main protagonist's journey towards peace and reconciliation following the sudden death of her son. The expressionistic use of colour accentuates the film's emotional undertow, while Almodóvar's seamlessly constructed narrative glides from the pain of bereavement to the acceptance of identity as a fluid state, all the while drawing on references from Federico García Lorca and Tennessee Williams to Douglas Sirk, Alfred Hitchcock and *All About Eve* (1950).

TiVo debuts in the United States, offering audiences the ability to record television programmes on to a hard drive.

Legendary film-maker Stanley Kubrick dies soon after completing his final film *Eyes Wide Shut*.

1999

Beau travail, Claire Denis, France

This adaptation of Herman Melville's *Billy Budd* (1888), transposes the action from the high seas to the coast of Djibouti and among a cadre of battle-ready French Foreign Legion soldiers. Claire Denis's visually rapturous film explores the tension that arises through the illicit, repressed desires of Denis Lavant's Chief Adjutant Galoup for a striking young recruit. Employing excerpts from Benjamin Britten's opera of Melville's novella and treating military exercises like beautiful dance routines, Denis's elliptical drama is a singular achievement in the French director's prodigious body of work.

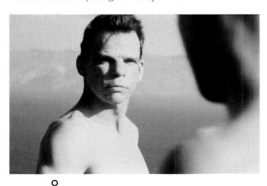

Crouching Tiger, Hidden Dragon (Wo hu cang long), Ang Lee, China/Hong Kong/Taiwan/USA

In the 1990s, Ang Lee proved himself a skilled film-maker at drawing out the nuances of human relationships across cultures. His paean to the *wuxia* (martial hero) film highlights his artistry as an action director. The narrative encompasses the search for a treasured sword, a decades-long rivalry between bitter foes and a young woman's desire to break free from the shackles of patriarchy. Lee's film is a whirlwind of stunningly choreographed set pieces, breathless storytelling and heightened emotion.

The dot-com bubble, which saw excessive investment and speculation in internet companies, rapidly begins to deflate, causing huge losses.

Vladimir Putin is elected President of Russia.

2000

6

—

THE DIGITAL
SCREEN

Historians looking for an event that signified the world's entry into the 21st century will likely point to the attack co-ordinated by the Islamist terrorist group al-Qaeda on 11 September 2001. Two passenger planes were flown into the World Trade Center towers in Manhattan, another made the Pentagon in Virginia its target and a fourth crashed into a field in Pennsylvania after passengers acted to prevent further destruction. This led to a military response from the United States that expanded into a protracted conflict, whose effects continue to tremor around the world.

The events of 9/11 resulted in numerous films that dramatized what took place, while others reflected upon them. In the years after the attacks, films such as *World Trade Center* and *United 93* (both 2006) focused on that day. Others, including *The Hamburg Cell* (2004) and *Charlie Wilson's War* (2007) looked to the past and the paths that led to the attacks, while quieter dramas such as *Reign Over Me*, *Grace Is Gone* (both 2007) and *The Space Between* (2010) approached the events from a more personal perspective. Iranian and Afghan directors also weighed in, representing the oppression of life under the Taliban and the period following it in films such as Mohsen Makhmalbaf's *Kandahar* (*Safar e Ghandehar*, 2001), Samira Makhmalbaf's *At Five in the Afternoon* (*Panj é asr*, 2003) and Siddiq Barmak's *Osama* (2003).

The resulting military conflicts, from the response against al-Qaeda, a wider operation against the Taliban in Afghanistan and the ensuing war in Iraq, saw a wide spectrum of cinematic treatments, ranging from *Jarhead* (2005) to *The Hurt Locker* (2008), *Green Zone* (2010), *American Sniper* (2014) and *Billy Lynn's Long Halftime Walk* (2016). Some films, such as *Lions for Lambs* (2007) and *Fair Game* (2010) explored the political machinations involved in the conflicts, while *Syriana* (2005), *Rendition* (2007) and *Body of Lies* (2008) dramatized the activities of intelligence agencies and big business in a region where religious extremism collides with the rapaciousness of the oil industry and international interests willing to take any measures in order to increase their control over the supply of natural resources.

The role of films in the ongoing conflicts often attracted controversy. None more so than *Zero Dark Thirty* (2012). Director Kathryn Bigelow and writer Mark Boal's follow-up to their Oscar-winning *The Hurt Locker* examined the hunt for the mastermind behind the attacks, al-Qaeda founder Osama bin Laden, and suggested that vital information had been gleaned through the use of enhanced interrogation techniques. Critics of the US government's permitted use of torture throughout the Afghanistan and Iraq conflicts criticized the film, arguing that it had produced no such result. Documentary film-maker Alex Gibney, who had examined the impact of torture by US forces and their allies in his Oscar-winning documentary *Taxi to the Dark Side* (2007), was one of *Zero Dark Thirty's* sternest critics.

Gibney represented a new era in documentary. The form had previously been a staple of television, or mainly played in specialized or art-house cinemas. But in the early 2000s, a shift took place. Key to this was Michael Moore. His first film *Roger & Me* (1989) detailed the devastating economic impact of General Motors closing its plant in

PREVIOUS PAGE. *Black Panther* (2018), Ryan Coogler, USA
Created in 1966 by Stan Lee and Jack Kirby, Black Panther (aka T'Challa) was the first Marvel superhero of African descent. The film adaptation represented the first superhero blockbuster to feature an almost entirely black cast.

ABOVE. *At Five in the Afternoon* (*Panj é asr*, 2003), Samira Makhmalbaf, Iran
The first film to be shot in Afghanistan after the NATO invasion of the country, Samira Makhmalbaf's drama focuses on a young woman desperate to receive an education in post-Taliban society.

his home town of Flint, Michigan and was a success. He perfected his combination of searing polemic, satire and staged stunts with *Bowling for Columbine* (2002), which examined gun culture in the United States. He attracted controversy at the 2003 Academy Awards for his criticism of the George W. Bush administration and the invasion of Iraq during his Best Documentary Award acceptance speech for the film. However, that paled in comparison to the response his film *Fahrenheit 9/11* (2004) received. Premiering at the Cannes Film Festival, where it was awarded the Palme d'Or, *Fahrenheit 9/11* presented a scathing critique of the Bush administration's response to 9/11 and the conflict in Iraq. The film represented one of the many documentaries that tackled the conflict, from *Control Room* (2004), *Why We Fight* (2005), *Iraq in Fragments* (2006), *No End in Sight* (2007) and *Standard Operating Procedure* (2008) to *Restrepo*, *The War You Don't See* (both 2010) and *The Unknown Known* (2013). Moore's film is also notable for its box-office success, earning more than $200 million globally on its initial release from a budget of $6 million.

Greater audience interest in documentaries saw their presence in mainstream cinemas increase. A sizeable proportion focused on environmental issues, from highlighting specific stories, such as the devastation wreaked on Lake Victoria, Tanzania in *Darwin's Nightmare* (2004) to the global perspective of films such as *An Inconvenient Truth* (2006). But the variety proved as diverse as narrative cinema, spanning the globe and every aspect of past and present life. From the account of Philippe Petit's walk between the two World Trade Center towers in 1974 in *Man on Wire* (2008) and Joshua Oppenheimer's unusual way of exploring Indonesia's genocidal past in *The Act of Killing* (2013), to acclaimed grande dame of non-fiction film Agnès Varda and street artist JR's singular portrait of contemporary France *Faces Places* (*Visages villages*, 2017).

Focus intensified on the economic disparity in societies around the world. The corporate malfeasance that led to the collapse of the Enron energy company in 2001 and the Worldcom telecommunications company in 2002 stand as harbingers of the economic rout after the stock-market crash of 2008, symbolizing a world that separates the super-wealthy from the rest of its population. Documentary and fiction film tackled these events, notably in Alex Gibney's forensically detailed *Enron: the Smartest Guys in the Room* (2005) and Adam McKay's satirical *The Big Short* (2015), an adaptation of Michael Lewis's account of the financiers who saw the 2008 crash coming. Cinema around the world grappled with the impact of inequality, from Ken Loach's searing portrait of disadvantaged lives in *I, Daniel Blake* (2016) to Bong Joon-ho's satire *Parasite* (*Gisaengchung*, 2019).

Cinema provided escapism from these events, as it had during moments of hardship in the 20th century. Fantasy came in the form of Peter Jackson's epic trilogies *The Lord of the Rings* (2001–03) and *The Hobbit* (2012–14). James Cameron had to delay his space fantasy *Avatar* (2009) for more than a decade to develop the effects needed to realize the world and inhabitants of the planet Pandora. Like his *Titanic* (1997), *Avatar* was the most expensive film made at that time and became the biggest film at the box office.

Mexican film-maker Guillermo del Toro also excelled with evocations of fantasy universes. Emerging with *Cronos* (1993), an original take on the vampire myth, he has ventured into the blockbuster arena with *Blade II* (2002), *Hellboy* (2004) and *Pacific Rim* (2013), but his greatest success has come from merging imagined worlds with a strong allegorical undertow. *The Devil's Backbone* (*El espinazo del diablo*, 2001) and *Pan's Labyrinth* (*El laberinto del fauno*, 2006) both explore Spain's fascist past. The former is a ghost story that unfolds in a remote boys' school during the Spanish Civil War (1936–39), while the latter is a baroque fantasy horror set in General Francisco Franco's victorious regime, in which a young girl suppresses the everyday horror around her by conjuring up an imagined world of fairies and monsters. Del Toro had more

success at the 2018 Academy Awards with his tender romance set in the Cold War (1947–91) *The Shape of Water* (2017), which won four Oscars including Best Picture and Best Director.

Fantasy of a superhero kind also reigned at the global box office throughout the 2000s. The golden age of comic books spanned a period marked by the rise of fascism, global conflict and increasing tensions prompted by the Cold War. The era saw the creation of Superman, Batman, Captain America and Wonder Woman. Over time, these figures would become part of the Marvel and DC Comics universes. Their journey to the big screen was not without its hiccups. For every *Superman* (1978) or *Batman* (1989), there were a glut of poorly produced sequels and spin-offs. However, the appearance of *X-Men* (2000) and *Spider-Man* (2002) not only announced

BELOW. *Pan's Labyrinth* (*El laberinto del fauno*, 2006), **Guillermo del Toro, Mexico** The richly detailed imagined world of a young girl lies in stark contrast to a despotic regime in Guillermo del Toro's Spanish fantasy.

TOP. *Drive* (2011), Nicolas Winding Refn, USA
Nicolas Winding Refn's thriller set in Los Angeles is a throwback to the work of Michael Mann and Walter Hill in the 1980s, while Ryan Gosling's protagonist recalls the stoic, silent characters beloved by French film-maker and actor Jean-Pierre Melville.

ABOVE. *Antichrist* (2009), Lars von Trier, Denmark/Germany/France/Sweden/Italy/Poland
Lars von Trier attracted controversy for his portrait of the emotionally and physically tortuous relationship of a grieving couple who seek solitude and solace in a rural retreat.

the arrival of a new generation of superhero films, they revelled in the advances in visual effects to showcase their powers. They were followed by Christopher Nolan's *Batman Begins* (2005), which hinted at the darker route that some superhero films would take. But it was Jon Favreau's *Iron Man* (2008) that saw the superhero film shift gear, placing the Marvel Cinematic Universe stand alongside the *Star Wars* (1977–2019), *James Bond* (1962–) and *Harry Potter* (2001–11) series as one of the most successful franchises in cinema.

As these commercial behemoths dominated the global box office, world cinema continued to flourish. The Romanian New Wave became one of the key movements of this era. Although many of the film-makers associated with the label shunned it, there was a specific style and similar thematic concerns that drew these films together. Another loosely defined group came under the banner of New French Extremity, which was linked through its transgressive themes. It included Claire Denis's *Trouble Every Day* (2001), Gaspar Noé's *Irreversible* (*Irréversible*, 2002), Catherine Breillat's *Romance* (1999), Bruno Dumont's *Twentynine Palms* (2003), Virginie Despentes and Coralie Trinh Thi's *Baise-moi* (2000), Leos Carax's *Pola X* (1999) and Philippe Grandrieux's *Sombre* (1998). They explored the body politic in the late 20th and early 21st century, finding a way to shock audiences into consciousness and drawing as much from the world of horror as the aesthetics of art-house cinema.

Other European directors followed a similar path, with Lars von Trier leading the way. His combination of beauty and repellence was evident in films such as *Antichrist* (2009) and *Melancholia* (2011), while his *Nymphomaniac* (2013) diptych and the brutal *The House That Jack Built* (2018) tested audiences' tolerance levels. If Lukas Moodysson's debut *Show Me Love* (*Fucking Åmål*, 1998) drew comparisons with Ingmar Bergman, later films such as *Hole in My Heart* (*Ett hål i mitt hjärta*, 2004) and *Container* (2006) edged closer to the nihilism present in the work of the New French Extremity directors. Elsewhere, the penchant for graphic violence evident in Nicolas Winding Refn's early Danish crime dramas *Pusher* (1996) and *Bleeder* (1999) continued in his larger-scale, US productions. Refn's *Drive* (2011), a taut adaptation of James Sallis's acclaimed novel of 2005, offered up a scintillating retro-portrait of Los Angeles that drew as much on Walter Hill's *The Driver* (1978) and Michael Mann's *Thief* (1981) as it did the cool elegance of Jean-Pierre Melville's *Le samouraï* (1967). Refn's later fashion world thriller *The Neon Demon* (2016) is a showcase for his perspective on the world.

As the 2000s progressed, digital cinema dominated the production process, from shooting through to exhibition. Some high-profile directors – Steven Spielberg and Christopher Nolan in particular – continued to fight for the importance of shooting on film. Many others embraced the new technology for the benefits it brought, from significantly reduced costs to increased mobility – including the ability to shoot a feature-length film with a smartphone. At the same time, the prevalence of streaming services threatened the existence, or for some people even the need, of cinemas. The desire to watch films will unlikely diminish but how people watch is radically changing.

2001-2002

War on terror. Shortly after his inauguration as the 43rd President of the United States on 20 January 2001, George W. Bush is advised by the Central Intelligence Agency (CIA) that there is a high risk of an attack on US soil by members of the al-Qaeda militant Islamist organization. In June, German intelligence advises that commercial planes may be used as weapons in an attack, with more information supplied by Jordan a month later, identifying the operation codename as 'The Big Wedding'. On 11 September, four planes are hijacked after leaving airports in Boston, Newark and near Washington, D.C. Two are flown into the World Trade Center towers in Manhattan. One hits the Pentagon in Virginia. The fourth crashes into a field in Pennsylvania after passengers and crew try to regain control of the plane. Within a month, Operation Enduring Freedom starts, with US forces leading an international invasion into Afghanistan. The next year, Bush signs the Homeland Security Act into law.

Apple launches Mac
OS X, its next generation
operating system.

Annual DVD sales outstrip
VHS for the first time.

○ *Spirited Away (Sen to Chihiro no kamikakushi*, 2001),
Hayao Miyazaki, Japan
Spirited Away is Hayao Miyazaki's eighth feature as writer and
director. It tells the story of a young girl who, when moving home
with her parents, happens upon a world of ghosts and spirits. With
echoes of *Alice's Adventures in Wonderland* (1865), the film is
a wildly inventive fantasy that affirms Studio Ghibli's reputation
as one of the world's leading animation houses. Like Miyazaki's
Princess Mononoke (*Mononoke-hime*, 1997), the film blends
computer animation with traditional hand-drawn techniques.
It becomes the first anime to win an Academy Award.

2001

Russian Ark (*Russkiy kovcheg*, 2002), Aleksandr Sokurov, Russia

An unnamed guide accompanies a French traveller through the rooms of St Petersburg's Winter Palace, describing its role in history, as characters from different eras pass around them. An extraordinary technical accomplishment and a landmark in the development of digital film-making, Aleksandr Sokurov's docudrama slips through the three centuries of the palace's existence in a single, unedited take. A cast of more than 2,000 performers and three orchestras appear throughout the film, which was the first to be shot using uncompressed high-definition video.

An **epidemic** of severe acute respiratory syndrome (SARS) breaks out in Guangdong Province, China.

Charges against the Central Park Five are dropped after convicted murderer Matias Reyes confesses to the crime. The story of the wrongly convicted youths and the racial tensions surrounding the case would form the basis of a documentary in 2012 by Ken Burns and dramatized series by Ava DuVernay in 2019.

City of God (*Cidade de Deus*, 2002), Fernando Miereilles and Kátia Lund, Brazil

City of God charts the growth of organized crime in the Cidade de Deus suburb of Rio de Janeiro between the 1960s and 1980s. Fernando Miereilles and co-director Kátia Lund chose youths from favelas to play the film's protagonists, working with them in acting workshops to prepare. The resulting drama is a kinetic, furiously paced portrait of lives afflicted by poverty, drugs, violence and crime.

2002

2003-2004

Shock and awe. The US government had adopted a more aggressive policy towards Iraq before the 9/11 attacks. After the invasion of Afghanistan, intelligence is compiled to present an argument that the Saddam Hussein regime is in possession of weapons of mass destruction. Retired US Marine and future US Senator Jim Webb warns: 'Those who are pushing for a unilateral war in Iraq know full well that there is no exit strategy if we invade and stay.' On 20 March 2003, Operation Iraqi Freedom – the Iraq War – begins. Webb's words soon ring true and the successful overthrow of the Hussein regime gives way to chaotic rule in the country. Peter Jackson completes his first J. R. R. Tolkien trilogy with the release and Oscars success of *The Lord of the Rings: The Return of the King* (2003). Mel Gibson directs the most successful non-English language film at the box office with the controversial *The Passion of the Christ* (2004).

Elephant, Gus Van Sant, USA

The massacre at Columbine High School in 1999 partly inspired Gus Van Sant's account of a shooting in a school. Rather than heighten the drama surrounding the shooting, Van Sant presents a lyrical portrait of teenage life torn apart by violence. Winner of the Palme d'Or at the Cannes Film Festival, *Elephant* is the second part of Van Sant's 'Death' trilogy, after *Gerry* (2003) and preceding *Last Days* (2005). The film's title is an homage to Alan Clarke's drama of the same name of 1989, whose minimalist style influenced Van Sant.

The Space Shuttle *Columbia* disintegrates as it attempts to re-enter the Earth's atmosphere over Texas, killing all on board.

The War in Darfur begins, resulting in a massive humanitarian crisis.

2003

Moolaadé, Ousmane Sembène, Senegal/France/ Burkina Faso/Cameroon/Morocco/

Ousmane Sembène's final film is a searing indictment of the practice of female genital mutilation. Unfolding in a rural village in Burkina Faso, _Moolaadé_ depicts a woman's battle to prevent her daughter and a group of younger girls from undergoing the dangerous procedure. Sembène's film plays out like a fable, but it is strident in its position, suggesting that honouring tradition is a noble pursuit, but never at the expense of progress.

Mark Zuckerberg creates the Facebook social-media platform.

2004

Fahrenheit 9/11, Michael Moore, USA

After the success of _Bowling for Columbine_ (2002), Michael Moore took aim at the Bush administration for its response to the attacks of 11 September 2001. Initially ridiculing President Bush's immediate response, offering an alternative interpretation of the footage showing him reading to a group of young school children as he is informed of the attacks, Moore's film shifts from satire to outrage. It is one of the earliest of many documentaries to detail the cost of the Iraq invasion.

LEFT. *Parasite (Gisaengchung,* 2019), Bong Joon-ho, South Korea
The first South Korean film to win the Palme d'Or at Cannes and the first non-English language film ever to win the Best Picture Academy Award, *Parasite* satirizes economic disparity in modern-day Seoul. The film resonated with a larger global audience, which embraced it enthusiastically.

SOUTH KOREAN CINEMA

The involvement of South Korean corporations in supporting its film industry in the early 1990s paved the way for a generation of film-makers to emerge by the end of the decade. They in turn supported home-grown talent that made Korean cinema a vital presence on the world stage.

The first Korean films, the feature *Loyal Revenge* (*Uirijeok Gutu*) and documentary *Scenes of Kyongsong City*, premiered in October 1919. If the growth of the national film industry was slow, it gathered pace from the late 1950s, producing a golden age that saw the release of acclaimed films such as *The Housemaid* (*Hanyo,* 1960) and *The Stray Bullet* (*Obaltan*, 1961). But a restrictive government in the 1970s witnessed heavy censorship and tightening controls, which were not fully relaxed until the early 1990s. That era saw business conglomerates, known as chaebol, increase their involvement in film production. This was drastically reduced following the Asian financial crisis of 1997, but by that time a new generation of film-makers were making their presence felt.

The commercial breakthrough for South Korean cinema came with *Shiri* (1999), a high-octane homage to the kind of stylized action film Tony Scott had been producing in Hollywood, as well as the kinetic bullet ballets of John Woo, Ringo Lam and Johnnie To. Its narrative tapped into tensions between North and South Korea, and its success at home and abroad helped rejuvenate the industry.

Two film-makers emerged who balanced artistry with commercial success and had a wider appeal. Park Chan-wook's breakthrough feature *Joint Security Area* (*Gongdong gyeongbi guyeok JSA*, 2000), a thriller that details an investigation into an incident along the demilitarized zone, broke domestic box-office records. But it was his *Vengeance* trilogy that raised his profile internationally. *Sympathy for Mr Vengeance* (*Boksuneun naui geot*, 2002), the international hit *Oldboy* (*Oldeuboi*, 2003) and *Lady Vengeance* (*Chinjeolhan geumjassi*, 2005) established Park's reputation for complex explorations of guilt and desire, which he continued to mine with *Thirst* (*Bakjwi*, 2009), his English-language debut *Stoker* (2013) and *The Handmaiden* (2016).

Bong Joon-ho's balance of humour, satire and moral ambivalence are evident in his directorial debut *Barking Dogs Never Bite* (*Flandersui gae*, 2000), but his police procedural *Memories of Murder* (*Salinui chueok*, 2003) and sci-fi adventure *The Host* (*Gwoemul*, 2006) established his reputation. After the quietly impressive *Mother* (*Madeo*, 2009), Bong made two international features with *Snowpiercer* (2013) and *Okja* (2017), before returning to Korea to make *Parasite* (*Gisaengchung*, 2019) whose global success, both critically and commercially, has made it a landmark in Korean film.

At the same time, other film-makers have broadened the landscape of Korean film, attracting critical acclaim, if not always the lion's share of the box office. Im Kwon-taek had been directing films since the early 1960s but in the 2000s he helped cement the importance of Korean cinema with *Drunk on Women and Poetry* (*Chihwaseon*, 2002), a portrait of a 19th-century painter, and the gangster drama *Low Life* (*Haryu insaeng*, 2004). With his graphic *The Isle* (*Seom*, 2000), Kim Ki-duk shocked audiences. But his *Spring, Summer, Autumn, Winter... and Spring* (*Bom Yeoareum Gaeul Gyeoul Geurigo Bom*, 2003), *3-Iron* (*Bin-jip*, 2004), *Arirang* (2011) and Venice Film Festival's Golden Lion winner *Pietà* (2012), showcased the prolific film-maker's range. On a quieter note, Hong Sang-soo's first features *The Day a Pig Fell into the Well* (*Daijiga umule pajinnal*, 1996) and *The Power of Kangwon Province* (*Kangwon-do ui him*, 1998) and his Rotterdam Film Festival winner *Right Now, Wrong Then* (*Ji-geum-eun-mat-go-geu-ddae-neun-teul-li-da*, 2015) highlight a director adept at capturing the spontaneity of everyday life. Lee Chang-dong's *Green Fish* (*Chorok mulkogi*, 1997) and *Burning* (*Beoning*, 2018) have seen him acclaimed as one of the most distinctive voices in Korean and world cinema.

2005-2006

Social media arrives. In February 2005, three former PayPal employees, Chad Hurley, Steve Chen and Jawed Karim, launch the online video-sharing platform YouTube. On 23 April, Karim posts the first film on the site. Entitled *Me at the zoo*, the 18-second video is a nondescript recording of Karim describing the elephants stood behind him. In terms of social media, it is the equivalent of the Lumière brothers' films, albeit more widely seen: by mid 2020, it had more than ninety-nine million views. Beta testing for the site begins shortly after Karim's film appears and by the time it is launched officially in December 2005 it receives eight million views a day. Individuals and organizations upload a wide variety of home-made films, promotional material or archive footage. In turn, viewers can comment on and like or dislike the uploaded material. In 2006, Google acquired YouTube for $1.65 billion.

Brokeback Mountain, Ang Lee, USA

Ang Lee's moving drama was adapted from Annie Proulx's acclaimed short story by novelist Larry McMurtry and Diana Ossana. It details the love affair between cowboys Ennis Del Mar and Jack Twist between 1963 and 1983. Grappling with a romance that transgresses heterosexual norms, the film explores the anguish of characters forced to accede to the conventions of marriage and family life in order to hide their true feelings. A critical and commercial success, it is a landmark in LGBTQI+ Cinema.

○ *The Child* (*L'enfant*), Jean-Pierre and Luc Dardenne, France

Jean-Pierre and Luc Dardenne's second Palme d'Or-winning film after their celebrated breakthrough drama *Rosetta* (1999) continues their naturalistic style of cinema, engaging with social issues and shining a light on inequality. Their focus here is a young couple, Bruno and Sonia, who find themselves parents. Desperate to make some money, Bruno decides on an action that will tear them apart. The Dardennes' unshowy directorial style, always intimate but never obtrusive, draws intense performances from Jérémie Renier, Déborah François and cast while never descending into cliché or melodrama.

The Kyoto Protocol, expanding on the United Nations Framework Convention on Climate Change, goes into effect.

Pope John Paul II dies. He is replaced by Pope Benedict XVI.

The world's population reaches 6.5 billion.

2005

FROM THE DIRECTOR OF
'THE BOURNE SUPREMACY' & 'BLOODY SUNDAY'

UNITED
93

www.united93movie.co.uk   www.workingtitlefilms.com   www.uip.co.uk

***United 93*, Paul Greengrass, USA/UK**

The exact details of what happened aboard
the fourth US plane overtaken by hijackers
on 11 September 2001 will never be known,
but Paul Greengrass's harrowing drama
attempts to imagine how the passengers
succeeded in foiling the attackers' plans,
but at the cost of all aboard flight United 93.
Eschewing sensationalism in favour of a
minute-by-minute realism, Greengrass's film
is unbearably tense, but never exploitative.
It honours a group of people whose bravery
cost their lives but saved many others.

Saddam Hussein is
sentenced to death
and executed on
30 December.

Daniel Craig is the
sixth official James
Bond in *Casino Royale*.

2006

2007–2008

A new cinema. The success of Cristi Puiu's *The Death of Mr Lazarescu* (*Moartea domnului Lăzărescu*, 2005), Corneliu Porumboiu's *12:08 East of Bucharest* (*A fost sau n-a fost?*) and Cătălin Mitulescu's *The Way I Spent the End of the World* (*Cum mi-am petrecut sfârsitul lumii*, both 2006) at the 2005 and 2006 Cannes Film Festivals launches what becomes known as the Romanian New Wave. Employing a minimalist style and often featuring long takes, the films explore everyday Romanian life during and after the Nicolae Ceauşescu regime. The films, with their with mordant humour, are often uncompromising accounts of the corrupting nature of power and frequently critical of Romania's emergence as a modern democracy. Other directors to emerge include Cristian Nemescu with *California Dreamin'* (2007), Adrian Sitaru with *Hooked* (*Pescuit sportiv*, 2008), Radu Jude with *The Happiest Girl in the World* (*Cea mai fericită fată din lume*, 2009) and Radu Muntean with *Tuesday, After Christmas* (*Marti, după Crăciun*, 2010).

There Will Be Blood, Paul Thomas Anderson, USA

Paul Thomas Anderson's fifth feature is a loose adaptation of Upton Sinclair's novel *Oil!* (1927). The film is a stark critique of unfettered capitalism, centring on Daniel Plainview, a gold prospector who discovers oil on his land and becomes a successful businessman. But his ruthlessness makes him a solitary figure, with only his adopted son to keep him company. The brilliance of Anderson's film, outside of Daniel Day-Lewis's mesmerizing performance, lies in its combination of virtuosic film-making and storytelling verve.

Steve Jobs unveils the first iPhone.

Netflix commences its streaming service.

2007

4 Months, 3 Weeks and 2 Days (*4 luni, 3 saptamâni si 2 zile*), Cristian Mungiu, Romania

Young student Găbiţa is pregnant and asks her friend Otilia to accompany her to have an abortion. However, this is Romania in 1987, still under the control of Nicolae Ceauşescu, where such procedures are illegal. Cristian Mungiu's second feature, which was awarded the Palme d'Or at the Cannes Film Festival, is a compelling portrait of a society whose citizens lack freedom in both their public and personal lives, and perfectly characterized the style of a new generation of Romanian film-makers.

The Large Hadron Collider, a high-energy particle accelerator and the largest machine in the world, begins operating.

Global financial markets crash following the depreciation in the US sub-prime mortgage market.

The Dark Knight, Christopher Nolan, USA

Christopher Nolan returned to Gotham for the second entry in *The Dark Knight* (2005–12) trilogy. Its source material notwithstanding, it resembles a precision-made crime thriller, as evinced by the opening sequence's bank heist. What it has in common with other caped crusader films prior to *Batman Begins* (2005) is a fascination with the Joker, whose antics here are played less for laughs than as a desire for mayhem, mirroring the atmosphere of a post-9/11 world.

2008

THE CINEMATIC THEME PARK

The battle between art and commerce in cinema has raged from its inception. The rise of the modern blockbuster since the 1970s has seen it expand from a few summer titles to a heavily populated calendar of year-round releases that dominate global cinemas. This has led to a division between supporters of the various franchises and those less convinced of their virtues.

The franchise film has existed since the earliest feature films. If a film was popular, producers and studios sought ways to earn further profits. The result was usually to repeat the trick or, at least, identify the elements that worked and tweak them in the hope of repeating the success. British academic Steve Neale called it 'repetition and difference'.

An early example was French film-maker Louis Feuillade's crime film serial *Fantômas* (1913–14). It proved so popular he created more crime dramas with *The Vampires* (*Les vampires*, 1915) and *Judex* (1916). Universal Pictures and Warner Bros' monster and gangster series of the early 1930s reflect the response of an industry to the popularity of a product, whereas the *Tarzan* (1932–48) and *Thin Man* (1934–47) series presented a character rather than genre- or thematically-linked series of films, not dissimilar to the *James Bond* (1962–) franchise, which itself presaged the rise of the modern blockbuster.

If *Jaws* (1975) led the way for the summer tentpole hit, the *Star Wars* (1977–2019) series laid the groundwork for most of the successful big-budget

commercial releases of the 2000s. Aside from the return of that space saga across two separate trilogies, the modern blockbuster is mostly comprised of adventures whose origins lie in another commercial market. The *Harry Potter* (2001–11) adventures, like *The Chronicles of Narnia* (2005–10), *Percy Jackson* (2010–13) and *The Hunger Games* (2012–) series followed the most conventional route, being based on popular novels. By contrast, the *Pirates of the Caribbean* (2003–17) series originated with a popular Disney theme-park attraction. Michael Bay's *Transformers* (2007–17) action films had their origins in the Hasbro toy series, which had already been an animated film in 1986.

Although superhero films were intermittently popular, their fortunes changed dramatically in the early 2000s. While the DC Comics adaptations have varied between the critical and commercial success of Christopher Nolan's *The Dark Knight* (2005–12) trilogy and the more lacklustre DC Extended Universe adventures, the cultural and commercial landscape of mainstream cinema has been dominated by the success of the Marvel Cinematic Universe franchise, beginning with *Iron Man* (2008).

Taken together, along with the thrills of *Avatar* (2008) and its upcoming sequels, as well as the continuing *Fast & Furious* (2001–) entries, these films make up a significant proportion of the film industry's annual box office. However, they divide critics, with some suggesting such films amount to little more than theme park rides, albeit enabled by gifted artists and technicians. A polemic by US film-maker Martin Scorsese in *The New York Times*, published around the time of his effects-laden but starkly different crime drama *The Irishman* (2019), expressed concern that 'the most ominous change has happened stealthily and under cover of night: the gradual but steady elimination of risk'. Nevertheless, with sequel after sequel still slated for release, these effects-driven, extraordinarily lucrative cinematic rides appear unlikely to stop any time soon.

OPPOSITE BELOW. *Black Panther* (2018), Ryan Coogler, USA
The main characters of Ryan Coogler's African and American adventure are black, making it a major cultural event, beyond the remit of the superhero genre.

BELOW. *Harry Potter and the Prisoner of Azkaban* (2004), Alfonso Cuarón, UK/USA
Director Alfonso Cuarón made the third *Harry Potter* film the darkest and most satisfying entry in the series, balancing thrills with a playful intelligence.

2009–2010

A box-office behemoth. James Cameron releases *Avatar* in 2008 and it surpasses his previous record with *Titanic* (1997) in being the most expensive film ever made and the biggest box-office success. *Avatar* is the biggest film to employ 3D technology. The technique had been in existence for decades, even enjoying a golden era in the early 1950s. But with his documentary *Ghosts of the Abyss* (2003), Cameron merged HD 3D technology with the IMAX format. Although 3D becomes another potential revenue stream through the 2000s it has as many critics as it does supporters. Subsequent directors such as Werner Herzog (*Cave of Forgotten Dreams*, 2010), Wim Wenders (*Pina*, 2011), Ang Lee (*Life of Pi*, 2012) and Alfonso Cuarón (*Gravity*, 2013) attempt to push the parameters of 3D technology, but for the most part it remains a staple of mainstream entertainment. At the 82nd Academy Awards, *Avatar* loses to *The Hurt Locker* (2008) for Best Picture and Director, and Kathryn Bigelow is the first woman to win the latter accolade.

The White Ribbon (*Das weisse Band*), Michael Haneke, Germany/ Austria/France/Italy/Canada

On the eve of the First World War (1914–18), a series of strange events unfold in a rural northern German village. What lies behind these acts is something few are willing to acknowledge. Pushing the 'sins of the parents' maxim to the extreme, Michael Haneke's beautifully shot black and white drama perfectly encapsulates his 'cinema of insistent questions' rather than one of answers. The result, like his film *Hidden* (*Caché*, 2005), is a mystery wrapped up in a morality play.

Barack Obama is sworn in as the 44th President of the United States, becoming the first African American to hold the position.

Slumdog Millionaire (2008) is the first movie shot mainly in digital to win the Academy Award for Best Cinematography.

2009

The Social Network, David Fincher, USA

Aaron Sorkin's Oscar-winning adaptation of Ben Mezrich's book *The Accidental Billionaires: The Founding of Facebook, a Tale of Sex, Money, Genius, and Betrayal* (2009) is directed by David Fincher as a slow-burn thriller in the style of his earlier *Se7en* (1995) and *Zodiac* (2007). The body count may be zero but there is plenty of blood in the boardroom as Fincher's forensic gaze examines Mark Zuckerberg's creation of the networking site and his ascent from a dorm room in Harvard to being head of a multinational.

WikiLeaks publishes a vast trove of leaked documents relating to US involvement in Afghanistan.

Iranian film-maker Jafar Panahi is sentenced to six years' house arrest and a twenty-year ban on film-making, which does not stop him continuing to write and direct films including *This Is Not a Film* (*In film nist*, 2011) and *Taxi Tehran* (*Taxi*, 2015).

Somewhere, Sofia Coppola, USA

Ennui is a difficult state of mind to convey to a cinema audience, particularly when it is experienced by a Hollywood star with few difficulties in his life. But this is a world Sofia Coppola knows well. Stephen Dorff's Johnny Marco drifts aimlessly through his life, but on reconnecting with his daughter he finds the possibility of redemption. Like all of Coppola's films, *Somewhere* is beautifully shot and Marco's journey is undercut with knowing humour.

2010

2011–2012

The Arab Spring. Following the Green Movement protests in Iran during 2009, a rising tide of opposition to autocratic rule in the Arab world gradually gains traction. Fundamental to its spread is the use of social media to corral supporters of change, to warn of potential dangers and to promote the cause of campaigners around the region. It is particularly effective in Tunisia and Egypt. Platforms such as Facebook enable news sources other than official media outlets to broadcast internationally. Social media helps organize action in a way that had previously been difficult with popular uprisings. The power and limitations of these tools is clear in the series of films and documentaries made about the uprisings, from Iranian-German film-maker Ali Samadi Ahadi's *The Green Wave* (2010) to Egyptian film-makers Jehane Noujaim's *The Square* (*Al midan*, 2013) and Mohamed Diab's *Clash* (*Eshtebak*, 2016).

South Korean director Park Chan-wook shoots his Berlin Film Festival-winning short *Night Fishing* (*Paranmanjang*) on an Apple iPhone 4.

Studios start selling the distribution rights of films to streaming platforms, so the window between cinema releases and their availability for home viewing reduces.

○ *The Tree of Life*, **Terrence Malick, USA**
Terrence Mallick's film unfolds across three distinct narrative strands. In one, Sean Penn's architect Jack O'Brien finds himself adrift in the modern world. In the longest section, Jack is the eldest sibling growing up with his family in 1950s Texas, then, at one point, the film segues into a dazzling 20-minute history of the planet. Beginning with a quote from the Book of Job and open to a variety of interpretations, Malick's visionary epic is studio film-making at its most ambitious.

2011

A Separation (Jodaeiye Nader az Simin), Asghar Farhadi, Iran
A compassionate portrait of life in contemporary Tehran, Asghar Farhadi's drama focuses on Simin and Nader, a couple with an eleven-year-old daughter, whose conflicting priorities see them separate. Matters worsen when Nader is involved in an altercation with the woman employed to look after his ailing father. Promoting Farhadi to the front rank of world directors, *A Separation* was the first Iranian film to win an Academy Award. The film-maker would win another one for *The Salesman (Forushande, 2016)*.

Vladimir Putin is elected President of Russia.

Barack Obama is re-elected for his second term as President of the United States.

Pixar's *Brave* becomes the studio's first major animation release to feature a female lead protagonist.

2012

Holy Motors, Leos Carax, France
The former *Cinéma du look* director's first film since the divisive *Pola X* (1999), Leos Carax's fifth feature is a wildly imaginative tableaux of stories revolving around the various characters played by Denis Lavant and seemingly engaged with the digitization of our everyday lives. Like a surrealist film, scenes do not follow on from each other in any recognizable narrative progression so much as portray a chaotic world whose facades hide the strangest activities. The result is mesmerizing and more than a little mad.

ABOVE. *Uncle Boonmee Who Can Recall His Past Lives*, (*Loong Boonmee raleuk chat*, 2010), Apichatpong Weerasethakul, Thailand
Part of a larger artwork exploring memory, transformation and death within Thai culture, *Uncle Boonmee's* seductive imagery blurs the line between reality and a spirit world.

SLOW CINEMA

Neither a genre, movement or wave, and unencumbered by national boundaries or running time, slow cinema is an increasingly popular style of film-making. Its minimalism contrasts with commercial cinema and echoes the work of directors of the silent era.

OPPOSITE. *Winter Sleep* (*Kis Uykusu*, 2014), Nuri Bilge Ceylan, Turkey
Nuri Bilge Ceylan's film adapts a short story by Anton Chekhov and elements of Fyodor Dostoyevsky's novel *The Brothers Karamazov* (1880). The drama unfolds in an austere landscape and witnesses its protagonist's life unravel.

If the commercial blockbuster is a cinema of perpetual motion, a rolling stone of fast cuts and torrent of action sequences, its antithesis is the loose assemblage of quietly meditative films that come under the banner of 'slow cinema'. It generally denotes films with little outward action that employ long takes, either with a static or slowly moving camera. Or, as British critic Jonathan Romney observed, it is a style that 'downplays event in favour of mood, evocativeness and an intensified sense of temporality'. In his time as a critic before becoming a film-maker, Paul Schrader employed the phrase 'transcendental style'. He used it to describe the work of Carl Theodor Dreyer, Yasujirō Ozu and Robert Bresson, three precursors to the growing number of contemporary film-makers who adopt this style.

Although there are no specific rules that define slow cinema, the observational style of Italian Neorealism and Parallel Cinema are key influences, as these films opt to record the minutiae of everyday life. Emphasis lies more with the passing of time than with activity. It is evident in the inexorable movement of

Japanese film-maker's Kenji Mizoguchi's camera in films such as *The Life of Oharu* (*Saikaku ichidai onna*, 1952), allowing the viewer to witness the anguish of his female characters and their years of suffering. Time is of the essence in Italian film-maker Michelangelo Antonioni's breakthrough films *L'avventura* (1960), *The Night* (*La notte*, 1961) and *L'cclisse* (1962), as it is in French film-maker Chantal Ackerman's *Jeanne Dielman, 23, quai du Commerce, 1080 Bruxelles* (1975). It is through the attention paid to the banality of Jeanne's everyday routine that the viewer understands the reasons for her actions in the film's final stages.

Ackerman's film is also free of the conventions of a normal running time. At 200 minutes, it is a long film. Others such as Hungarian film-maker Béla Tarr and Filipino writer-director Lav Diaz – whose body of work averages six hours but whose films can stretch to ten – have produced longer films, not so much to test an audience's endurance but to emphasize the passing of time. Greek film-maker Theo Angelopoulos's most acclaimed film *The Travelling Players*

(*O thiasos*, 1975), runs just shy of four hours, which allows the viewer to engage with time in relation to history and the impact of events upon its characters.

However, slow cinema need not solely be defined by a film's length. In Russian film-maker Aleksandr Sokurov's *Mother and Son* (*Mat i syn*, 1997) the relationship between the film's eponymous characters unfolds within a visually sublime world over the course of 70 minutes, while Italian film-maker Michelangelo Frammartino's portrait of rural life and rumination on transmigration, *Le quattro volte* (2010), is only marginally longer.

Recent film-makers to embrace slow cinema include Turkey's Nuri Bilge Ceylan whose painterly style draws upon the beauty of the Anatolian landscape and grittier urban locations as a backdrop to forensic examinations of his character's lives, Thailand's Apichatpong Weerasethakul who draws on myth, sexuality and the tropical climate of his country to create a heady mix of the spiritual and carnal, along with Portugal's Pedro Costa, whose work gives voice to the dispossessed.

2013–2014

Rebellion and repression. In early 2014, Ukraine's Euromaidan movement, keen to build greater ties with the European Union and reduce the influence of Russia, erupts. Elected president Viktor Yanukovych is ousted in the Ukrainian Revolution of Dignity. The revolt sends fissures through the country and the Crimea, with aid from the Russian Federation, splits away. Reports arrive from north-east Nigeria of an assault on a school and the kidnapping of 276 female students, raising the international profile of Islamist terrorist group Boko Haram. If film-makers in Ukraine mainly capture events through a series of controversial documentaries such as *Maidan* (2014), *Winter on Fire* and *The Russian Woodpecker* (both 2015), the rise of Islamic fundamentalism in Africa is presented in dramas such as Abderrahmane Sissako's *Timbuktu* (2014). Like Steve McQueen's important Academy Award winner *12 Years a Slave* (2013), Sissako's film is a startling portrait of mindless cruelty.

Jorge Mario Bergoglio of Argentina is elected as the 266th pope. He is the first Jesuit, and the first cardinal from both the Americas and the southern hemisphere to be pontiff. He takes the name 'Francis'.

Former CIA employee Edward Snowden discloses classified information regarding mass surveillance being carried out by the National Security Agency and its allies.

Documentary short *Inocente* is the first crowdfunded film to win an Oscar and is followed by a slew of features whose budget is partly raised through crowdfunding.

The Wolf of Wall Street, Martin Scorsese, USA

With its conveyor-belt delivery of sex and profanity, Martin Scorsese's journey through the life and larceny of Jordan Belfort, an ex-Wall Street trader who made a fortune channelling other people's money through penny stocks, offers up a compelling, at times discomforting, but often hilarious portrait of avarice. Unlike Oliver Stone's *Wall Street* (1987), which adopts a lofty moralistic tone, Scorsese accepts Belfort's actions are wrong without signposting. Instead, his film shows why someone might choose to revel in such behaviour.

2013

Leviathan (Leviafan), Andrey Zvyagintsev, Russia

The protagonist of Andrey Zvyagintsev's stately and beautifully composed satire is a temperamental car mechanic whose life in a small coastal town is turned upside down when his land is expropriated by the mayor in order to build a new, larger church. Refusing to acquiesce, his attempts to seek redress for his complaints place him at the mercy of the Church and state. Inspired by the Book of Job, *Leviathan* is a bleak portrait of Vladimir Putin's Russia.

Sony Pictures is hacked by a group thought to be affiliated to North Korea in response to the studio's release of the satirical comedy *The Interview*.

The Grand Budapest Hotel, Wes Anderson, USA/Germany

Presented as a story told within three flashbacks, Wes Anderson's exquisite, perfectly crafted and designed comedy is an homage to the writings of Stefan Zweig. The bulk of the narrative details the friendship between the eponymous hotel's concierge Gustave H. and the lobby boy Zero Moustafa who will one day be the property's owner. The narrative is deliciously labyrinthine and the populous cast colourful, none more so than Ralph Fiennes's irrepressible Gustave, whose performance echoes the flamboyant antics of the great silent comedians.

2014

2015-2016

Mobile technology. Camera mobility was an essential element for capturing footage during the Second World War (1939–45), and the technology that was developed influenced subsequent feature film-making. Digital technology dramatically increases the mobility of high-quality cameras, eventually working its way into smartphones. Everyone is a film-maker, which proves vital in the increase of citizen journalism around the world. It also impacts commercial film-making. Ilya Naishuller's *Hardcore Henry* (2015) is entirely shot using a GoPro camera. In the same year, Sean Baker's trans drama *Tangerine* is filmed using three iPhone 5S smartphones. Steven Soderbergh, whose career shifts between high-end Hollywood productions and more low-key projects that experiment with form and technology, enters the fray with his thriller *Unsane* (2018), shot with an iPhone 7 Plus, and follows it with the basketball drama *High Flying Bird* (2019), shot on an iPhone 8 equipped with an anamorphic lens.

***Son of Saul (Saul fia)*, László Nemes, Hungary**

With a narrative that echoes some of the testimonies that appeared in Claude Lanzmann's *Shoah* (1985), László Nemes's intense drama unfolds in Auschwitz-Birkenau towards the end of the Second World War (1939–45). Saul is a *Sonderkommando*, a Jew with orders to corral arrivals into the gas chambers and then dispose of their bodies. Shot almost entirely in extreme close-up, the horrors of what Saul witnesses can only be heard and imagined, the sounds and images just out of focus conjuring up a hellish vision.

In Paris, two gunmen force their way into the offices of the French satirical weekly newspaper *Charlie Hebdo*, killing twelve people.

2015

Toni Erdmann, Maren Ade, Germany/Austria/Monaco/Romania/France/Switzerland

A rarity at the Cannes Film Festival – a comedy in the main competition that many critics were hoping would scoop the top award – Maren Ade's film ambitiously encompasses droll social satire, a portrait of dysfunctional family life whose denouement is genuinely and deservedly moving, and a critique of the contemporary workplace. Through its portrait of a young executive's distress at her prankster father's sudden arrival from Germany at her home in Romania, Ade's film questions the universal and personal impact of big business in people's lives.

The leak of the Panama Papers, a collection of 11.5 million documents revealing the tax-avoidance practices of individuals and businesses around the world, results in various investigations and resignations by politicians.

The UK votes to leave the European Union in a referendum.

Donald J. Trump is elected as the 45th President of the United States.

Moonlight, Barry Jenkins, USA

Based on Tarell Alvin McCraney's unpublished semi-autobiographical play *In Moonlight Black Boys Look Blue* and with a screenplay written by director Barry Jenkins, *Moonlight* chronicles the life of a young African American through three stages in his life: a prepubescent Little, the teen Chiron and twenty-something Black, all of whom have to deal with a crack-addicted mother. With its expressive use of colour and music, Jenkins's film undermines lazy stereotypes to present a portrait of a young man as a knot of neuroses and doubts.

2016

2017–2018

Time's up. Jodi Kantor and Megan Twohey of *The New York Times*, and Ronan Farrow for *The New Yorker*, publish accounts of Oscar-winning Hollywood film producer Harvey Weinstein's behaviour towards women, including accusations of sexual assault and harassment, which would lead to his conviction and imprisonment in 2020. The phrase 'Me Too' was coined by sexual-harassment survivor and activist Tarana Burke in 2006 as a way to draw women who had similar experiences together. In 2017, the hashtag #MeToo was used by actor Alyssa Milano in a similar way, suggesting 'If all the women who have been sexually harassed or assaulted wrote "Me too" as a status, we might give people a sense of the magnitude of the problem.' The revelations about Weinstein prompt other women to come forward, both in the entertainment and media industry, and across other professions. In 2018, the Time's Up movement is formed to battle sexual harassment.

Get Out, Jordan Peele, USA

Jordan Peele rejuvenates the US horror film and undermines the conventions of the liberal-conservative divide with his politically astute, whip-smart satire. An African American photographer is invited by his white girlfriend to her family's home for the weekend. Although the presence of African American house staff unsettles him, he realizes too late the motives behind his hosts' cordiality. Peele's film, which received an Academy Award for Best Original Screenplay, is a masterclass in the use of genre tropes to explore the experience of being black in the United States.

Walt Disney Company acquires a majority stake in 21st Century Fox, including the 20th Century Fox film studio. Following its acquisition of Pixar, Marvel Entertainment and Lucasfilm, this makes it one of the most powerful studios in the world.

2017

Cold War (*Zimna wojna*), Paweł Pawlikowski, Poland/France/UK

Like his Academy Award-winning film *Ida* (2013), Paweł Pawlikowski's 1950s-set drama is shot in crisp monochrome and, although brief, carries with it the weight of recent history. Wiktor is one of two musicologists travelling around Poland in search of singers for a state-sponsored folk-music ensemble. He encounters Zula and the affair they embark on stretches across countries and decades. Loosely based on his parents' relationship, Pawlikowski's film captures the intensity of love and longing, while perfectly integrating his characters into the turbulent events of post-war Eastern Europe.

Roma, Alfonso Cuarón, Mexico

After the technical virtuosity of his *Gravity* (2013), Alfonso Cuarón returns to his native Mexico and the events of his youth, capturing the energy and air of revolution that pervaded the country's capital city during the early 1970s. Set in the Colonia Roma neighbourhood, where Cuarón grew up, the film is told from the perspective of the indigenous live-in housemaid Cleo. Featuring his signature long takes, Cuarón's film – which he also shot – is a compelling account of lives intertwined through personal and political forces.

A Fantastic Woman (*Una Mujer Fantástica*, 2017) by Chilean director Sebastián Lelio is the first film featuring a transgender performer in the lead role to win an Academy Award.

Cinemas open in Saudi Arabia for the first time since 1983 with *Black Panther* chosen as the first to be screened.

Crazy Rich Asians is the first US studio film since Wayne Wang's *The Joy Luck Club* (1993) to star Asian American actors in leading roles.

2018

2019-PRESENT

A locked-down world. In late 2019, a virus believed to emanate from a wet market in the Chinese province of Wuhan, Hubei Province starts to spread. By December, its main mode of transmission is between humans. Over the course of the next three months, the virus spreads across the world, prompting governments to lock down trade, travel and the movement of citizens. This results in a stock-market crash. In early March 2020, the World Health Organization declares COVID-19 a pandemic. Like any other industry, the film business comes to a standstill. For the first time since 1968, the Cannes Film Festival is cancelled. However, some festivals move online. This development, combined with the launch of Disney's own streaming channel, the successful streaming-only release of Universal Pictures' *Trolls World Tour* (2020) and other films that were originally planned to open theatrically but turn instead to online releasing, encourages a rethink of the way people watch new releases.

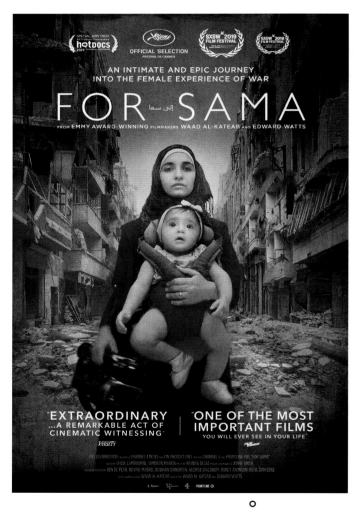

For Sama, Waad Al-Kateab and Edward Watts, UK/Syria/USA

In 2012, Waad Al-Kateab was a marketing student at the University of Aleppo when the Syrian uprising began with a series of student demonstrations. She began filming the events, continuing over the next five years as the situation in the country and her adopted city became more desperate. At the same time she married and gave birth to a daughter, to whom the film is addressed. Although harrowing, *For Sama* is a film of depthless compassion and in an age when everyone carries around a portable camera with them, underpins the importance of citizen journalists.

Disney's remake of *The Lion King* (1994) is trumpeted by the studio as the first fully computer-generated live-action feature.

2019

Uncut Gems, Ben and Joshua Safdie, USA

Like Martin Scorsese's similarly nervy *After Hours* (1985), the Safdie brothers' anxiety-inducing journey into the heart of New York's diamond business is a frenetically paced character study of a man who exists on the precipice of chaos. Adam Sandler throws himself into the role of Howard Ratner, a gem specialist whose addiction to everything in life finds him in hock to colleagues and shady members of the mob. By turns sleazy and exuberant, *Uncut Gems* is a quintessential New York film.

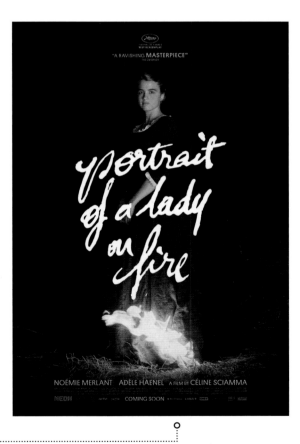

Portrait of a Lady on Fire (*Portrait de la jeune fille en feu*), Céline Sciamma, France

The three previous features from writer and director Céline Sciamma were contemporary portraits of childhood and adolescence. Her first period drama continues her exploration of gender and identity, through the prism of the growing intimacy between an artist and her subject. Tensions between the artist and the woman, who at first has no idea her new companion is to paint her, soon give way to passion. Sciamma's subtlety in direction is reflected in the performances, which make the denouement all the more powerful.

The Best Picture Oscar goes to a non-English language film for the first time. The Cannes Palme d'Or winner Bong Joon-ho's *Parasite* (*Gisaengchung*, 2019) is the first film to win both accolades since the US drama *Marty* (1955).

The United States and the Taliban sign a conditional peace agreement, and the United States begins withdrawing troops from Afghanistan.

The International Criminal Court authorizes an Afghanistan war crimes inquiry and allows US troops to be investigated.

2020

THE FUTURE

Cinema turned 125 years old in 2020. Compared to other art forms, it is still a youth. Yet, with the development of technology in the digital age, some doubt its future. However, it is not the first instance of time being called on the seventh art and its magic continues to surprise.

Digital technology has transformed cinema. As a tool in post-production, it has enabled film-makers to create past and future worlds, or to embellish upon the present. Visual effects can transform every element within the frame, creating fantastical backdrops or adding to real ones. Whereas film-makers from Giovanni Pastrone and D. W. Griffith to William Wyler and David Lean oversaw the construction of life-sized sets for their epics, for *Gladiator* (2000) Ridley Scott was able to create huge edifices and populate them with thousands of spectators through digital means. The integration of footage shot on location and images created in post-production is seamless, as seen in Christopher Nolan's *Inception* (2010), where the streets of Paris are transformed into an Escher-like conundrum. But visual effects are not employed solely to transport audiences to worlds they could only previously dream of. They can also make the most subtle adjustments. If a period drama is shooting on location, a director has a choice of removing all contemporary objects while filming or leaving them in the shot in order to have them airbrushed out in post-production.

Technological advances have impacted performance. The transformations of Andy Serkis into Gollum for *The Lord of the Rings* (2001–03) and Caesar for *The Planet of the Apes* (2011–17) trilogies are a marvel of performance capture. As is the de-ageing of Robert De Niro, Al Pacino and Joe Pesci for *The Irishman* (2019). What these films share is the use of state-of-the-art effects in the service of the script; the tools are not used to dazzle audiences so much as accentuate the emotional journeys of these characters. With Martin Scorsese's decades-spanning gangster saga, visual effects allowed him to emphasize the toll the characters' criminal activities have had over the course of their lives, in a way that casting actors of different ages for the same role could never achieve.

OPPOSITE. *The Irishman* (2019), Martin Scorsese, USA
Combining 35 mm and digital shooting, along with a state-of-the-art de-ageing process, Martin Scorsese presented a bleak portrait of lives in crime.

RIGHT. *Tangerine* (2015), Sean Baker, USA
With its vibrant use of colour, offering a different portrait of life on the streets of Los Angeles, *Tangerine* displayed the potential of smartphone film-making.

Digital technology has democratized the making of films. Once prohibitively expensive, the means to shoot a film are available to anyone. Whereas video in the 1980s and 1990s often lacked the sensitivity of celluloid when it came to light variances, modern cameras are adept at coping with changing environmental conditions and are mobile enough to reduce the need for a large crew. There has been an increase in the number of films made with smartphone cameras. Sean Baker's *Tangerine* (2015) was not only the most high-profile early example of a feature shot with a smartphone, its portrait of a trans sex worker hunting down her pimp boyfriend on the streets of Los Angeles was evidence that the freedom allowed by digital technology also extends to the narratives being filmed.

Documentary has benefited the most from these advances. *Burma VJ* (2008) showed how hand-held video cameras and the internet enabled video journalists to smuggle footage of human rights abuses in Burma out of the country to director Anders Østergaard in Denmark. Meanwhile, *Five Broken Cameras* (2011) detailed how co-director and camera operator Emad Burnat used advances in technology to capture the precariousness of life in the West Bank village of Bil'in. Since then, uprisings in Arab countries have underpinned the importance of citizen journalists and how smartphone technology can capture footage that a film crew might not. The speed at which such footage is disseminated is greater than ever before. Within minutes of George Floyd's death at the hands of Minneapolis police officers in May 2020, footage of the incident travelled around the world via social-media sites. The subsequent footage from demonstrations around the world coalesced people from diverse backgrounds into a larger movement for change.

The way people watch films is one of the biggest transformations to have taken place since 2010. Until then people were limited to watching films in a specific place – in a cinema or wherever a TV and video/DVD player was located. It then became possible for people to watch a film via a laptop while travelling, or via a smartphone or tablet at any point in their daily life. Some films are available day-and-date, ready for streaming or downloading the moment they open in cinemas. People do not have to go to the cinema to get the full 3D experience, as home-entertainment systems offer state-of-the art visuals that bring the cinema experience into the home. However, the thrill of cinema does not just lie in the spectacle of the big screen but in the shared experience of it. To watch a horror film or a comedy in a packed auditorium is a different experience to watching it at home. The shared experience, of laughing, being thrilled, scared, moved or shocked by a film is what makes it essential.

Cinema, or the art of film-making, is no less adventurous than it once was. There is Chinese film-maker Bi Gan's *Long Day's Journey into Night* (*Diqiu zuihou de yewan*, 2018), an exploration of memory whose second half comprises a breathtaking 59-minute single take projected in 3D. *Varda by Agnès* (*Varda par Agnès*, 2019) is the final film by the great French film-maker and is a unique take on personal history and celebration of a medium that is at its best when erasing the limitations placed upon it. British film-maker Mark Jenkin's mesmerizing *Bait* (2019) draws on experimental and early cinema to conjure up a singular portrait of a fractured, post-Brexit United Kingdom. French film-maker Mati Diop's *Atlantics* (*Atlantique*, 2019) examines the dangers of economic migrancy while combined with a

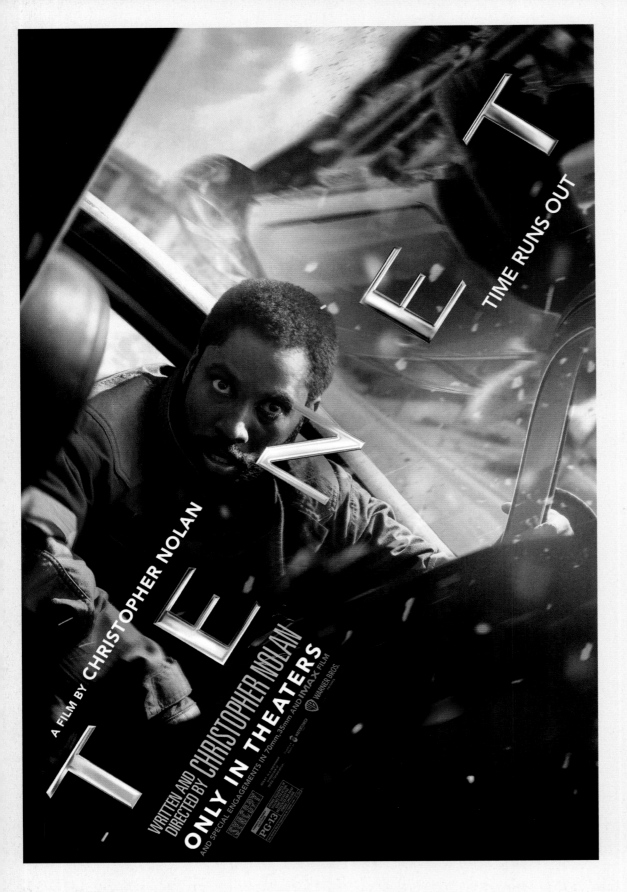

LEFT. *Tenet* (2020),
Christopher Nolan, USA
Director Christopher Nolan's
action spectacular follows the
style of his films *Memento*
(2000), *Inception* (2010) and
Interstellar (2014) in playing
with space and time.

ghost story to present a haunting portrait of youth in contemporary Senegal. These films could be watched on a phone, tablet, laptop or flat-screen TV. However, their impact will likely be lessened compared with the experience of seeing them in a cinema, where every detail is writ large and the responses of other audience members can be heard and felt.

Whether films can prompt change in the world has been a point of discussion for decades. Certainly, film as propaganda has proven effective in the past. However, on occasions it has proven unerringly prescient. In 2011, Steven Soderbergh's thriller *Contagion* opened in cinemas. It detailed a deadly virus that emanated from a live food market in China before spreading, through human contact, around the world. In late 2019, a similar, all-too-real virus began to spread its way around the world, threatening the lives of millions and bringing daily life to a standstill.

For the first time in the medium's history, cinemas around the world closed, film production stopped and festivals such as South by Southwest, Tribeca and Cannes had no choice but to cancel their events, with some moving their festivals online. As the first wave of the virus receded in summer 2020, cinemas began to reopen. Christopher Nolan's *Tenet* became the first major release to premiere. But audiences were still required to distance themselves.

However, misfortune can be the mother of invention. Some directors joined their cast and crew in a self-enforced lockdown in order to shoot a film. Other projects involved actors using their family and friends as their crew, advised remotely by a director, in order to film. Even drive-in events became fashionable once again. A writer may look back on the period impacted by COVID-19 as the moment cinema embarked on a new path, or inspired a generation to think about the way films are made and consumed. Cinema is part of the fabric of people's lives. The role it will play in the future is unclear, but the journey is likely to be just as exciting as it has been since the first moment that an audience saw moving images flicker across a screen.

BELOW. *Atlantics* (*Atlantique*, **2019), Mati Diop, France/ Senegal/Belgium**
Mati Diop became the first black female director to take part in the main competition at the Cannes Film Festival with *Atlantics*, which won the Grand Prix.

Best Picture

Academy Awards

The Academy's award for best film of the year has been renamed over the years. At the first ceremony, which took place in 1929 at the Roosevelt Hotel in Hollywood, it was referred to as Outstanding Picture. It was changed to Outstanding Production at the third ceremony in 1930. For the 14th edition of the awards in 1942, rewarding the films of 1941, it was renamed Outstanding Motion Picture, only to change again three years later to Best Motion Picture. Finally, it became known as the Best Picture award from the 35th edition in 1963.

The years listed below cover the period of eligibility for the films. The awards ceremony itself took place early the following year. For example, *Parasite* (*Gisaengchung*) was released in 2019 but received the Best Picture award on 9 February 2020.

Year	Title	Director	Country
1927/28	*Wings*	William A. Wellman	USA
1928/29	*The Broadway Melody*	Harry Beaumont	USA
1929/30	*All Quiet on the Western Front*	Lewis Milestone	USA
1930/31	*Cimarron*	Wesley Ruggles	USA
1931/32	*Grand Hotel*	Edmund Goulding	USA
1932/33	*Cavalcade*	Frank Lloyd	USA
1934	*It Happened One Night*	Frank Capra	USA
1935	*Mutiny on the Bounty*	Frank Lloyd	USA
1936	*The Great Ziegfeld*	Robert Z. Leonard	USA
1937	*The Life of Emile Zola*	William Dieterle	USA
1938	*You Can't Take It With You*	Frank Capra	USA
1939	*Gone with the Wind*	Victor Fleming	USA
1940	*Rebecca*	Alfred Hitchcock	USA
1941	*How Green Was My Valley*	John Ford	USA
1942	*Mrs Miniver*	William Wyler	USA
1943	*Casablanca*	Michael Curtiz	USA
1944	*Going My Way*	Leo McCarey	USA
1945	*The Lost Weekend*	Billy Wilder	USA
1946	*The Best Years of Our Lives*	William Wyler	USA
1947	*Gentleman's Agreement*	Elia Kazan	USA

1948	*Hamlet*	Laurence Olivier	UK
1949	*All the King's Men*	Robert Rossen	USA
1950	*All About Eve*	Joseph L. Mankiewicz	USA
1951	*An American in Paris*	Vincente Minnelli	USA
1952	*The Greatest Show on Earth*	Cecil B. DeMille	USA
1953	*From Here to Eternity*	Fred Zinnemann	USA
1954	*On the Waterfront*	Elia Kazan	USA
1955	*Marty*	Delbert Mann	USA
1956	*Around the World in 80 Days*	Michael Anderson	USA
1957	*The Bridge on the River Kwai*	David Lean	UK/USA
1958	*Gigi*	Vincente Minnelli	USA
1959	*Ben-Hur*	William Wyler	USA
1960	*The Apartment*	Billy Wilder	USA
1961	*West Side Story*	Robert Wise and Jerome Robbins	USA
1962	*Lawrence of Arabia*	David Lean	UK
1963	*Tom Jones*	Tony Richardson	UK
1964	*My Fair Lady*	George Cukor	USA
1965	*The Sound of Music*	Robert Wise	USA
1966	*A Man for All Seasons*	Fred Zinnemann	UK
1967	*In the Heat of the Night*	Norman Jewison	USA
1968	*Oliver!*	Carol Reed	UK
1969	*Midnight Cowboy*	John Schlesinger	USA
1970	*Patton*	Franklin J. Schaffner	USA
1971	*The French Connection*	William Friedkin	USA
1972	*The Godfather*	Francis Ford Coppola	USA
1973	*The Sting*	George Roy Hill	USA
1974	*The Godfather Part II*	Francis Ford Coppola	USA
1975	*One Flew Over the Cuckoo's Nest*	Miloš Forman	USA
1976	*Rocky*	John G. Avildsen	USA
1977	*Annie Hall*	Woody Allen	USA
1978	*The Deer Hunter*	Michael Cimino	USA
1979	*Kramer vs. Kramer*	Robert Benton	USA
1980	*Ordinary People*	Robert Redford	USA
1981	*Chariots of Fire*	Hugh Hudson	UK
1982	*Gandhi*	Richard Attenborough	UK/India

1983	*Terms of Endearment*	James L. Brooks	USA
1984	*Amadeus*	Miloš Forman	USA/France/Czechoslovakia/Italy
1985	*Out of Africa*	Sydney Pollack	USA/UK
1986	*Platoon*	Oliver Stone	USA/UK
1987	*The Last Emperor*	Bernardo Bertolucci	UK/Italy/France
1988	*Rain Man*	Barry Levinson	USA
1989	*Driving Miss Daisy*	Bruce Beresford	USA
1990	*Dances with Wolves*	Kevin Costner	USA
1991	*The Silence of the Lambs*	Jonathan Demme	USA
1992	*Unforgiven*	Clint Eastwood	USA
1993	*Schindler's List*	Steven Spielberg	USA
1994	*Forrest Gump*	Robert Zemeckis	USA
1995	*Braveheart*	Mel Gibson	USA
1996	*The English Patient*	Anthony Minghella	USA/UK
1997	*Titanic*	James Cameron	USA
1998	*Shakespeare in Love*	John Madden	USA/UK
1999	*American Beauty*	Sam Mendes	USA
2000	*Gladiator*	Ridley Scott	USA /UK/Malta/Morocco
2001	*A Beautiful Mind*	Ron Howard	USA
2002	*Chicago*	Rob Marshall	USA/Germany/Canada
2003	*The Lord of the Rings: The Return of the King*	Peter Jackson	New Zealand
2004	*Million Dollar Baby*	Clint Eastwood	USA
2005	*Crash*	Paul Haggis	USA/Germany
2006	*The Departed*	Martin Scorsese	USA
2007	*No Country for Old Men*	Joel and Ethan Coen	USA/Mexico
2008	*Slumdog Millionaire*	Danny Boyle	UK/France/USA
2009	*The Hurt Locker*	Kathryn Bigelow	USA
2010	*The King's Speech*	Tom Hooper	UK/USA/Australia
2011	*The Artist*	Michel Hazanavicius	France/Belgium/USA
2012	*Argo*	Ben Affleck	USA/UK
2013	*12 Years a Slave*	Steve McQueen	UK/USA
2014	*Birdman or (The Unexpected Virtue of Ignorance)*	Alejandro G. Iñárritu	USA
2015	*Spotlight*	Tom McCarthy	USA
2016	*Moonlight*	Barry Jenkins	USA
2017	*The Shape of Water*	Guillermo del Toro	USA/Canada
2018	*Green Book*	Peter Farrelly	USA/China
2019	*Parasite (Gisaengchung)*	Bong Joon-ho	South Korea

Palme d'Or

Cannes Film Festival

Cannes has seen its main prize change name over the years. A festival took place in 1939, in response to Italy's fascist government's meddling with the Venice Film Festival in 1938. The Second World War (1939–45) halted subsequent editions. It returned in 1946, since referred to as the first edition. That year a prize was shared among eleven entries from around the world. In 1947, it was shared among five entries. Afterwards, it conformed to a standard of deciding one or two top films. There were no editions in 1948 and 1950 because of financial problems. The 1968 edition was closed by film-makers in support of the student and worker demonstrations in across France. The 2020 edition was suspended – and partially moved online, albeit without a competition section – as a result of the COVID-19 pandemic.

The main prize was initially known as the Grand Prix du Festival International du Film. In 1955, it became the Palme d'Or. It was renamed the Grand Prix in 1964 and then changed back to the Palme d'Or in 1975.

Year	Title	Director	Country
1939	*Union Pacific*	Cecil B. DeMille	USA
1949	*The Third Man*	Carol Reed	UK
1951	*Miss Julie (Fröken Julie)*	Alf Sjöberg	Sweden
	Miracle in Milan (Miracolo a Milano)	Vittorio De Sica	Italy
1952	*The Tragedy of Othello: The Moor of Venice*	Orson Welles	USA
	Two Cents Worth of Hope (Due soldi di speranza)	Renato Castellani	Italy
1953	*The Wages of Fear (Le salaire de la peur)*	Henri-Georges Clouzot	France/Italy
1954	*Gate of Hell (Jigoku-mon)*	Teinosuke Kinugasa	Japan
1955	*Marty*	Delbert Mann	USA
1956	*The Silent World (Le monde du silence)*	Jacques Cousteau and Louis Malle	France/Italy
1957	*Friendly Persuasion*	William Wyler	USA
1958	*The Cranes Are Flying (Letyat zhuravli)*	Mikhail Kalatozov	Soviet Union
1959	*Black Orpheus (Orfeu Negro)*	Marcel Camus	France/Brazil
1960	*La dolce vita*	Federico Fellini	Italy/France
1961	*The Long Absence (Une aussi longue absence)*	Henri Colpi	France
	Viridiana	Luis Buñuel	Mexico/Spain

1962	*Keeper of Promises (O Pagador de Promessas)*	Anselmo Duarte	Brazil
1963	*The Leopard (Il gattopardo)*	Luchino Visconti	Italy
1964	*The Umbrellas of Cherbourg (Les parapluies de Cherbourg)*	Jacques Demy	France
1965	*The Knack...And How to Get It*	Richard Lester	UK
1966	*A Man and a Woman (Un homme et une femme)*	Claude Lelouch	France
	The Birds, the Bees and the Italians (Signore e signori)	Pietro Germi	Italy
1967	*Blow-Up*	Michelangelo Antonioni	UK/Italy
1969	*If....*	Lindsay Anderson	UK
1970	M*A*S*H	Robert Altman	USA
1971	*The Go-Between*	Joseph Losey	UK
1972	*The Working Class Goes to Heaven (La classe operaia va in paradiso)*	Elio Petri	Italy
	The Mattei Affair (Il caso Mattei)	Francesco Rosi	Italy
1973	*The Hireling*	Alan Bridges	UK
	Scarecrow	Jerry Schatzberg	USA
1974	*The Conversation*	Francis Ford Coppola	USA
1975	*Chronicle of the Years of Fire (Chronique des années de braise)*	Mohammed Lakhdar-Hamina	Algeria
1976	*Taxi Driver*	Martin Scorsese	USA
1977	*Padre Padrone*	Paolo and Vittorio Taviani	Italy
1978	*The Tree of Wooden Clogs (L'albero degli zoccoli)*	Ermanno Olmi	Italy
1979	*Apocalypse Now*	Francis Ford Coppola	USA
	The Tin Drum (Die Blechtrommel)	Volker Schlöndorf	Germany
1980	*All That Jazz*	Bob Fosse	USA
	Kagemusha	Akira Kurosawa	Japan
1981	*Man of Iron (Czlowiek z zelaza)*	Andrzej Wajda	Poland
1982	*Missing*	Costa-Gavras	USA
	Yol	Yılmaz Güney and Serif Gören	Turkey
1983	*The Ballad of Narayama (Narayama bushikō)*	Shohei Imamura	Japan
1984	*Paris, Texas*	Wim Wenders	Germany
1985	*When Father Was Away on Business (Otats na službenom putu)*	Emir Kustirica	Yugoslavia
1986	*The Mission*	Roland Joffé	UK
1987	*Under the Sun of Satan (Sous le soleil de Satan)*	Maurice Pialat	France
1988	*Pelle the Conqueror (Pelle Erobreren)*	Bille August	Denmark/Sweden

1989	*Sex, Lies, and Videotape*	Steven Soderbergh	USA
1990	*Wild at Heart*	David Lynch	USA
1991	*Barton Fink*	Joel and Ethan Coen	USA
1992	*The Best Intentions (Den goda viljan)*	Bille August	Sweden
1993	*Farewell, My Concubine (Ba wang bie ji)*	Chen Kaige	China/Hong Kong
	The Piano	Jane Campion	New Zealand/Australia/France
1994	*Pulp Fiction*	Quentin Tarantino	USA
1995	*Underground (Podzemlje)*	Emir Kustirica	FR Yugoslavia
1996	*Secrets & Lies*	Mike Leigh	UK
1997	*Taste of Cherry (Ta'm e guilass)*	Abbas Kiarostami	Iran
	The Eel (Unagi)	Shohei Imamura	Japan
1998	*Eternity and a Day (Mia aioniotita kai mia mera)*	Theo Angelopoulos	Greece
1999	*Rosetta*	Jean-Pierre and Luc Dardenne	Belgium
2000	*Dancer in the Dark*	Lars von Trier	Denmark
2001	*The Son's Room (La stanza del figlio)*	Nanni Moretti	Italy
2002	*The Pianist*	Roman Polanski	Poland/France/Germany/UK
2003	*Elephant*	Gus Van Sant	USA
2004	*Fahrenheit 9/11*	Michael Moore	USA
2005	*The Child (L'enfant)*	Jean-Pierre and Luc Dardenne	Belgium
2006	*The Wind That Shakes the Barley*	Ken Loach	Ireland/USA
2007	*4 Months, 3 Weeks and 2 Days (4 luni, 3 saptamâni si 2 zile)*	Cristian Mungiu	Romania
2008	*The Class (Entre les murs)*	Laurent Cantet	France
2009	*The White Ribbon (Das weisse Band)*	Michael Haneke	Germany/Austria
2010	*Uncle Boonmee Who Can Recall His Past Lives (Loong Boonmee raleuk chat)*	Apichatpong Weerasethakul	Thailand
2011	*The Tree of Life*	Terrence Malick	USA
2012	*Amour*	Michael Haneke	France/Austria
2013	*Blue Is the Warmest Colour (La vie d'Adèle)*	Abdellatif Kechiche (shared with lead actors Adèle Exarchopoulos and Léa Seydoux)	France/Belgium
2014	*Winter Sleep (Kis Uykusu)*	Nuri Bilge Ceylan	Turkey
2015	*Dheepan*	Jacques Audiard	France
2016	*I, Daniel Blake*	Ken Loach	UK
2017	*The Square*	Ruben Östlund	Sweden
2018	*Shoplifters (Manbiki kazoku)*	Hirokazu Kore-eda	Japan
2019	*Parasite (Gisaengchung)*	Bong Joon-ho	South Korea

Further Reading

Altman, Rick. *The American Film Musical*, Indiana University Press, 1988.

Anderson, Joseph L. and Donald Ritchie. *The Japanese Film: Art and Industry*, Princeton University Press, 1982 edition.

Andrew, J. Dudley. *The Major Film Theories*, Oxford University Press, 1976.

Andrew, Geoff. *Stranger Than Paradise: Maverick Film-makers in Recent American Cinema*, Prion Books, 1998.

Barr, Charles. *All Our Yesterdays: 90 Years of British Cinema*, British Film Institute, 1986.

Barr, Charles. *English Hitchcock*, Cameron & Hollis, 1999.

Bazin, André. *What is Cinema? Volume 1*, University of California Press, 1967.

Bazin, André. *What is Cinema? Volume 2*, University of California Press, 1971.

Bergman, Ingmar. *The Magic Lantern*, Hamish Hamilton, 1987.

Berry, Chris and Mary Ann Farquhar. *China on Screen: Cinema and Nation*, Columbia University Press, 2006.

Biskind, Peter. *Easy Riders, Raging Bulls: How the Sex-Drugs-and-Rock 'N Roll Generation Saved Hollywood*, Simon & Schuster, 1998.

Biskind, Peter. *Down and Dirty Pictures: Miramax, Sundance and the Rise of Independent Film*, Bloomsbury Publishing, 2005.

Bogdanovich, Peter. *Who the Devil Made It? Conversations with Legendary Film Directors*, Alfred A. Knopf, 1997.

Bondanella, Peter. *Italian Cinema: From Neorealism to the Present*, Bloomsbury Publishing, 1983.

Bordwell, David. *Planet Hong Kong: Popular Cinema and the Art of Entertainment*, Harvard University Press, 2000.

Bordwell, David. *Reinventing Hollywood: How 1940s Filmmakers Changed Movie Storytelling*, University of Chicago Press, 2017.

Bordwell, David, Janet Staiger and Kristin Thompson. *The Classical Hollywood Cinema: Film Style and Mode of Production to 1960*, Routledge, 1988.

Bordwell, David, Kristin Thompson and Jeff Smith. *Film Art: An Introduction*, McGraw-Hill Education, 2019. 12th edition.

Bowser, Pearl, Jane Gaines and Charles Musser (eds.). *Oscar Micheaux & His Circle: African-American Filmmaking and Race Cinema of the Silent Era*, Indiana University Press, 2001.

Bresson, Robert. *Notes on the Cinematographer*, Éditions Gallimard, 1975.

Brownlow, Kevin. *The Parade's Gone By*, Secker & Warburg, 1968.

Buñuel, Luis. *My Last Breath*, Jonathan Cape, 1983.

Burch, Noël. *Theory of Film Practice*, Secker & Warburg, 1973.

Cavell, Stanley. *The World Viewed: Reflections on the Ontology of Film*, Harvard University Press, 1980.

Clee, Paul. *Before Hollywood: From Shadow Play to the Silver Screen*, Clarion Books, 2005.

Clover, Carol. *Men, Women, and Chain Saws: Gender in the Modern Horror Film*, Princeton University Press, 1993.

Cohan, Steve and Ina Rae Hark (eds.). *The Road Movie Book*, Routledge, 1997.

Cook, Pam. *The Cinema Book*, British Film Institute, 1985.

Cousins, Mark. *The Story of Film*, Pavilion Books, 2004.

Cousins, Mark and Kevin Macdonald (eds.). *Imagining Reality*, Faber & Faber, 2006.

Cox, Alex. *10,000 Ways to Die*, Oldcastle Books, 2009.

Dabashi, Hamid. *Close Up: Iranian Cinema Past, Present and Future*, Verso, 2001.

Davies, Steven Paul. *Out at the Movies : A History of Gay Cinema*, Kamera Books, 2016.

Diawara, Manthia. *African Cinema: Politics & Culture*, Indiana University Press, 1992.

Diawara, Manthia. *Black American Cinema*, Routledge, 1993.

Doherty, Thomas. *Pre-Code Hollywood: Sex, Immorality, and Insurrection in American Cinema, 1930–1934*, Columbia University Press, 1999.

Doherty, Thomas. *Projections of War: Hollywood, American Culture, and World War II*, Columbia University Press, 1996.

Dunne, John Gregory. *The Studio*, Straus & Giroux, 1969.

Durgnat, Raymond. *Films and Feelings*, MIT Press, 1971.

Dyer, Richard. *Heavenly Bodies: Film Stars and Society*, British Film Institute, 1986.

Dyer, Richard. *Stars*, British Film Institute, 1979.

Eisenstein, Sergei. *Film Form*, Harcourt, Brace, 1949.

Eisenstein, Sergei. *The Film Sense*, Harcourt, Brace, 1947.

Elsaesser, Thomas. *Fassbinder's Germany: History, Identity, Subject*, Amsterdam University Press, 1996.

Elsaesser, Thomas. *New German Cinema: A History*, Rutgers University Press, 1989.

Elsaesser, Thomas. *Weimar Cinema and After: Germany's Historical Imaginary*, Routledge, 2000.

Evans, Robert. *The Kid Stays in the Picture*, Hyperion, 1994.

Ezra, Elizabeth. *Georges Méliès*, Manchester University Press, 2000.

Farber, Manny. *Farber on Film: The Complete Film Writings of Manny Farber*, Library of America, 2009.

Farber, Manny. *Negative Space: Manny Farber on the Movies*, Da Capo Press, 1998. Expanded edition.

Finler, Joel W. *The Hollywood Story*, Octopus Books, 1988.

Fischer, Lucy. *Shot/Countershot: Film Tradition and Women's Cinema*, BFI Cinema, 1989.

Förster, Annette. *Women in the Silent Cinema: Histories of Fame and Fate*, Amsterdam University Press, 2017.

Fraser, Nick. *Say What Happened: A Story of Documentaries*, Faber & Faber, 2019.

Frayling, Christopher. *Sergio Leone: Something to Do with Death*, Faber & Faber, 2000.

Friedrich, Otto. *City of Nets: A Portrait of Hollywood in the 1940s*, University of California Press, 1986.

Fujiki, Hideaki and Alistair Phillips (eds.). *The Japanese Cinema Book*, BFI Publishing, 2020.

Godard, Jean-Luc (ed. Tom Milne). *Godard on Godard*, Secker & Warburg, 1972.

Gokulsing, K. Moti and Wimal Dissanayake. *From Aan to Lagaan and Beyond: A Guide to the Study of Indian Cinema*, Trentham Books, 2012.

Goldman, William. *Adventures in the Screen Trade: A Personal View of Hollywood and Screenwriting*, Warner Books, 1983.

Grant, Peter S. and Chris Wood. *Blockbusters and Trade Wars: Popular Culture in a Globalized World*, Douglas & McIntyre, 2004.

Guerrero, Ed. *Framing Blackness: The African American Image in Film*, Temple University Press, 1993.

Gunning, Tom. *D. W. Griffith and the Origins of American Narrative Film: The Early Years at Biograph*, University of Illinois Press, 1993.

Gunning, Tom, Giovanna Fossati, Joshua Yumibe and Jonathon Rosen. *Fantasia of Color in Early Cinema*, Amsterdam University Press, 2015.

Harris, Mark. *Pictures at a Revolution: Five Movies and the Birth of the New Hollywood*, Canongate Books, 2008.

Haskell, Molly. *From Reverence to Rape: The Treatment of Women in the Movies*, New English Library, 1975.

Hecht, Herman (ed. Ann Hecht). *Pre-cinema History: Encyclopaedia and Annotated Bibliography of the Moving Image Before 1896*, Bowker-Saur, 1993.

Hillier, Jim (ed.). *Cahiers du Cinéma. Volume 1: The 1950s: Neo-realism, Hollywood, New Wave*, Routledge, 1996.

Isenberg, Noah. *Weimar Cinema: An Essential Guide to Classic Films of the Era*, Columbia University Press, 2008.

Issa, Rose and Sheila Whittaker (eds.). *Life and Art: The New Iranian Cinema*, National Film Theatre/British Film Institute, 1999.

Jackson, Kevin (ed.). *Schrader on Schrader & Other Writings*, Faber & Faber, 1990.

Kael, Pauline. *Going Steady*, Little, Brown and Company, 1970.

Kael, Pauline. *Kiss Kiss Bang Bang*, Calder & Boyars, 1970.

Kael, Pauline. *Reeling*, Little, Brown and Company, 1977.

Kael, Pauline. *When the Lights Go Down*, Little, Brown and Company, 1980.

Kantor, Jodi and Megan Twohey. *She Said: Breaking the Sexual Harassment Story that Helped Ignite a Movement*, Bloomsbury Circus, 2019.

Kazan, Elia. *Elia Kazan: A Life,* Pan Books, 1989.

Kelly, Richard T. *The Name of this Book is Dogme95*, Faber & Faber, 2000.

Kitses, Jim. *Horizons West: Studies in Authorship in the Western*, Thames & Hudson, 1969.

Kolker, Robert. *A Cinema of Loneliness*, Oxford University Press, 1980.

Kracauer, Siegfried. *From Caligari to Hitler: A Psychological History of the German Film*, Princeton University Press, 1947.

Kuhn, Annette. *Women's Pictures: Feminism and Cinema*, Verso, 1982.

Lee, Sangjoon. *Rediscovering Korean Cinema*, University of Michigan Press, 2019.

Leyda, Jay. *Kino: A History of the Russian and Soviet Cinema*, Allen & Unwin, 1960.

Lim, Song Hwee and Julian Ward. *The Chinese Cinema Book*, Palgrave Macmillan, 2011.

Mackendrick, Alexander. *On Film-making : An Introduction to the Craft of the Director*, Faber & Faber, 2004.

Maltby, Richard. *Hollywood Cinema: An Introduction*, Blackwell Publishers, 1995.

Massood, Paula J. *Black City Cinema: African American Urban Experiences In Film*, Temple University Press, 2003.

McFarlane, Brian. *An Autobiography of British Cinema*, Methuen Publishing, 1997.

Mulvey, Laura. *Visual and Other Pleasures*, Palgrave, 1989.

Murphy, David and Patrick Williams. *Postcolonial African Cinema: Ten Directors*, Manchester University Press, 2007.

Murray, Scott. *The New Australian Cinema*, Elm Tree Books, 1980.

Musser, Charles. *Thomas A. Edison and His Kinetographic Motion Pictures*, Rutgers University Press, 1995.

Napper, Lawrence. *Silent Cinema: Before the Pictures Got Small*, Columbia University Press, 2017.

Naremore, James. *More Than Night: Film Noir in Its Contexts*, University of California Press, 2008. Expanded edition.

Neale, Stephen. *Genre*, British Film Institute, 1996.

Overby, David (ed.). *Springtime in Italy: A Reader on Neo-realism*, Archon Books, 1978.

Pack, Susan. *Film Posters of the Russian Avant-Garde*, Taschen, 2017.

Perkins V. F. *Film as Film: Understanding and Judging Movies*, Penguin, 1972.

Phillips, Ray. *Edison's Kinetoscope and Its Films: A History to 1896*, Greenwood Press, 1997.

Pierson, John. *Spike, Mike, Slackers & Dykes: A Guided Tour across a Decade of American Independent Cinema*, Hyperion, 1998.

Popple, Simon. *Early Cinema: From Factory Gate to Dream Factory*, Wallflower Press, 2003.

Powell, Michael. *A Life in Movies: An Autobiography*, Heinemann, 1986.

Rahbaran, Shiva. *Iranian Cinema Uncensored: Contemporary Film-makers Since the Islamic Revolution*, I. B. Tauris, 2016.

Rangan, Baradwaj. *Dispatches From the Wall Corner: A Journey Through Indian Cinema*, Tranquebar Press, 2014.

Rich, B. Ruby. *New Queer Cinema: The Director's Cut*, Duke University Press, 2013.

Robb, Brian J. *Silent Cinema*, Kamera Books, 2010.

Rosenbaum, Jonathan. *Movie Wars: How Hollywood and the Media Limit What Movies We Can See*, A Cappella Books, 2002.

Ross, Lillian. *Picture: A Story About Hollywood*, Rinehart, 1952.

Salt, Barry. *Film Style and Technology: History & Analysis*, Starword, 1983.

Sarris, Andrew. *The American Cinema: Directors and Directions 1929–1968*, Dutton, 1968.

Schatz, Thomas. *The Genius of the System: Hollywood Filmmaking in the Studio Era*, Metropolitan Books, 1988.

Schikel, Richard. *D. W. Griffith: An American Life*, Proscenium Publishers, 1984.

Shone, Tom. *Blockbuster: How the Jaws and Jedi Generation Turned Hollywood into a Boom-town*, Free Press, 2004.

Sitney, P. Adams. *Visionary Film: The American Avant Garde 1943–2000*, Oxford University Press, 2002.

Srivastava, Manoj. *Wide Angle: History of Indian Cinema*, Notion Press, 2016.

Stevenson, Jack. *Dogme Uncut: Lars von Trier, Thomas Vinterberg, and the Gang that Took on Hollywood*, Santa Monica Press, 2004.

Stross, Randall E. *The Wizard of Menlo Park: How Thomas Alva Edison Invented the Modern World*, Three Rivers Press, 2008.

Tarkovsky, Andrei. *Sculpting in Time: Reflections on the Cinema*, The Bodley Head, 1986.

Thomson, David. *The Big Screen: The Story of the Movies and What They Did to Us*, Penguin, 2013.

Thomson, David. *The New Biographical Dictionary of Film: Sixth Edition*, Knopf Publishing Group, 2014.

Thomson, David. *The Whole Equation: A History of Hollywood*, Abacus, 2006.

Truffaut, François. *Hitchcock*, Simon & Schuster, 1967.

Vachon, Christine. *A Killer Life: How An Independent Film Producer Survives Deals and Disasters in Hollywood and Beyond*, Limelight Editions, 2007.

Vogel, Amos. *Film as a Subversive Art*, Random House, 1974.

Westwell, Guy. *War Cinema: Hollywood on the Front Line*, Wallflower Press, 2006.

Williamson, Judith. *Deadline at Dawn : Film Writings, 1980–90*, Marion Boyars Publishers, 1992.

Wollen, Peter. *Signs and Meaning in the Cinema*, Secker & Warburg, 1969.

Wood, Jason. *The Faber Book of Mexican Cinema*, Faber & Faber, 2006.

Wood, Robin. *Hitchcock's Films*, A. S. Barnes & Co, 1965.

Wood, Robin. *Hollywood From Vietnam to Reagan…And Beyond*, Columbia University Press, 2003.

Zhen, Ni. *Memoirs of the Beijing Film Academy: The Genesis of China's Fifth Generation*, National Publishers of Japan, 1995.

Zhen, Zhang. *An Amorous History of the Silver Screen: Shanghai Cinema, 1896–1937*, University of Chicago Press, 2006.

About the Author

Ian Haydn Smith is the author of *The Short Story of Film*, *The Short Story of Photography*, *Selling the Movie: The Art of the Film Poster*, *Cult Filmmakers* and *Cult Writers*, as well as *Wim Wenders* and *New British Cinema: From Submarine to 12 Years a Slave* (both with Jason Wood).

From 2007 to 2013, he was the editor of the annual *International Film Guide*, an overview of world cinema, the film industry and festivals. Since 2011, he has been the editor of *Curzon Magazine*. He is also the update editor of *1001 Movies You Must See Before You Die*.

As a broadcaster, Haydn Smith has appeared on the BBC, Sky and international media outlets. He has also overseen a series of international arts programmes and lectured on film literature and photography for the British Council. He lives in north London.

Index

Page numbers in **bold** indicate illustrations.

Picture Credits

The publishers would like to thank the museums, artists, archives and photographers for their kind permission to reproduce the works featured in this book. Every effort has been made to trace all copyright owners but if any have been inadvertently overlooked, the publishers would be pleased to make the necessary arrangements at the first opportunity.

Key: top = t; bottom = b; left = l; right = r; centre = c; top left = tl; top right = tr; centre left = cl; centre right = cr; bottom left = bl; bottom right = br

2 Hugh Rooney / Eye Ubiquitous / Alamy Stock Photo **7** AF Fotografie / Alamy Stock Photo **8 t** North Wind Picture Archives / Alamy Stock Photo **8 b** Andrew Barker / Alamy Stock Photo **9** Dmytro Razinkov / Alamy Stock Vector **10-11** Sean Pavone / Alamy Stock Photo **12** Stig Alenäs / Alamy Stock Photo **13** andrew parker / Alamy Stock Photo **14** dave stamboulis / Alamy Stock Photo **15** Michael Winters / Alamy Stock Photo **16** KENAN KAYA / Alamy Stock Photo **17 t** Jack Sullivan / Alamy Stock Photo **17 b** Derek Croucher / Alamy Stock Photo **18** David Muenker / Alamy Stock Photo **19 t** Universal Images Group North America LLC / DeAgostini / Alamy Stock Photo **19 b** HomoCosmicos / Alamy Stock Photo **20** Constantinos Iliopoulos / Alamy Stock Photo **21 l** PRISMA ARCHIVO / Alamy Stock Photo **21 r** isa özdere / Alamy Stock Photo **22 t** Luc Novovitch / Alamy Stock Photo **22 b** Sean Pavone / Alamy Stock Photo **24** Craig Hallewell / Alamy Stock Photo **25 t** Leonid Andronov / Alamy Stock Photo **25 b** B.O'Kane / Alamy Stock Photo **26** Norbert Nagel (CC BY-SA 3.0) **27 t** Ludovic Maisant / Hemis / Alamy Stock Photo **27 b** juan moyano / Alamy Stock Photo **28** eFesenko / Alamy Stock Photo **29** Sean Pavone / Alamy Stock Photo **30** Sergey Borisov / Alamy Stock Photo **31 t** Oliver Christie / Alamy Stock Photo **31 b** Todor Yankov / Zoonar GmbH / Alamy Stock Photo **32** Roger Coulam / Alamy Stock Photo **33 l** Vincenzo Lombardo / robertharding / Alamy Stock Photo **33 r** eye35.pix / Alamy Stock Photo **34** Angelo Hornak / Alamy Stock Photo **35** Hercules Milas / Alamy Stock Photo **36** Zev Radovan / www.BibleLandPictures.com / Alamy Stock Photo **37 t** Heinz L.Boerder (CC BY-SA 3.0) **37 b** Windmill Books / Universal Images Group North America LLC / Alamy Stock Photo **38** Ivan Vdovin / Alamy Stock Photo **39 l** Ondřej Žváček (CC BY-SA 3.0) **39 r** Chris Mellor / Alamy Stock Photo **41 t** Carole Raddato (CC BY-SA 2.0) **41 b** CrniBombarder (public domain) **42** Sarah Williams / Alamy Stock Photo **43 l** Katja Kreder / imageBROKER / Alamy Stock Photo **43 r** Nourry Richard/SCOPE-IMAGE / Alamy Stock Photo **44 t** Karl Johaentges / Look / Alamy Stock Photo **44 b** PF-(sdasm3) / Alamy Stock Photo **45** Konstantin Kalishko / Alamy Stock Photo **46** Nikolay Sivenkov / Alamy Stock Photo **47** Jan Wlodarczyk / Alamy Stock Photo **48** Top Photo / Asia Photo Connection / Henry Westheim Photography / Alamy Stock Photo **49 l** Neil Turner via Getty Images **49 r** David Keith Jones / Alamy Stock Photo **50** Andrew Shiva / Wikipedia / CC BY-SA 4.0 **51 t** Wiiii (CC BY-SA 3.0) **51 b** Jon Arnold Images Ltd / Alamy Stock Photo **52** Volha Kavalenkava / Panther Media GmbH / Alamy Stock Photo **53** Ben Pipe / robertharding / Alamy Stock Photo **54** Gerald Hänel / StockFood GmbH / Alamy Stock Photo **55 t** Flore Lamoureux / India Picture / Arcaid Images / Alamy Stock Photo **55 b** Rose Araya-Farias / Heritage Image Partnership Ltd / Alamy Stock Photo **56** Don Douglas / Alamy Stock Photo **57 t** Bertrand Gardel / Hemis / Alamy Stock Photo **57 b** P Tomlins / Alamy Stock Photo **58** Frank Bach / Alamy Stock Photo **59 t** funkyfood London - Paul Williams / Alamy Stock Photo **59 b** Bernard Gagnon (CC BY-SA 3.0) **60** Tm (public domain) **61** akg-images / De Agostini Picture Lib. / A. Dagli Orti **62** PRISMA ARCHIVO / Alamy Stock Photo **63 t** kostas koufogiorgos / Alamy Stock Photo **63 b** David Angel / Alamy Stock Photo **64** Wolfgang Kaehler/LightRocket via Getty Images **65 l** Florian Monheim / Bildarchiv Monheim GmbH / Alamy Stock Photo **65 r** Kumar Sriskandan / Alamy Stock Photo **67 t** Jose Fuste Raga / mauritius images GmbH / Alamy Stock Photo **67 b** Ian Dagnall / Alamy Stock Photo **68** Sergi Reboredo / Alamy Stock Photo **69 l** Sean Pavone / Alamy Stock Photo **69 r** kravka / Alamy Stock Photo **70** Adam Burton / Alamy Stock Photo **71 t** Paul Melling / Alamy Stock Photo **71 b** Felix Lipov / Alamy Stock Photo **72** Egmont Strigl / imageBROKER / Alamy Stock Photo **73** akg-images / A.F.Kersting **74** Michael Runkel / robertharding / Alamy Stock Photo **75 l** Heritage Image Partnership Ltd / Alamy Stock Photo **75 r** giuseppe masci / Alamy Stock Photo **76** Alan Novelli / Alamy Stock Photo **77 l** Alex Ramsay / Alamy Stock Photo **77 r** Francisco Martinez / Alamy Stock Photo **78** GTW / imageBROKER / Alamy Stock Photo **79** JOHN KELLERMAN / Alamy Stock Photo **80** Alvesgaspar (CC BY-SA 4.0) **81 t** Daniel Vorndran / DXR (CC BY-SA 3.0) **81 b** Ben Pipe / robertharding / Alamy Stock Photo **82-83** Arnaud Chicurel / Hemis / Alamy Stock Photo **84** S. Forster / Alamy Stock Photo **85** Daniel Schoenen / imageBROKER / Alamy Stock Photo **86** Angelo Hornak / Alamy Stock Photo **87** Eric VANDEVILLE/Gamma-Rapho via Getty Images **88 l** Tom Uhlman / Alamy Stock Photo **88 r** Sean Pavone / Alamy Stock Photo **89** Ekrem Canli (CC BY-SA 3.0) **90** Riccardo Bianchini / Alamy Stock Photo **91 l** Hugh Rooney / Eye Ubiquitous / Alamy Stock Photo **91 r** Angelo Hornak / Alamy Stock Photo **92** Michal Sikorski / Alamy Stock Photo **93 t** Ian G Dagnall / Alamy Stock Photo **93 b** Ian G Dagnall / Alamy Stock Photo **94** Art Collection 3 / Alamy Stock Photo **95 t** Nikolay Vinokurov / Alamy Stock Photo **95 b** Fine Art Images / Heritage Image Partnership Ltd / Alamy Stock Photo **96 t** Julian Elliott / robertharding / Alamy Stock Photo **96 b** Peter Thompson / Heritage Image Partnership Ltd / Alamy Stock Photo **98** Peter Probst / Alamy Stock Photo **99 l** M@rcel / Alamy Stock Photo **99 r** Didier Descouens (CC BY-SA 4.0) **100** Angelo Hornak / Alamy Stock Photo **101 t** Stefano Valeri / Alamy Stock Photo **101 b** Azoor Travel Photo / Alamy Stock Photo **102** Lucas Vallecillos / Alamy Stock Photo **103** Mariordo (Mario Roberto Durán Ortiz) (CC BY-SA 4.0) **104** Dave Zubraski / Alamy Stock Photo **105 l** Luise Berg-Ehlers / Alamy Stock Photo **105 r** Taras Vyshnya / Alamy Stock Photo **106** Benh LIEU SONG (CC BY-SA 3.0) **107 l** Ggia (CC BY-SA 3.0) **107 r** Marco Saracco / Alamy Stock Photo **108 t** Pat Tuson / Alamy Stock Photo **108 b** neville morgan / Alamy Stock Photo **110** Didier Descouens (CC BY-SA 4.0) **111 t** GRANT ROONEY PREMIUM / Alamy Stock Photo **111 b** Marcok (CC BY-SA 3.0) **112** Didier Descouens (CC BY-SA 4.0) **113 l** UNESCO (CC BY-SA 3.0 IGO) **113 r** Alex Ramsay / Alamy Stock Photo **114 t** eye35.pix / Alamy Stock Photo **114 b** Martin Jung / imageBROKER / Alamy Stock Photo **116** Sandra Antonella Parodi (CC BY-SA 4.0) **117 t** Arthur Greenberg / Alamy Stock Photo **117 b** Jeff Whyte / Shutterstock.com **118** Benjamin Matthijs Lichtwerk via Getty Images **119 l** EVREN KALINBACAK / Alamy Stock Photo **119 r** Nikreates / Alamy Stock Photo **120** Nacho Calonge / Alamy Stock Photo **121 l** Martin Jung / imageBROKER / Alamy Stock Photo **121 r** © Karel de Grendre /ASK Images / Alamy Stock Photo **122 t** Arnaud Chicurel / Hemis / Alamy Stock Photo **122 b** Stephane Lemaire / Hemis / Alamy Stock Photo **124 l** René Mattes / Hemis / Alamy Stock Photo **124 r** JOHN BRACEGIRDLE / Alamy Stock Photo **125** Rod Clement / Alamy Stock Photo **126 l** Guillaume Louyot / Alamy Stock Photo **126 r** Wiki alf (public domain) **127** Timothy Valentine (CC BY-SA 2.0) **128** debra millet / Alamy Stock Photo **129** aerial-photos.com / Alamy Stock Photo **130** John Mitchell / Alamy Stock Photo **131 t** YAY Media AS / Alamy Stock Photo **131 b** Daniel Schwen (CC BY-SA 4.0) **132 l** Lankowsky / Alamy Stock Photo **132 r** Thomas Ledl (CC BY-SA 4.0) **133** Marius745 (CC BY-SA 4.0) **134** Aw58 (CC BY-SA 4.0) **135** Arnaud Chicurel / Hemis / Alamy Stock Photo **136** Erich Teister / Zoonar GmbH / Alamy Stock Photo **137 t** De Agostini Picture Library / A. Dagli Orti / Bridgeman Images **137 b** Dallas and John Heaton / Stock Connection Blue / Alamy Stock Photo **138–139** Francois Roux / Alamy Stock Photo **140** eye35.pix / Alamy Stock Photo **141** Thomas Robbin / imageBROKER / Alamy Stock Photo **142** Ian Dagnall / Alamy Stock Photo **143** Russell Kord / Alamy Stock Photo **144** Justin Kase z12z / Alamy Stock Photo **145 l** Paul Seheult / Eye Ubiquitous / Alamy Stock Photo **145 r** NiKreative / Alamy Stock Photo **146** JOHN KELLERMAN / Alamy Stock Photo **147 t** Chiswick Chap (CC BY-SA 3.0) **147 b** S.d.touro (CC BY-SA 4.0) **148** Neale Clark / robertharding / Alamy Stock Photo **149** eye35.pix / Alamy Stock Photo **150** A. Savin (Free Art License) **151 l** aerial-photos.com / Alamy Stock Photo **151 r** Jean-Christophe Benoist (CC BY-SA 3.0) **152** Herb Bendicks / Alamy Stock Photo **153 t** Mihael Grmek (CC BY-SA 3.0) **153 b** Camille Gévaudan (CC BY-SA 3.0) **154 l** Alessio Damato (CC BY-SA 3.0) **154 r** ICP / incamerastock / Alamy Stock Photo **155** nattanai chimjanon / Alamy Stock Photo **156 t** Granger Historical Picture Archive / Alamy Stock Photo **156 b** Classic Image / Alamy Stock Photo **158** Hon Lau - Dublin / Alamy Stock Photo **159 t** Mick Rock / Cephas Picture Library / Alamy Stock Photo **159 b** Paul Harris / John Warburton-Lee Photography / Alamy Stock Photo **160 l** Michael Howell / Alamy Stock Photo **160 r** Schoening / Arco Images GmbH / Alamy Stock Photo **161** Ian Dagnall / Alamy Stock Photo **162** Artokoloro Quint Lox Limited / Alamy Stock Photo **163** Adrian Baker / Alamy Stock Photo **164** Diego Grandi / Alamy Stock Photo **165 t** LianeM / Alamy Stock Photo **165 b** W. Buss / Universal Images Group North America LLC / DeAgostini / Alamy Stock Photo **166 t** Guillem Lopez / Alamy Stock Photo **166 b** Peter Durant / Arcaid Images / Alamy Stock Photo **167** Ned Goode / Historic American Buildings Survey (Library of Congress) **168** Augustus Welby Northmore Pugin, Ryerson and Burnham Libraries, The Art Institute of Chicago **169** Chris Pancewicz / Alamy Stock Photo **170** Inge Johnsson / Alamy Stock Photo **171 t** Rene Mattes / mauritius images GmbH / Alamy Stock Photo **171 b** Philip Scalia / Alamy Stock Photo **172** Valeriya Popova / Alamy Stock Photo **173 t** Ian Dagnall / Alamy Stock Photo **173 b** Alex 'Florstein' Fedorov (CC BY-SA 4.0) **174** History and Art Collection / Alamy Stock Photo **175** Norbert Probst / imageBROKER / Alamy Stock Photo **176** Robert K. Chin – Storefronts / Alamy Stock Photo **177 l** Angelo Hornak / Alamy Stock Photo **177 r** Nattee Chalermtiragool / Alamy Stock Photo **178** Stephen Coyne / Alamy Stock Photo **179 t** Michael Weber / imageBROKER / Alamy Stock Photo **179 b** Daniel Case (CC BY-SA 3.0) **180** Archive World / Alamy Stock Photo **181** Historic Architecture and Landscape Image Collection, Ryerson and Burnham Archives, The Art Institute of Chicago **182** Sean Pavone / Alamy Stock Photo **183 l** North Wind Picture Archives / Alamy Stock Photo **183 r** Vincenzo Lombardo / robertharding / Alamy Stock Photo **184** Dorling Kindersley ltd / Alamy Stock Photo **185 l** Alan John Ainsworth/Heritage Images/Getty Images **185 r** Francois Roux / Alamy Stock Photo **186** Chicago History Museum, USA / Bridgeman Images **187** FL Historical 1A / Alamy Stock Photo **188–189** travelpix / Alamy Stock Photo **190** Serhii Chrucky / Alamy Stock Photo **191** Carol M. Highsmith Archive, Library of Congress **192** Cameron Davidson / Westend61 GmbH / Alamy Stock Photo **193** John Zukowsky **194** Beyond My Ken (CC BY-SA 4.0) **195 l** Sean Pavone / Alamy Stock Photo **195 r** Jackdude101 (CC BY-SA 4.0) **196** Thomas Wolf (CC BY-SA 3.0 DE) **197 t** Ariadne Van Zandbergen / Alamy Stock Photo **197 b** Thomas A. Heinz / Arcaid Images / Alamy Stock Photo **198 t** Julian Krakowiak / Alamy Stock Photo **198 b** Grant Smith-VIEW / Alamy Stock Photo **200** Sorin Colac / Alamy Stock Photo **201 t** Thomas Robbin / imageBROKER / Alamy Stock Photo **201 b** Peter Eltham (CC BY-SA 3.0) **202** Alamy **203 l** Šarūnas Burdulis (CC BY-SA 2.0) **203 r** Scott Goodno / Alamy Stock Photo **204** A. Savin (Free Art License) **205** © Freunde der Weissenhofsiedlung e.V. **206** Popow / blickwinkel / Alamy Stock Photo **207 l** Mara Brandl / imageBROKER / Alamy Stock Photo **207 r** Martin Bond / Alamy Stock Photo **208** Ian Dagnall / Alamy Stock Photo **209 t** travelpix / Alamy Stock Photo **209 b** Misc / GFC Collection / Alamy Stock Photo **210** Schütze / Rodemann / Bildarchiv Monheim GmbH / Alamy Stock Photo **211 l** Chris Gascoigne / Alamy Stock Photo **211 r** Daderot (CC0 1.0) **212** Julie g Woodhouse / Alamy Stock Photo **213 t** Onda Turnosa / Alamy Stock Photo **213 b** Spaces Images / Mint Images Limited / Alamy Stock Photo **214** Michael Nitzschke / imageBROKER / Alamy Stock Photo **215** ullstein bild via Getty Images **216** Thant Zaw Wai / Alamy Stock Photo **217 l** Carol M. Highsmith Archive, Library of Congress **217 r** Karl F. Schöfmann / imageBROKER / Alamy Stock Photo **218** JLImages / Alamy Stock Photo **219 t** vdbvsl / Alamy Stock Photo **219 b** Jorge Salcedo / Shutterstock.com **220** © Bill Bachmann / Alamy Stock Photo **221** Hermann Dobler / imageBROKER / Alamy Stock Photo **222–223** Ana Flašker / Alamy Stock Photo **224** Gert Kreutschmann/ullstein bild via Getty Images **225** STOCKFOLIO® / Alamy Stock Photo **226** Paul Brown / Alamy Stock Photo **227** Thomas Robbin / imageBROKER / Alamy Stock Photo **228 l** Rick Buettner / Alamy Stock Photo **228 r** Sergey Dzyuba / Alamy Stock Photo **229** Sean Pavone / Alamy Stock Photo **230** Dietrich Burgmair / Alamy Stock Photo **231 t** Batchelder / Alamy Stock Photo **231 b** Elisa Locci / Alamy Stock Photo **232** Bernard O'Kane / Alamy Stock Photo **233** Niels Quist / Alamy Stock Photo **234** Bill Brooks / Alamy Stock Photo **235 t** Nathan Willock-VIEW / Alamy Stock Photo **235 b** bdstockphoto / Alamy Stock Photo **236** Architect´s Eye / Alamy Stock Photo **237 l** © Ralf Roletschek **237 r** Taxiarchos228 (Free Art License) **238** Carol M. Highsmith Archive, Library of Congress **239 l** Hugh Rooney / Eye Ubiquitous / Alamy Stock Photo **239 r** akg-images / Bildarchiv Monheim **240** Gilles Targat / Photo 12 / Alamy Stock Photo **241 t** Philip Scalia / Alamy Stock Photo **241 b** Archivio Storico della Biennale di Venezia - ASAC © Antonio Martinelli **242** Peter Bennett / Citizen of the Planet / Alamy Stock Photo **243** John Elk III / Alamy Stock Photo **244 t** ivoivanov / F1online digitale Bildagentur GmbH / Alamy Stock Photo **244 b** Mathias Beinling / Alamy Stock Photo **245** Classic Image / Alamy Stock Photo **246** Viennaslide / Alamy Stock Photo **247 l** Ken Wolter / Alamy Stock Photo **247 r** View Stock / Alamy Stock Photo **248 t** George Rose/Getty Images **248–249** Geoffrey Taunton / Alamy Stock Photo **250** STEPHEN FLEMING / Alamy Stock Photo **251 t** Aardvark / Alamy Stock Photo **251 b** Sean Pavone / Alamy Stock Photo **252** Alan Copson / robertharding / Alamy Stock Photo **253 l** archipix / Alamy Stock Photo **253 r** John McKenna / Alamy Stock Photo **255 l** ilyas Ayub / Alamy Stock Photo **255 r** Simon Reddy / Alamy Stock Photo **256** adam eastland / Alamy Stock Photo **257 t** B.O'Kane / Alamy Stock Photo **257 b** BANANA PANCAKE / Alamy Stock Photo **258** Stuart Black / Alamy Stock Photo **259 t** James Doro / Alamy Stock Photo **259 b** Donaldytong (CC BY-SA 3.0) **260** Francois Roux / Alamy Stock Photo **261** ARV / Alamy Stock Photo **262 l** Raga Jose Fuste / Prisma by Dukas Presseagentur GmbH / Alamy Stock Photo **262 r** Amy Cicconi / Alamy Stock Photo **263** Michael Ventura / Alamy Stock Photo **264 l** © Adrian Smith + Gordon Gill Architecture/Jeddah Economic Company **264 r** Serhii Chrucky / Alamy Stock Photo **265** hapabapa via Getty Images

Front Cover: *Parasite* (*Gisaengchung*), South Korea (2019)
© JRC, Inc / Alamy Stock Photo

Page 2: *The Blue Angel* (*Der blaue Engel*, 1930), Germany
© World History Archive / Alamy Stock Photo

First published in the United States of America in 2021 by
Thames & Hudson Inc., 500 Fifth Avenue,
New York, New York 10110

© 2021 Quarto Publishing plc

This book was designed and produced by
Quintessence, an imprint of The Quarto Group
The Quarto Group
The Old Brewery
6 Blundell Street
London N7 9BH

Editor   Carol King
Designer   Michelle Kliem
Production Manager Charlotte Oliver
Publisher   Samantha Warrington

Library of Congress Control Number 2020939957

ISBN 978-0500-02369-3

Printed in Singapore

Be the first to know about our new releases,
exclusive content and author events by visiting
thamesandhudson.com
thamesandhudsonusa.com
thamesandhudson.com.au